FOUNDING EDITOR
Rasheed Araeen

EDITOR
Richard Appignanesi

ASSISTANT EDITORS
Richard Dyer, Adele Tan

MANAGING EDITOR
Yvie Andrews

EDITORIAL BOARD
Ali Nobil Ahmad, Jorella Andrews,
Annie Coombes, Anthony Downey,
Raimi Gbadamosi, Amna Malik,
Leon Wainwright

ADVISORY COUNCIL
Rustom Bharucha *Calcutta, India*
Guy Brett *London, UK*
Iain Chambers *University of Naples, Italy*
David Craven *Uni of New Mexico, USA*
Sean Cubitt *Uni of Melbourne, Australia*
Denis Ekpo *Uni of Port Harcourt Nigeria*
Ihab Hassan *University of Wisconsin-Milwaukee, USA*
Janis Jefferies *Goldsmiths, University of London, UK*
Geeta Kapur *New Delhi, India*
Tabish Khair *Aarhus Universitet, Denmark*
Vinay Lal *University of California, Los Angeles, USA*
José-Carlos Mariategui *Lima, Peru*
Ian McLean *Uni of Western Australia, Perth*
Laura Mulvey *Birkbeck College, University of London, UK*
Gerardo Mosquera *Havana, Cuba*
Benita Parry *University of Warwick, UK*
Howardena Pindell *Stony Brook University, New York, USA*
Mario Pissarro *ASAI, Uni of Cape Town, South Africa*
Gene Ray *Berlin, Germany*
John Roberts *Uni of Wolverhampton, UK*
Gayatri Spivak *Columbia University, New York, USA*
Julian Stallabrass *Courtauld Institute, London, UK*
Victor Tupitsyn *Paris/Moscow*
Stephen Wright *Paris, France*
Slavoj Zizek *Institute for Social Sciences, Uni of Ljubljana, Slovenia*

EDITORIAL ADDRESS
Third Text, 2G Crusader House,
289 Cricklewood Broadway,
London NW2 6NX, UK
Tel: +44 (0)20 8830 7803
E-mail: thirdtext@btconnect.com

THIRD TEXT
CRITICAL PERSPECTIVES ON CONTEMPORARY ART & CULTURE

98 VOLUME 23 ISSUE 3 MAY 2009

SPECIAL ISSUE: MEDIA ARTS: Practice, Institutions and Histories
Guest Editors: José-Carlos Mariátegui, Sean Cubitt and Gunalan Nadarajan

José-Carlos Mariátegui, Sean Cubitt and Gunalan Nadarajan	Social Formations of Global Media Art	217
Laura U Marks	Taking a Line for a Walk, from the Abbasid Caliphate to Vector Graphics	229
Maree Mills	Pou Rewa: The Liquid Post, Maori Go Digital?	241
Nina Czegledy and Andrea Szekeres	Agents for Change: The Contemporary Art Centres of the Soros Foundation and C^3	251
Olga Goriunova	Old Contexts for New: Media Cultures (in Russia)	261
Eduardo de Jesus	Electronic Image: Identities and the Experience of Globalisation in the International Festival of Electronic Art – *Videobrasil*	269
Ernesto Calvo and María José Monge	New Technologies in Central American Contemporary Art: A Partial Archaeology and Some Critical Appreciations from the Institutional Realm	281
Mauricio Delfín and Miguel Zegarra	Electronic Art in Peru: The Discovery of an Invisible Territory in the Country of the Incas	293
Pi Li	Chinese Contemporary Video Art	303
Hannah Feldman	Excavating Images on the Border	309
Marcus Neustetter	Analogue and Digital Anecdotes and Artworks from South Africa	323
Ravi Sundaram	Revisiting the Pirate Kingdom	335
Contributors		347

Founded in 1987, *Third Text* is published by Routledge on behalf of Black Umbrella with financial assistance of the Arts Council England.

Black Umbrella is a registered charity, no. 11108974, governed by a board of trustees: Marjorie Allthorpe-Guyton, René Gimpel, Merryl Wyn Davies, Elinor Jansz, Francesco Manacorda, Lord Bhikhu Parekh, Ziauddin Sardar (Chair), David Thorp

SUBSCRIPTION INFORMATION

Third Text is a learned journal internally refereed by its editorial board and is published by Routledge Journals Taylor & Francis, 4 Park Square, Milton Park, Abingdon, Oxfordshire, OX14 4RN, UK.
Tel: +44 (0)207 017 6000; Fax: +44 (0)207 017 6336

All research articles published in this journal have undergone peer review based on initial editorial screening.

Annual subscription rates 2009
Volume 23, 6 issues, ISSN 0952–8822
Institutional rate (includes free online access): £343/$522/€416
Personal rate (print only): £88/$147/€117
Online only (plus tax where applicable): £326/$496/€395

A subscription to the print edition includes free access for any number of concurrent users across a local area network to the online edition, ISSN 1475–5297. Subscriptions purchased at the personal rate are strictly for personal, non-commercial use only. The reselling of personal subscriptions is prohibited. Personal subscriptions must be purchased with a personal cheque or credit card. Proof of personal status may be requested.

Third Text (USPS permit no. 018158) is published bi-monthly, in January, March, May, July, September and November. The 2009 US institutional subscription price is $522. Periodicals postage paid at Jamaica, NY, by US Mail Agent Air Business Ltd, c/o Priority Airfreight NY Ltd, 147-29 182nd Street, Jamaica, NY 11413, USA.

US Postmaster: Please send address changes to CTTE, Air Business Ltd, c/o Priority Airfreight NY Ltd, 147-29 182nd Street, Jamaica, NY 11413, USA

For a complete and up-to-date guide to Taylor & Francis journals and books publishing programmes, and details of advertising in our journals, visit our website: http://www.tandf.co.uk

Dollar rates apply to subscribers in all countries except the UK and the Republic of Ireland where the pound sterling rate applies. If you are unsure which rate applies to you please contact Customer Services in the UK. All subscriptions are payable in advance and all rates include postage. Journals are sent by air to the USA, Canada, Mexico, India, Japan and Australasia. Subscriptions are entered on an annual basis, i.e. January to December. Payment may be made by sterling cheque, dollar cheque, international money order, National Giro, or credit card (Amex, Visa, Mastercard).

Ordering information:
USA, Canada: Routledge Journals, Taylor & Francis, Inc., 325 Chestnut Street, 8th Floor, Philadelphia, PA 19106, USA Tel: + 1 800 354 1420; Fax: + 1 215 625 2940. **UK/Europe/Rest of World:** T&F Customer Services, T&F Informa UK Ltd, Sheepen Place, Colchester, Essex, CO3 3LP, UK. Tel: +44 (0)207 0175544; Fax: +44 (0)207 0175198. **WWW:** http://www.tandf.co.uk; **E-mail:** tf.enquiries@tfinforma.com

The print edition of this journal is typeset by Genesis Typesetting Limited, Rochester, Kent and printed on ANSI conforming acid free paper by Hobbs the Printers, UK.

Copyright © Third Text (2009). All rights reserved. No part of this publication may be reproduced, stored, transmitted, or disseminated, in any form, or by any means, without prior written permission from Taylor & Francis, to whom all requests to reproduce copyright material should be directed, in writing.

Taylor & Francis and *Third Text* make every effort to ensure the accuracy of all the information (the 'Content') contained in its publications. However, Taylor & Francis and *Third Text* and its agents and licensors make no representations or warranties whatsoever as to the accuracy, completeness or suitability for any purpose of the Content and disclaim all such representations and warranties whether express or implied to the maximum extent permitted by law. Any views expressed in this publication are the views of the authors and are not the views of Taylor & Francis and *Third Text*.

Taylor & Francis grants authorisation for individuals to photocopy copyright material for private research use, on the sole basis that requests for such use are referred directly to the requestor's local Reproduction Rights Organisation (RRO). The copyright fee is $25 exclusive of any charge or fee levied. In order to contact your local RRO, please contact: International Federation of Reproduction Rights Organisations (IFRRO), rue du Prince Royal, 87, B-1050 Brussels, Belgium, e-mail: ifrro@skynet.be; Copyright Clearance Center Inc., 222 Rosewood Drive, Danvers, MA 01923, USA, e-mail: info@copyright.com; Copyright Licensing Agency, 90 Tottenham Court Road, London, W1P 0LP, UK, e-mail: cla@cla.co.uk. This authorisation does not extend to any other kind of copying by any means, in any form, for any purpose other than private research use.

Copyright. It is a condition of publication that authors assign copyright or licence the publication rights in their articles, including abstracts, to Third Text. This enables us to ensure full copyright protection and to disseminate the article, and of course the Journal, to the widest possible readership in print and electronic formats as appropriate. Authors may, of course, use the article elsewhere *after* publication without prior permission from Third Text, provided that acknowledgement is given to the Journal as the original source of publication, and that Third Text is notified so that our records show that its use is properly authorised. Authors retain a number of other rights under the Third Text rights policies documents. These policies are referred to at http://www.tandf.co.uk/journals/authorrights.pdf for full details. Authors are themselves responsible for obtaining permission to reproduce copyright material from other sources.

Social Formations of Global Media Art

José-Carlos Mariátegui, Sean Cubitt and Gunalan Nadarajan

INTRODUCTION

Though digital media date back to the 1940s and digital arts to the 1950s, it is only since the mass marketing of personal digital technology in the mid-1980s and the arrival of the world wide web in the early 1990s that social science researchers have begun to ask themselves what is the relation between new media and development, and particularly how relations between the First and the Third World become restructured.[1] Though many of the technologies may seem similar, their effects on diverse groups of people are qualitatively as well as quantitatively different, very often reflecting the differential access and distribution of such technologies. This is the case of the use of new media in emergent areas of the world, particularly when related to culture and arts. This special issue of *Third Text* aims to analyse new media art practice in recent decades and asks whether it has provided a source for new cultural and social practices. While individual practitioners have produced thousands of innovations, the purchase of such innovations in the wider culture depends on their distribution and publicity: for this reason, we have elected to trace the histories not of individual artists but of networks and social formations, most of them created by artists and cultural workers devoted to establishing longer-term impacts than single artworks usually can.

The term 'institution' is problematic. On the one hand, in the political philosophy stemming from Michel Foucault, institutions appear as regulators of exchange, instruments of oppression and guardians of what can or cannot be legitimately thought. Such institutions exercise rule, through discipline or control, in the interests of what in the twenty-first century need to be understood as numerically tiny cosmopolitan elites, who are also the class to whom wealth accrues, and who are the taste-setters for the global art market. On the other hand, institutions such as artist-run spaces and organised networks can be considered counter-institutions, aligned neither with the state nor with corporations, but operating as organised forms of civic life in the public sphere.[2] In recent decades, such institutions have

---

1. Arturo Escobar, 'Welcome to Cyberia: Notes on the Anthropology of Cyberculture', *Current Anthropology*, 35:3, p 211; Manuel Castells, *The Rise of the Network Society*, Blackwell, Oxford, 2000

2. Ned Rossiter, *Organized Networks: Media Theory, Creative Labour, New Institutions*, Institute of Network Cultures/NAi Publishers, Amsterdam, 2006

included very loose, open networks without fixed memberships or structures, perhaps most famously those associated with the anti-globalisation protest movements. This ambiguity in the meaning of the word is important because it is reflected in the kinds of practice that self-organised new media institutions engage in. However, as is clear from several contributions to the *Third Text* special issue 'Whither Tactical Media?' (no 94), new media practices frequently frustrate and reformulate the term. So it is better to opt for the less loaded term 'social formation', which captures the tenuous and temporary nature of such formations that are still structurally coherent enough to act with some common intentionality.

New media art practice, or at least its computing-related precedents, started in the 1950s and 1960s as a means of experimenting with both concepts and the core technical apparatus. The term 'electronic art' became a popular way to refer to this type of art, identifying it closely with the media used. Throughout this formative period and to some extent beyond, there were two particular emphases: on the one side a critical relation to television and mass media; and, on the other, a positive relation between art, science and technology.[3] The 1990s also brought a shift in the dissemination of non-Western cultures, not least in the realm of new media art, opening a dialogue for democratic and open exchange. Nevertheless, over the years, some of these exchanges and initial critical perspectives became institutionalised (in the negative sense) in formal discourses that lost their initial value as agents for change. Current access to information about non-Western critical discourse and the proliferation of collaborative global projects to some extent owes its existence to communication and media technologies developed initially in the West. But like institutional structures, these technologies are not only replicated but also remixed to become new cultural forms (and not just standard formats).

In the case of new media art, the notion of 'video creation', for example, gained widespread circulation in creative production, offering a licence to play – literally – with the moving image and to explore its possibilities by means of the technological artefact. For artists gaining experience with a new medium, such play results in technological flexibility and 'meaning-in-use', the derivation of new kinds of meanings from the new medium itself. A user utilises a given technology not only as originally designed, but also by inventing (programming) new uses that were not initially identified by their original designers. This is the case of what also is defined as the 'localisation or 'tropicalisation' of a technology, and by Norman Girvan as 'indigenisable technologies', that is, those which are neither black boxes which cannot be modified to suit local conditions, nor those which militant development experts define as indigenous, but those whose black boxes can be opened and made relevant to local users.[4] The user is not only a practitioner but a designer, and the resulting technology expresses a level of malleability. However, technology is not infinitely malleable; its level of flexibility depends to a large degree on the level of interconnectedness and configuration of the technological artefact.[5]

THE CURRENT (PAST) DISCOURSE

For the last decade, a decisive cultural practice in the use of new technologies has been emerging in underdeveloped countries. Recent studies

3. Sean Cubitt, *Videography: Video Media as Art and Culture*, St Martin's Press, New York, 1993; Richard Wise and Jeanette Steemers, *Multimedia: A Critical Introduction*, Routledge, London–New York, 2000

4. Norman Girvan, *Cooperation in Science and Technology: An Agenda 2000 for the South*, South Centre, Kingston, Jamaica, 1994

5. Wanda J Orlikowski, 'Using Technology and Constituting Structures: A Practice Lens for Studying Technology in Organizations', *Organization Science*, 4:11, 2000, pp 404-28; Jannis Kallinikos, 'Reopening the Black Box of Technology Artifacts and Human Agency', 23rd International Conference on Information Systems, Barcelona, 15–17 December 2002

have tried to show the development of artistic and cultural practices in the light of globalisation.[6] In many such recent accounts it is becoming evident that the technological muse plays a decisive role, for example in new senses of belonging fostered through networked access to the languages, cultures and political activities of migrants' home countries. Evaluations of the effects of such access differ widely from positive to negative visions. The potentiality of digital technologies reminds us how the 'low-tech' can provide the basis for critique of the 'high-tech' (in the same way that there is a critique of Western culture from non-Western perspectives). However, in many of these discussions the uses of technology are treated as a given and this assumption is connected with a narrow approach to technology, which defines it as autonomous from society and value-neutral.[7] By observing how artists and others are dealing with the technological apparatus, and thereby radically changing our definition of artistic practice towards a more social perspective, we can also challenge this autonomous, neutral vision of technology inherited from the West.

As technologies become more widely disseminated, globalisation needs to be interpreted as a process whereby imported ideas, concepts and artefacts are indigenised or tropicalised. In this respect people may adapt information and communication technologies (ICTs) for their own purposes to generate value that is meaningful, beyond any specific national or multilateral agenda. Implicit in this reading of indigenised, tropicalised technologies is the principle that technologies are not given, but are the product of both design and use. Technology is, then, made out of cultural processes; and since culture is at its heart dynamic and emergent, so too are information and communications technologies that evolve as appropriations in local contexts to suit local people's imperatives, both cultural and pragmatic.

Nevertheless, if we take up this conceptualisation of technology naively, without regard to its actual implementation in social formations, issues in the alignment between nation-state objectives and the practice itself may become problematic. For example, concepts of citizenship do not fit neatly or figure prominently in the everyday network communications and exchanges of people around the world. This ambivalence over citizenship challenges many presumptions about equality of access to technologies.[8]

Postcolonial theory can be used as a lens to understand how powerful economic, social and cultural influences affect the development of technologies and their use in local contexts, particularly where traditional institutional concepts prevail.[9] A key argument to take into consideration is that during the late 1980s and early 1990s, less emphasis was put on the actual consequences of technology. As the standardisation processes were being deployed, the idea of using the internet for democratic enhancement was at its highest. This was the principle on which many technology-oriented organisations were established.[10] There was the myth that technology, in a plausible future, was going to resolve many issues in underdeveloped societies in the same way it had in the developed world. The argument rested on two premises. First, since the foundation of US aid programmes in the 1950s, the theory was that because the West had progressed from agriculture to industrialisation and thence to the finance and information economies, developing

6. Nikos Papastergiadis, *Complex Entanglements: Art, Globalisation and Cultural Difference*, Rivers Oram Press, Malden, MA, 2003; Gerardo Mosquera, Jean Fisher et al, *Over Here: International Perspectives on Art and Culture*, New Museum of Contemporary Art, MIT Press, Cambridge, MA, 2004

7. Escobar, op cit, 1994

8. Jodi Dean, Jon W Anderson et al, *Reformatting Politics: Information Technology and Global Civil Society*, Routledge, New York, 2006

9. M S Adam and M D Myers, 'Have you got anything to declare? Neo-Colonialism, Information Systems, and the Imposition of Customs and Duties in a Third World Country: Organizational Information Systems in the Context of Globalization', IFIP TC8, TC9/WG8.2/WG9.4. 'Working Conference on Information Systems Perspectives and Challenges in the Context of Globalization, Athens, Greece', Kluwer, 2003

10. Saskia Sassen, *Cities in a World Economy*, Pine Forge Press, London–Thousand Oaks, CA, 2006

nations of necessity had to follow the same 'modernisation' path. The second is characterised by Robert Hunter Wade as tractorisation,[11] the theory that since Western agriculture was successful and had lots of tractors, all that developing agricultural nations needed was more tractors. Wade accuses the United Nations Development Programme (UNDP) and other development agencies of applying the same logic to computers, with very probably the same result: fields full of unmaintained tractors ill-equipped for tropical conditions; schools and libraries with unopened boxes of computers, or computers used only for word processing and games; or computers simply dumped for lack of interest or anyone to maintain them. Western institutions – and corporations like Microsoft, Cisco Systems and Dell who have major development projects – constantly repeat this error in their collaborations with non-Western settings and practitioners, applying network solutions from the West with no concept of how their rigidity and complexity fail to match the often fuzzy, vague and ad hoc arrangements of business and public life in the non-West. Even some non-profit projects that come from the West, such as the One-Laptop-Per-Child (OLPC) initiative, do not seem – at least from their initial implementation – to take into consideration the context in which these machines are used. By means of a piece of standardised hardware and software, the OLPC intends to make children learn and collaborate in places with no internet connection and where there are other more complex contextual problems yet to be solved. Questions of whether this is appropriate technology, whether it can truly be indigenised, and whether it may also generate generational and other conflict have scarcely been addressed by its proselytisers.

The majority of development policies aimed at integrating developing nations into globalisation have been based around such standardised frameworks. In the case of new media, globalisation typically arrived as part of a local intervention and was not formally considered within a discourse about social formations. Local cultural organisations, founded prior to the arrival of internet and digital technologies, confronted the issue of new media from an ambiguous position due to its hybrid and de-localised nature, as well as its artistic background. From one side there was clear evidence of local participation and use of technologies in new ways, offering new visions and hybridities that questioned established discourses. From the other side, as internet connectivity evolved, many joined in simply because they did not want to be left behind or excluded from global activities and projects. These orientations were confirmed by the association of sustainability with information and computer technologies for development (ICT4D) by the UNDP in its 2001 Human Development Report,[12] *Making New Technologies Work for Human Development*. In this context, new media art had potentially new areas to work in, and new ways to intervene in policy discussions on ICT and development.

Much development discourse concerning media is based on the idea that technological leapfrogs would enable underdeveloped societies to catch up thanks to new technologies, a concept typically operationalised at the level of infrastructure. We would like to argue that a socio-technical approach to information infrastructure better explains the case by thinking of it as an ecology of systems that emerges from the interaction between people,[13] activities and structures. In this approach infrastructures are seen

11. Robert Hunter Wade, 'Bridging the Digital Divide: New Route to Development or New Form of Dependency?', in Global Governance, October-December, 8:4, 2002, pp 443–66

12. UNDP, *Human Development Report 2001: Making New Technologies Work for Human Development*, United Nations Development Programme, New York, 2001

13. L S Star and K Ruhleder, 'Steps Toward an Ecology of Infrastructure: Design and Access for Large Information Spaces', Information Systems Research, 7:1, 1996, pp 111–34

not merely as technical, but as the norms, social formations and conventions that enable practices. At the same time, in recent years the cultural agenda has also changed from the idea that culture is an elitist consumption towards its consideration in development and social programmes.[14]

Socialising the idea of infrastructure and embracing culture as development process both fostered the current institutional interest in new media art. At the same time it is important to recognise the 'expediency' of culture analysed by George Yúdice, for whom cultural interventions funded by development agencies (and to a great extent arts funding in the West shares this agenda) must not only achieve significant aesthetic 'goals' but provide employment, replace failing education systems by inculcating new skills, and counter the desocialising results of missing social programmes lost to IMF restrictions on state-supported welfare. When the demand by funders that the whole process be apolitical is added to this burden, the most intense innovations are required.[15]

Thus we believe that, alongside the institutionalisation of ICT, reconsidered in terms of a socio-technical procedure, we also need to understand how people get involved with the use of particular technologies, for example, by recycling its use into new forms. Marcus Neustetter mentions in his article how people are embracing technology more than we think, knowing that it gives them access to a variety of services. Though this approach to technology can mimic the old centre-out model of publishing and media, making the user a one-way media receiver; when people raise questions about the capacities of the technology, there is the potential to develop dialogic values that were previously unavailable.

NEW MEDIA VICINITIES

Although many representations could provide a focus for discussions of new media, in the case of video and electronic art in the non-Western world, a particularly fruitful one is that of the city which the discourse of new media art has tried to abstract as an 'Other' space. There is no doubt that, after decades of migratory displacement, the megacities such as São Paulo, Mexico City or Delhi are not merely similar to any modern city: they also become portrayers of the ideas and desires of their inhabitants. As Néstor García Canclini comments: 'as a result of this kind of situation, national cultures lose their influence in the social definition of identity, and new modes of definition are accepted'.[16] In this sense, local culture acts as a repository of popular narrative, creating a space where modernity and tradition converge through day-to-day practice.

Eduardo de Jesús, in this issue, points out how in many underdeveloped countries television is still a very important instrument in social life. New media occupy a more peripheral position, but as a result can promote alternative ways of using the media. On the one hand, new media have to escape from the conventional formats that dominate the mass media. On the other, they give access to the means of production. Both tactics depend on whether or not there are resources, where by 'resources' we mean the socio-technical networks of skills, policies and cultural orientations that make alternative social formations so central to new media in the developing world. We still believe that true originality lies in the work that does not enslave itself to the Western mainstream,

14. Vijayendra Rao and Michael Walton, *Culture And Public Action*, Stanford University Press, Stanford, CA, 2004

15. George Yúdice, *The Expediency of Culture: Uses of Culture in the Global Era*, Duke University Press, Durham, NC, 2003

16. Néstor García Canclini, *Hybrid Cultures: Strategies for Entering and Leaving Modernity*, trans Christopher L Chiappari and Silvia L López, University of Minnesota Press, Minneapolis, Minnesota, 1995

but we recognise work which also plays with it as a way of reconstructing an indigenised, tropicalised image. We are also embarking on a completely global phenomenon in the distribution of information. Not only have the channels for its diffusion expanded, thanks to the internet, but both the size of and the interconnections between cities that gather people into globalised groups are growing at much the same rate.[17] When successful non-Western artists become trapped by the system of mainstream art, one of the most convincing temptations for them is that of scale. Ten years ago, the scarcity of technology required either the loan of equipment to artists or the provision of centres where they could work for periods of time. These 'media labs' and similar centres in many instances also became institutionalised, not least through their effective monopoly on the means of artistic production. Today this picture has been challenged. Projects require socialised, even gregarious, human resources far more than facilities and equipment in order to make them happen. In her article in this issue, Olga Goriunova notes that the net.art scene in Russia was initially supported by social formations, such as Moscow MediaArtLab. But, as she asserts, many of these initiatives carried an impregnated deterministic and instrumentalist ideology that made evident a limited and limiting interpretation of technology.

The absence of an uninterrupted, lived tradition of critical inquiry into and artistic engagement with technology led to the spread of a certain ideology regarding media or digital media which can be characterised as deterministic, instrumentalist and essentialist. Even when the origins of technologies are considered to be social, their effects are believed to spring from the technologies rather than from their complex uses. Since Kant and Hegel, technologies have been defined as having a teleology other than themselves: unlike living creatures, for whom the goal – to live – is intrinsic, the purposes of technologies are external to themselves – to carry out whatever they were designed to do. Technology is also described in essentialist terms in that the designed purpose is held to override every attempt at repurposing. Technology is still usually regarded today as a black-box phenomenon, either more or less neutral, incapable of playing any significant role in original creation or cultural life at large; or alternatively as vicious, inhuman and destructive of civilization. We renounce these models and argue that technology has no essence, not even in the sense of Martin Heidegger's claim that 'the essence of technology is nothing technological'.[18] Nor is it determining of what people do with it. Given these conditions, we reject the notion that technology 'is' good or evil: it is as much a part of the human ecology as climate, water, soil, animals and the laws of physics. Taking this perspective, contemporary Russian culture, for example, is unprepared to accept technological forms of art or even of technology culturally as not merely an information channel but as what informs, shapes and structures our world, and in turn is informed, shaped and structured by it. This perspective is reinforced by consideration of how video art was conceived in China, a country in which art has been seen as utilitarian and functionalist. Pi Li reminds us that video is a communication channel, and in China, thanks to the medium's ease of use, its widespread adoption and familiar mode of communication, it became a conduit for art that reflected its audience. In this it differed from the initial uses of video art in the West, as a critique of the medium of television. In China

17. Saskia Sassen, Foreword, in *Reformatting Politics: Information Technology and Global Civil Society*, J Dean, J W Anderson and G Lovink, Routledge, New York, pp vii-xiii, 2006

18. Martin Heidegger, 'The Question Concerning Technology', in *The Question Concerning Technology and Other Essays*, trans William Lovitt, Harper & Row, New York, 1977, pp 3–35

video became popular because of its richness and diversity, and, to a great extent, the empowering capacity of the technological medium.

Arturo Escobar criticises post-development literature as having romanticised local traditions and local social movements, ignoring the fact that the local is also embedded in global power relations and that many of the struggles of today are around access to information.[19] This is even more the case with media technologies, where global flows of programme formats and content are essential components of the broadcast and internet economies, as in the case of Rede Globo and Televisa, the Brazilian and Mexican multinational broadcast companies, of Al-Jazeera and BBC World satellite and internet services, and the vast if only semi-public world of news, video and photographic agencies like Visnews, Reuters and Magnum. As the de facto dominant communication media in the world today, TV and the internet – increasingly interwoven with each other and with mobile media – play a central role as distribution media for locally produced content which then serves a global market. We should note also the importance of technical standards bodies like the ISO, ITU and the IETF, responsible respectively for electrical and engineering standards, telecommunications standardisation and international pricing, and for the stabilisation of internet protocols and formats like html, xml or mpeg. A handful of operating systems dominate global computing – Windows, Mac OS/Unix and Linux. A single corporation, Cisco Systems, has effective control over the market for core devices such as switches and routers. If on the one hand this seems like a recipe for global homogenisation, it is also the ground on which complex retro-engineering and recombinant strategies have been and can be built, perhaps most notably in the FLOSS (Free Libre Open Source Software) movement and through mass participation projects like Project Gutenberg and Wikipedia. In this issue, Ravi Sundaram revisits the technology markets of Delhi to demonstrate the inventiveness of ordinary people, undaunted by all this standardisation, and the regimes of intellectual property and internet governance that accompany it. But questions remain. What information is available, and to whom? How is information processed from its universal Western technological mode into local cultural meanings? And when these new local meanings begin to articulate themselves, how, if at all, are they able to broadcast themselves either locally or back into some putative global commons?

NEW SOCIAL FORMATIONS AND NEW MEDIA PRACTICE

During the last decade many social formations in developing countries have claimed to be the voice of new media and culture. Not all of them had been particularly active or successful in their own countries. A common intention of many of these social formations was to become visible internationally by doing projects specifically designed to be recognised outside their country. This is a sign and a consequence of globalisation, particularly in large cities. For example, Videobrasil, a group based in São Paulo, works with artists from Lebanon and is developing projects in South Africa. This decontextualised process, though it demonstrates a will to open up to new cultures by bypassing the metropolitan centres, has become part of an institutional setting,

19. Arturo Escobar, 'Beyond the Search for a Paradigm? Post-Development and Beyond', *Developments*, 43:4, 2000, pp 11–14

promoted by an international cultural scene that fosters cultural exchange among different non-Western groups in pursuit of novelty and creativity which it must often feel the metropolitan centres themselves can no longer provide. Though the idea of cultural exchange in itself may not seem bad, too often the emphasis falls on the exchange of culture as commodity exchange rather than as something that might bring a new meaning or outcome to the setting or the community in which it was deployed. Sometimes these initiatives become so delocalised that it may seem difficult to define a beneficiary group or audience. In such circumstances, cultural exchange becomes an object of consumption for connoisseurs, and its social repercussion is minimal.

Self-organising actors have in many instances brought a new way of thinking, introducing more Western-based concepts such as transparency and pluralism. Nina Czegledy and Andrea Szekeres described how the Soros Centers for Contemporary Arts supported culture in general and contemporary new media arts in particular through their network in Eastern Europe. Although the Soros Centers were conceived initially as institutionalising functions of donor capitalism, many of these art centres became key generators of new social formations, promoting flexibility, addressing topical issues, promoting new initiatives, and opening themselves to change at the hands of their users.

TECHNO-CULTURAL TRADITIONS

New media also offer a way of embracing tradition and modernity. Laura Marks, in this issue, argues that Islamic number science and its integration into Islamic art foreshadow the development of digital media in the twentieth century. The process is not unfamiliar. European and North American modernism has looted the supermarkets of colonised and indigenous cultures for more than a century. What is significant in our context is that Marks posits an absolute continuity between tradition and digital modernity in Islam. In her contribution, Maree Mills shows how video and digital media have enabled indigenous artists to engage with Maori philosophy. In a different case, in the Andean regions of Peru the use of video cameras have enabled not only the preservation of oral traditions in communities, but also, perhaps even more significantly, it has enabled those traditions to be diffused via a VHS or a DVD to other communities in which that knowledge was already lost. In both Maori and Quechua cases, as well as many more, the technological artefact is used as a way to preserve but also evolve traditions. Similarly, in Guatemala, whose indigenous population amounts to about eighty-five per cent of the total, a new use of technology in the arts, heavily based on performance and rituals related to their cultural traditions, has evolved. Understood as a tool for the construction of objective or instrumental knowledge, photography constructed the colonial Other as the object, rather than the subject of knowledge, whose own codes of visual communication were excluded from the process and deemed wholly known through an external visual discourse. In the case of Peru, as Delfín and Zegarra recount, there is a permanent struggle between, on one side, a patrimonialist discourse and vision of the territory, discursively fixed in the collective imaginary as the only path towards local legitimisation and international recognition; and on the other, a growing scenario of global aspirations related to digital paradigms and more critical research on recent memory. Curiously, while the former fixed vision may well be a reminiscence of the past, the latter runs the risk of succumbing to current techno-deterministic political agendas that come from the West. Technologies paradigmatically place the tools for cultural evolution in the hands of younger generations. Indigenous cultural reductionism can take the form of refusal to use non-traditional media as a mode of resistance to colonisation but, by enabling a new kind of cultural activism, it allows groups to become more autonomous in telling their stories, both to each other and where appropriate to potential allies in struggles such as that of the Zapatista peasants of Chiapas. At such points, tactical media become strategic and should be understood as a road to liberation: not merely resisting Western intellectual property but constructing peer-to-peer networks for sharing their ideas and productions.

The global art institution has its favourite 'Other' cities: São Paulo, Dakar, Havana and so on. In the intervening layer of regions, organisations may act as hub for a cluster of initiatives. This is distinct from those social formations which arrange cultural exchange for the delectation of the global market. For example, as Ernesto Calvo and María José Monge point out, Costa Rica is seen, particularly in the new media art scene, as one of the main activators of experimental work in Central America. New media art production in Costa Rica has acquired a significant role in the years since 2000. This phenomenon is inevitably associated with the promotion platform developed from within an institutional setting, the Contemporary Art and Design Museum. As the main hub of the Central American new media art scene, Costa Rica is also strategic: there is little interest in the artworld in what is happening in Nicaragua, Honduras or other Central American countries, but clustering several countries together does give greater opportunity to interconnect, to support small nations and language cultures, to provide instruction and material support. It is only as a result of these regional initiatives that international visibility becomes possible, and that visibility is secondary to the dynamic of regional cultural dialogue. These types of regional cluster are also a way of making visible troubles that are not usually so evident, if seen in a granular sense, but which when collected may not only become visible but meaningful to a broader audience. The same could be said of the work of Akram Zaatari in contemporary Lebanon, as Hannah Feldman describes it in her essay. Feldman mentions the importance of archives as cultural repositories that represent different experiential approaches to history and constructed identities performed by a multiplicity of buried desires. Such memory archives are in many cases situated in artist-originated social formations of the kinds described in this issue.

CONCLUSION: EMBRACING THE IDEA OF TRADITION AND MODERNITY

Institutionalisation is not always necessary. Indeed, sometimes, especially when dealing with dispersed groups of people, institutionalisation may seem far from compelling as a mode of operation and its outcomes too complicated to measure. It has been clear since Marx – to everyone not devoted to neo-liberal fundamentalism – that human activity, human creativity, is fundamentally social. This is the foundation of the theory of the general intellect, first mooted in Karl Marx's *Grundrisse*, and recently warmly debated among post-autonomist political philosophers in Italy and elsewhere. The sum total of human knowledge and skill never resides in a single individual but in the social. Social formations are ways of managing this common inheritance, either for the benefit of a small elite of owners, or for the general welfare of all, or at least of the largest number. The anarchy of the 'free' market produces neither an adequate living for all, nor innovation. As Paolo Virno argues, innovation is a devolved process: 'the task of the worker or of the clerk to some extent consists in actually finding, in discovering expedients, "tricks", solutions which ameliorate the organization of labour'.[20] What is specific to our post-Fordist period in history is that communication functions as a means of production. The question of who controls it is of the highest importance. This is why alternative forms of organisation in arts and cultural projects are of such significance, and why they risk being turned from radical innovation into the unpaid research and development of information capitalism. The analogy with the sourcing of aesthetic innovation in marginalised cultures need not be emphasised for readers of *Third Text*.

Even in densely populated cities, where the use of technology is much more intense, differences of wealth no longer determine access to communication. The inventiveness of a large proportion of the population challenges established companies and their commercial offerings. In that sense, the only way to encourage radical innovation, which is at least difficult to recuperate into the dominant forms of managerialism, must be based on the understanding that technological infrastructures embrace language, culture and the common inheritance of the general intellect. This alone provides the potential to think critically about the context and diverse uses of a technology in people's everyday existence: how it improves their lives, not by homogenising but by being open to diverse scenarios. A large city or the capital of an underdeveloped country may act as a threshold of possibilities; for example, in South Africa, people-interaction is much preferred to mediated interfaces, even if the latter offer greater convenience and efficiency. We can certainly assume that ICTs and culture, both elements embedded in new media, may not be a bad way to forge new local practices. However, the particular way organisations try to use them may become institutionalised and act as part of a broader globalising agenda, one which actively produces underdevelopment as a necessary element of the world system. In the case of new media, as a global and international development, a global agenda may suit a very narrow international elite and have little significance for local users, at which point its significance is diluted or destroyed.

The notion of the museum and of cultural spaces is also challenged by organisational appropriations of alternative spaces. The internet is one of these alternative spaces that, though it has been institutionalised in many of the cases we examine in this issue, still has the capacity to act as an experimental social formation, especially when access is offered and there is not an uncritically accepted agenda of 'how to use it'. Such

20. Paolo Virno, *A Grammar of the Multitude: For an Analysis of Contemporary Forms of Life*, trans Isabella Bertoletti, James Cascaito and Andrea Casson, Semiotext(e), Los Angeles, CA, 2004, p 63

access is not merely a matter of being able to sit down in front of a computer. It implies access to the inner workings of the machine, such that it can be adapted and indigenised. That in turn implies a sharing of expertise and a willingness to acquire it. Both sharing and will to acquire are themselves cultural issues. Where there is no reason to want to learn how to make computers do what we want, there is no motivation to learn about them. This chicken-and-egg situation is where the innovative organisational skills of many of our cases come into play. After an all too brief period of anarchy, the internet has increasingly settled into the one-way model of broadcasting which has dominated communications in the developing world for thirty years or more. In some respects, the internet may be understood as even more powerful, both because of its ability to recruit unpaid labour to provide content for corporately owned social networking sites like MySpace (Murdoch) and Flickr (Yahoo!) and YouTube (Google); and because of its technical base in the TCP/IP suite of tools, a regime of control which Alex Galloway describes as 'protocol',[21] a new mode of biopolitical management, one in which certain kinds of illegitimate actions are no longer disciplined or assimilated but are simply impossible.

In a series of lectures given towards the end of his life, Michel Foucault mooted the thesis that the 'disciplinary' mode of rule, typical of the transition to modernity, had been exchanged at some point during the nineteenth century for a new biopolitical order.[22] Where the old regime relied on the disciplining of individuals and the inculcation of discipline in each citizen, the new biopolitical order was a management of populations in the mass. The model of the old regime was the panopticon; that of the new was epidemiology and the regulations surrounding the control of biological life. Armed with the 'social physics' of statistical social science, and with actuarial risk-management techniques derived from the insurance industry, the biopolitical state aimed not at total regulation but at measurable success - for example in mortality rates – and on bracketing off previously unacceptable crimes or injuries as acceptable rates of criminality and accidents that could be ameliorated through various social instruments like media campaigns and neighbourhood watch schemes. Galloway's protocological rule moves one step further: certain kinds of criminality (for example the theft of intellectual property – critical to the new economy of the USA) become impossible due to control over the technical means of distribution. Meanwhile, these same infrastructures can be painted as, and indeed in many senses are, vehicles of a new kind of freedom. Galloway's point is that such freedom is always circumscribed, always permitted, always at the mercy of the power to control protocols. Of particular interest in our present context is that this new mode of power is the first truly to extend beyond national borders – the first genuinely global political regime.

Reflecting on a similarly Foucauldian analysis of freedom and control in network communications, Wendy Hui Kyong Chun argues that the translation of human language into software commands 'perpetuates master–slave relations … reduces freedom to control, language to program and commands'. But she concludes her reflections by arguing that 'These languages may not allow for polysemy – meaning can only be opened by rewriting the languages and their compilers – but the future remains open'.[23] Today more than ever, the internet and new

21. Alexander R Galloway, *Protocol: How Control Exists After Decentralization*, MIT Press, Cambridge, MA, 2004

22. Michel Foucault, *Society Must be Defended: Lectures at the Collège de France 1975–76*, eds Mauro Bertani and Alessandro Fontana, trans David Macey, Penguin, London, 2003; *The Birth of Biopolitics: Lectures at the Collège de France, 1978–1979*, ed Michel Senellart, trans Graham Burchell, Palgrave Macmillan, Basingstoke, 2004; *Security, Population, Territory: Lectures at the Collège de France 1977–1978*, Michel ed Senellart, trans Graham Burchell, Palgrave Macmillan, Basingstoke, 2007

23. Wendy Hui-Kyong Chun, *Control and Freedom: Power and Paranoia in the Age of Fiber Optics*, MIT Press, Cambridge, MA, p 297

media more generally are becoming much more malleable. It is in this sense that they retain the power to generate critical meanings.

Technology is socially adaptable. For that reason we can speak of 'new' technologies, despite their sixty years of history, when the dynamics of the apparatus allow users to tell suppressed stories and experience new narrative forms in groups with rich oral culture and social interaction. Capital treads a fine line in the management of innovation: too much innovation too quickly runs the risk of revolutionising not only techniques but the social organisations which are implicated in them. Media history teaches us that key innovations (sound, film, FM radio, Open Source) have been the objects of often successful attempts to stifle innovation in the interests of maintaining a profitable status quo. The irrationality of the market is everywhere apparent: given the current global financial crisis, news in January 2009 of US bank executives in the US paying themselves billion-dollar bonuses demonstrates that the hidden hand of the market is quite capable of slitting its own wrist. Capital fears innovation as much as it craves it. Satirising and sabotaging the major portals and e-businesses that dominate internet traffic is merely tactical; building alternatives to them in the form of peer-to-peer networks and new modes of organisation is strategic. The kinds of social and aesthetic projects analysed here not only awake interest in originality, but also contribute critical reflection on both the dominant culture and the emerging museumification of media art. The yearning to be incorporated into universality, to which the global standardisation of internet protocols appeals, is not a desire that can be diffused with a few pretty splash pages and a smattering of free speech ranters. Once awakened, that demand for universality is also a demand for universal justice and equal access not just to computers but to the wealth and power monopolised by the West. The best new media artefacts are not necessarily websites or installations: they may well be the artefacts of new organisational forms, linking local to global struggles, building solidarities. Such artefacts are ready to burst into new forms and to change forever the habits of use designed into our digital tools. Such resistant fragmentations are the enclaves of difference and change.

Taking a Line for a Walk,
from the Abbasid Caliphate to Vector Graphics

Laura U Marks

Une ligne pour le plaisir d'être ligne, d'aller, ligne. Points. Poudre de points. Une ligne rêve. On n'avait jusque-là jamais laissé rêver une ligne.

Henri Michaux on the art of Paul Klee[1]

The poet Michaux writes that never before Klee had a line been allowed to dream, to be a line for the pleasure of being a line. In fact the line had been permitted to dream quite extravagantly long before it celebrated its liberty in European painting, and also before it swirled on a phosphorescent screen.

This article looks at two kinds of dreaming line – the pen-stroke of Islamic calligraphy and the vector of computer graphics – and the points or pixels that rudely awakened them. In both cases there are implications for plasticity and politics. Islamic art cultivated new kinds of lines that seemed to take on lives of their own; it also found ways to discipline the line and subordinate it to the point. The history of Islamic calligraphy is shaped by profound philosophical, theological and even political debates over the relationship between the fixed point and the moving line. In computer art as well, a process of standardisation subsumed the lively line of vector graphics to the rigours of the pixel. The history of computer graphics retraces some of the contours of a debate that occurred 900 years ago.

This article is part of a larger project that proposes an Islamic genealogy of new media art. My research traces how principles of Islamic art travelled westward to inform the development of European abstraction, and then to re-flower in contemporary algorithmic artworks. One goal of this research is to underline historical and plastic connections between seemingly disparate practices. Another goal is to allow the history of Islamic art, and the Islamic philosophy, theology and science that accompany it, to pose questions to new media art; to offer an Islamic critique of new media art.

1. Henri Michaux, 'Aventures de lignes', *Oeuvres Complètes*, Gallimard, Paris, 2001, p 362

I have posited that several plastic qualities are shared by Islamic art and computer-based art.² In this article I examine one of these, namely an emphasis on performativity rather than representation. The work of art plays out in time, unfolding image from information and information from experience, in the performance of algorithmic instructions and/or the attentive recognition of observers.³ The relationship between point and line is performative, in that a line is drawn out from a point in duration: this might be the duration of sculpting wet stucco, of writing, of connecting points with light, or of the act of following such lines with one's eyes. When the line stops, or when the point dictates the movements of the line, the experience of duration is changed as well.

You may recognise in this lively line what Gilles Deleuze and Félix Guattari called the abstract line or nomad line which they found in art that does not tame the line into a contour: in Gothic art, taking up the thesis of art historian Wilhelm Worringer, and also in nomad art and children's art.

> Whereas the rectilinear – or 'regularly' rounded – Egyptian line is negatively motivated by anxiety in the face of all that passes, flows or varies, the nomad line is abstract in an entirely different sense, precisely because it has a multiple orientation and passes *between* points, figures and contours. It is positively motivated by the smooth space it draws, not by any striation it might perform to ward off anxiety and subordinate the smooth.⁴

Needless to say, the aniconism of Islamic art, or its tendency to avoid figurative representation, provides a healthy environment for abstraction, for lines to be free not to depict. The unsubordinated, lively line Deleuze and Guattari described was already undulating in Islamic art as early as the ninth century.

I begin this genealogy of the abstract line in the middle, in 1926. In *Point and Line to Plane*, Wassily Kandinsky suggested that the line itself is invisible; it is 'the trail left by the point in motion… It comes about through movement – indeed, by destroying the ultimately self-contained repose of the point.'⁵ This line destroys as it creates; it is a time-based line that has no existence independent of movement. In figurative art, the line serves representation or depiction, such as when it is a contour that defines a figure. Kandinsky describes a line that is free to become. We see the activities of this line in the modern paintings of the early twentieth century. In Kandinsky, the line is always struggling – sometimes smashed into a haptic smudge, sometimes striated into a geometric arc. In Klee the line takes leave of representation by turns stealthily, ironically, muscularly and diffidently. Klee himself wrote that he would like to 'take a line for a walk', and in his paintings and drawings, lines do get to stretch their legs and tentatively test their powers.

When defined not by position but by direction, lines become vectors, a vector being, in mathematics, a quantity that is wholly defined by magnitude and direction. Media historian Claus Pias suggests that the lively and destructive line of which Kandinsky wrote points forward to the vector of computer graphics.⁶ In vector graphics the line emanating from the centre of the monitor is actually a moving point that leaves behind it a trail of light as it connects one point to another. Here is the incarnation in phosphorus of Kandinsky's principle – a line that has only a momentary existence as a connection between points. Vector graphics

2. See Laura U Marks, 'Infinity and Accident: Strategies of Enfoldment in Islamic Art and Computer Art', *Leonardo*, 39:1, winter 2006, pp 37–42.

3. For the relationship between image, information and experience, please see my 'Enfolding and Unfolding: An Aesthetics for the Information Age', an interactive article produced in collaboration with designer Raegan Kelly, *Vectors: Journal of Culture and Technology in a Dynamic Vernacular*, 1:3, available at http://www.vectorsjournal.org.

4. Gilles Deleuze and Félix Guattari, '1440: The Smooth and the Striated', in *A Thousand Plateaus: Capitalism and Schizophrenia*, trans Brian Massumi, University of Minnesota Press, Minneapolis, 1987, pp 496–7

5. Wassily Kandinsky, *Point and Line to Plane*, trans Howard Dearstyne and Hilla Rebay, Dover Publications, New York, 1979 (first published 1926)

6. Claus Pias, 'Point and Line to Raster – On the Genealogy of Computer Graphics', in *Ornament and Abstraction*, ed Markus Brüderlin, Fondation Beyeler, Basel, 2001, pp 64–9

occur in their rawest form in oscilloscope and radar, those solidly analogue screen-based media whose moving points index physical locations or properties. Vector graphics can draw quickly in real time with very few data, making them ideal for the early computer arcade games. Vector graphics are now used in 3D animation software like Flash and drawing software like Illustrator. These programs are powerful for the speed and economy with which they draw contours in real time, as well as their scalability.[7]

The living–dying line of vector graphics is taken up poetically by Sean Cubitt who defines the vector in Deleuzian terms as a line that describes not being but becoming, not identity but mobile relationship.[8] Vector-based images are not beings but becomings, and their becoming is pulled by a certain directional force. The abstract line and its vector incarnation, in their directionality and continual movement, embody a kind of non-sentient will or non-organic life.

The television screen disciplined the vector into the raster, drawing the electron beam across the screen into 525 parallel lines (in NTSC video). The raster is an indentured vector, endlessly retracing the same paths like a tenant farmer ploughing the field season after season. The digital screen replaced even this time-based act of drawing with the mosaic-like array of pixels, converting the line to vector dots. The performative act of drawing was replaced by the all-at-once of an array of points.

With the exception of Flash-type graphics, vector graphics have been mostly surpassed by the pixel-based image. Both Pias and Cubitt note with regret the subsumption of the vector by the bit map, the real-time drawing on the computer screen by the discrete sample. Cubitt, the Deleuzian film scholar, sees the vector as a principle of narrative, which invents the future in a universe that is ultimately open. He sees the obsolescence of the vector as tragic at the level of narrative, as the vector's principle of becoming gives way to the fixed universe of what he calls neo-baroque cinema.[9] Pias, the modernist media historian, argues that vector graphics are the true modern art, being a direct effect of the action of the medium, while pixel-based images are tired old naturalistic illusionism.[10] He finds it a shame that the transparency of the vector-based screen, which allows us to see how it builds its image, gives way to the opacity of the pixel-based screen. In the vector was movement and performed real-time connection; in the pixel, connections are hidden, movement stops, and the resulting image cannot be considered any kind of living act.

In Islamic art, the fleeting immaterial nature of the line and the sense of the point pulling it along in a trajectory arrive to us recorded on stone, stucco, ceramic and paper; this can occur in both writing and the curvilinear abstraction of the arabesque. Looking at Islamic art compels me to redefine the vector as *the power of signification that propels a sign to have meaning for a certain receiver*. Islamic art is performative in that its vector, though supposedly coming from the divine to the human, is nonetheless activated by the human receiver.

During the flurry of building construction that took place in mid-ninth-century Iraq, a new style arose. Historians of Islamic art call it the 'bevelled style' or, because of one of its places of origin, the Third Samarra Style. This style evolved from the leaf and vine forms of Byzantine sculpture into a curvilinear abstract form that is both linear and sculptural.

7. Thanks to Keith Sanborn for setting me straight on vector graphics.

8. Sean Cubitt, *The Cinema Effect*, MIT Press, Cambridge, MA, 2004, pp 70–1

9. Ibid, p 249

10. Pias, op cit, p 68

When you look at it, as you can at the Pergamon Museum in Berlin, this form seems constantly to shift between figure and ground, space and void. Made of stucco, the Third Samarra Style shows the sure and sweeping movements of the craftsman, working while the material was still wet. Its line seems to possess a life of its own, a muscular, internal trajectivity. Art historians fall over themselves to qualify this style as the origin of the arabesque and other kinds of overall abstract ornament in Islamic art.[11]

The arabesque is a form in which line multiplies, branches and doubles back on itself, until it takes on an additional dimension: it almost becomes a plane. It gives the eye freedom to follow it in any direction, suggesting the possibility of infinite growth.[12] Computer art is also familiar with the shimmering fractal surface built by the activities of abstract lines. Beautiful and sophisticated examples can be found in the digital drawings of artist-programmer Mauro Annunziato, who uses genetic algorithms to create vectors that have self-organising, emergent 'behaviours'. Each line in Annunziato's digital print *Migration* (2000), in the series 'Artificial Societies', is programmed to grow and 'reproduce'. He describes the activity of a similar work as follows:

> An individual [a line] dies when it meets the trail of another individual. Otherwise it can die a natural death (depending on a mortality factor). One single individual can generate a son with similar genetic map but with a lower energy. This position is established to evoke plant growth: the *branch-sons* are thinner than the parent. The reproduction rate is regulated by a reproduction probability (fecundity). A minimal threshold of energy is required for reproduction.[13]

In the effort to live as long as possible, the vectors in *Migration* dart across space, seek uninhabited spaces in which to grow, produce offspring, and curl in on themselves. Like the Third Samarra Style and the Islamic arabesque, Annunziato's picture suggests an infinity of directions for the eye to follow and produces a shimmering surface that confounds the difference between figure and ground, space and void.

Islamic calligraphy shares many of the properties of the living line of the arabesque. Deleuze and Guattari passed over Islamic calligraphy in their genealogy of the abstract line, perhaps because they considered writing to be a disciplining of the line.[14] But that is not necessarily so.

11. One of the definitive assertions of the genealogy of the arabesque in the Third Samarra Style is Oleg Grabar, *The Formation of Islamic Art*, Yale University Press, New Haven–London, 1973 (revised and enlarged 1987), pp 187–9.

12. Ibid, p 188. Gülru Necipoğlu compares the Third Samarra style to primordial matter in *The Topkapi Scroll: Geometry and Ornament in Islamic Architecture*, Getty Center for the History of Art and the Humanities, Santa Monica, 1995.

13. Mauro Annunziato, 'The Nagual Experiment', *Proceedings of the First International Conference on Generative Art*, Milan, December 1998; available at http://www.plancton.com.

14. Deleuze and Guattari, op cit, p 497

Mauro Annunziato, *Migration,* 2000, digital print, collection of the artist, photo: Mauro Annunziato, courtesy of the artist

The many varieties, decorative functions and degrees of legibility of Islamic calligraphy show that its purpose is not limited to conveying a textual meaning. Written on skin or paper, carved in stone or woven in textile, these Arabic words become other things, lines that by turn communicate, embody and fly away.

Calligraphy and other kinds of abstract ornament possess the vector-like capacity to pull the worshipper toward the divine as though toward a magnet. Writing the Qur'an is a form of prayer, as it is repeating in time the words spoken by God. The calligrapher, as described by contemporary calligrapher Abdel Ghani Alani, must be both present and absent, as though daydreaming; as though the 'energy' that motivates the writing moves both from beyond the calligrapher and through him or her.[15] In so far as writing embodies the act of prayer, it is not a fixed symbol but the trace of a performative act. In Islam, according to art historian Oleg Grabar, what holds the community together is language, spoken or written, as it is the intermediary of prayer. Thus calligraphy and other kinds of ornament perform the space of worship.[16] In several ways, then, Islamic calligraphy can be considered the visible, living line of a community of faith – the vector that holds the community in a relation with God.

It is not a surprise to find one of the most compelling descriptions of the performativity of the vector halfway between iconophilic Europe and the aniconic Islamic world, in Byzantine art. The Emperor Constantine V (reign 741–775) denounced images as impious because they are *composed of lines, and hence finite*: 'If the icon draws the figure of the divine, it encloses the infinite within its line, which is impossible.'[17] Constantine's astonishing decree could be taken as justifying Islamic aniconism, for Islamic disapproval of making figural representations of divine beings also expresses a kind of artist's modesty in the face of the infinite. But, as Marie-José Mondzain writes, Eastern Christian religious icons were defended against Constantine's iconoclasm in so far as they were not discrete images (thus subject to idolatry) but indications of the *directionality* of divine intention, performed by the worshipping viewer. The icon, Mondzain writes, 'made in the image of [the "natural image" of] Christ, will no longer be expressive, signifying, or referential. It will not be inscribed within the space of a gap, but will *incarnate withdrawal itself.*'[18] The religious icon compels the worshipper to gaze into its absence, beyond it, towards the unknowable face of God. Icons, like Islamic calligraphy and ornament, are not images but *vectors* towards the divine.

All the vector-like artworks I have described, from the digital drawing to religious writing, maintain a latent performativity that can take place, even centuries later, on the part of the *subject* who unfolds the work.[19]

FIXING THE POINT

Around the time that the Third Samarra Style was being sculpted on palace walls, Islamic philosophers in Iraq were attempting to account for the smallest elements of matter, ie, atoms. These theoretical physicists were a sub-group of the *kalam* theologians who struggled to develop a

15. Abdel Ghani Alani, *L'Ecriture de l'écriture: Traité de calligraphie arabo-musulmane*, Editions Dervy, Paris, 2002, p 18 (my translation)

16. Oleg Grabar, *The Mediation of Ornament*, Princeton University Press, Princeton, 1992, pp 103–11

17. Marie-José Mondzain, *Image, Icon, Economy: The Byzantine Origins of the Contemporary Imaginary*, trans Rico Franses, Stanford University Press, Palo Alto, 2004, p 73

18. Ibid, pp 80–81 (my emphasis)

19. This attribution of intention to a work of art, or at least the capacity to communicate to its receiver how it may be perceived, is the *Kunstwollen* posited by Aloïs Riegl, the art historian who identified a continuity of the increasingly abstract line from Greek to Byzantine to Islamic art.

rationalist philosophy in keeping with the Qur'an and independent of Greek philosophy. Their thought had manifold philosophical and political ramifications, only a small aspect of which I examine here.[20] The atomists argued that matter, space, time and motion are all composed of indivisible minimal parts, and that the entire created world could be understood as a combination of these atoms and the accidents that occur to them. The Islamic atomists debated hotly whether atoms had magnitude and extension, generally concluding, in line with Epicurus' doctrine of minimal parts, that they do.[21] In the early eleventh century, Ibn Mattawayah of Basra argued that atoms measure space by occupying it, and that they are not triangular or round, but resemble a square; he seems, writes historian Alnoor Dhanani, to have meant a cube.[22] The smallest possible line is made of two atoms; the smallest possible surface, four; and three-dimensional space is filled by eight atoms.[23]

Atomist philosophy fuelled fiery theological debates. When God sustains the universe, went the argument of Baghdadi radical atomist al-Nazzam (d 845), He sustains it one atom at a time, one motion at a time, with the command 'Continue to exist!'. By contrast, the Basrian Mu'tazila argued that continuing to exist is one of the properties of things, and that God only commands them to cease to exist.[24] In both cases it is evident that the atomist philosophers held a radically performative view of the universe: nothing can be counted on to endure, so both existence and cessation are acts performed by God's command.

The Mu'tazili doctrine on the createdness of the Qur'an was established as dogma in 818, only to be revoked by caliph al-Mutawakkil in 847, after which point the popularity and advisability of rationalist philosophy plummeted in the Sunni world. Nevertheless, atomism continued to inform Islamic thought, even the mysticism of reformed rationalist al-'Ash'ari. It is notable, then, that in the ninth century a doctrine of minimal parts reigned across philosophy and theology. The theory of minimal parts conceived of reality as both discrete and continuous; its continuity is not due to some internal power but to divine grace; and there is no need, and indeed no possibility, of a part smaller than the atom.

A century later in Iraq, an important functionary was also turning his attention to the minimal part. In the early tenth century the Abbasid caliphate, like other burgeoning bureaucracies, needed an efficient and legible script in which to keep its documents in order. Ibn Muqla (885–939), geometer and vizier to the Abbasid court in Baghdad, is credited with having created a standardised, proportioned Arabic writing based on geometry, *al-khatt al-mansub*. The word *khatt* means both a line of writing and a line of communication, as in airline, telephone line and railroad line; so we might think of *al-khatt al-mansub* as a regulated vector. Arabic etymology also shows the connection between the street and Islamic law (*shari'a* is the word for both), the road, the way (both *tariq*), faith, and a mystical order (*tariqat*); the path (*sirat*) and the straight path of religious practice (*sirat al mustaqim*).[25] All these vector-like etymologies bring together movement along a line, correct collective practice, and the yearning for the divine. It seems, then, that proportioned writing is synechdotal of Sunni religious practice. The system did not necessarily cramp the calligrapher's style, but established limits in which an individual's style could appear to advantage[26] – much as each

20. For a summary of these debates, which were inextricably theological, philosophical and political, see the chapter 'The Early Rationalists' in Tilman Nagel, *The History of Islamic Theology: From Muhammad to the Present*, trans Thomas Thornton, Markus Wiener, Princeton, 2000.

21. Although the Mu'tazili atomists did not translate Greek texts (unlike the Islamic *falasifa*, or philosophers who developed the Greek tradition), Dhanani points out that their concept of the minimal part having extension was similar to that of Epicurus. The Greeks did not distinguish between physical and geometric space. While Aristotle argued that a line cannot be composed of points, Epicurus insisted that it can, because the minimal part has extension in space. Zeno of Sidon founded his paradox in this debate over the nature of the point. Alnoor Dhanani, *The Physical Theory of Kalām: Atoms, Space, and Void in Basrian Mu'tazili Cosmology*, E J Brill, Leiden–New York–Cologne, 1994, p 103

22. Ibid, p 115

23. Ibid, p 95

24. Ibid, pp 43–37

25. I thank David Simonowitz for pointing out these etymologies.

26. Hassan Massoudy with Isabelle Nitzer, *Calligraphie arabe vivante*, Flammarion, Paris, 1998, p 49

Abu'l Hasan, *'Alî ibn Hilal, known as Ibn al-Bawwab*, Qu'ran page, c 1000, Baghdad, courtesy of the Chester Beatty Library, Dublin

believer prays in his or her own way, even while following established practice.

Proportioned writing became the basis of templates for several different scripts, all of which are still in use.[27] This standardisation was based on multiples of the smallest mark, namely the cross-section of a reed pen, as a point, rhomboid in shape. This point becomes the basis of all other measurement. In Ibn Muqla's system, the straight line is defined as the trace that springs from a point.[28] The line arises from the point; the line is also, now, composed of a series of points. It is commonly said that if the point (which first shows up in the alphabet as the diacritical mark under the letter *beh*) is the mother of letters, the line (the letter *alif*) is the father.[29] This is so less because of its verticalness than because, rotated to form a circle, the *alif* describes the field of all possible letters in Ibn Muqla's standardisation of writing. We might say the line husbands or shepherds points in their field of activity. The line is latent in the point; the point is drawn out into a line in time. But, in systematised writing, nothing is smaller than the point.

Square atoms in philosophy. Square (or rhomboid) points in calligraphy. And now, square pixels in the contemporary screen. Each of these shapes is the basic unit of a potentially infinite extension. Yet, as a minimal part, it does not admit of internal extension. Standardisation stops at the point, and it is notable that the Arabic term for standardisation is *muqaf*, to fix or stop. There is infinite extension outward from

27. These include *naskhi, thoulthi, roqa, diwani,* and *farsi*. Ibid, pp 32–9

28. Alani, op cit, p 68

29. Ibid, p 70

the minimal part, and an infinite possibility of movement latent in the still point. No need to look for internal infinities. Standardised Arabic writing, based on the minimal part of the point, permitted an extensive infinity but not an intensive infinity or the infinitesimal.

THE POINT AND THE STATE

Critical historians of Islamic art and writing such as Brinkley Messick, Yasser Tabbaa, Gülru Necipoğlu, and Irene Bierman point out that standardised writing reinforced a general rationalisation of the state.[30] This occurred first secularly, as Ibn Muqla's system helped the Abbasid state to consolidate its power – a consolidation made easier by the introduction of paper, which, like every newly introduced bureaucratic technology, led to a proliferation in the production of bureaucratic documents. Subsequently, the standardisation of writing placed control of religious doctrine with the Abbasid state. Ibn Muqla, as vizier to three successive Abbasid caliphs, was called upon to produce a standardised recension of the Qur'an.[31] This second standardisation process had already begun during the Umayyad caliphate, when diacritical marks were added to the Qur'an in order to establish the vowels of each word, avoiding ambiguity. Tabbaa argues that the application of proportioned writing to the Qur'an under Ibn Muqla extended this process of control of doctrinal meaning; and that it was finally consolidated in the development of a more cursive but still clearly legible calligraphic style under Ibn Muqla's follower, the calligrapher Ibn al-Bawwab (d 1022).

The shapely *thuluth* and *nashki* texts that Ibn al-Bawwab developed began to appear all over the sacred texts of the Sunnis, both written in Qur'ans and carved in stone monuments;[32] they continue to be standard scripts. These styles showed up in the mosques of other Sunni states in what Tabbaa argues was a symbolic show of alliance with the Abbasid caliphate and against their common enemy, the Fatimids.[33] The statement that was increasingly communicated by the consolidating powers of the Sunni state was, 'Accept these truths as fundamental and do not question them'. This point was specifically concerned with the interpretation of the Qur'an. Those scholars who ultimately founded the Sunni tradition argued against excessive interpretation (*ijtihad*), with all its potential for quarrelling, and in favour of general public agreement on the meaning of the sacred text. For Sunni Islam of the Abbasid caliphate, standardised Arabic provided a sort of 'good enough infinity', capable of instilling awe and communicating grace while also remaining within a range of legibility that might be understood by all. Sunni Islam insisted that interpretation of the sacred text was no longer necessary; that infinite divine grace, the mystery of the divine, are to be found beyond the point – not within it.

The minimal part means there is no concept of the infinitesimal in standardised calligraphy; but it is capable of infinite extension. Especially under the Ottomans, the standard styles formed the basis of wonderfully fanciful and elaborate textual decorations, eg, the Ottoman *tughra* or state seal. Standardised calligraphy is also used to write quasi-figurative forms resembling tigers, birds, boats, and abstract patterns.

30. Yasser Tabbaa, *The Transformation of Islamic Art During the Sunni Revival*, University of Washington Press, Seattle–London, 2001; Gülru Necipoğlu, op cit; Irene A Bierman, *Writing Signs: The Fatimid Public Text*, University of California Press, Berkeley, 1998. Brinkley Messick demonstrates the close connections between writing and power in *The Calligraphic State: Textual Domination and History in a Muslim Society*, University of California, Berkeley, 1993. I must note that these political readings are viewed askance by more cautious or conservative historians of Islamic art. Sheila Blair, in her definitive, 681-page *Islamic Calligraphy*, takes issue with Tabbaa's argument and its adoption by Necipoglu, arguing that the evidence is inconclusive; Sheila S Blair, *Islamic Calligraphy*, Edinburgh University Press, Edinburgh, 2006, pp 174–7. I recognise these criticisms, yet I continue to find these authors' arguments convincing; I see the debate as one between the differing argumentative styles of social and traditional art history.

31. Tabbaa, op cit, pp 41–2

32. Ibid, pp 57–72

33. Ibid, pp 58–9

As Simon Yuill points out, contemporary information culture is like the information culture of the Abbasids in that both treat text as at once a communication and an aesthetic medium.[34] The politics of standardisation, based on the point, translates well to the world created by computers. There appears to be no question that digital computers work with discrete, minimal parts: the on and off signals, the bit and byte of information. If we ignore for the moment the fact that in a transistor-based digital computer each on signal represents a hurtling mass of millions of electrons, each off signal a relative dearth of electrons, then we can accept that there is nothing smaller than the on, off, and bit. The pixel, then, is the minimal visible part that corresponds to a minimal part of information. There is no inside to the pixel. This standard minimal part supports standardised systems, such as WYSIWYG applications, that do not seem particularly controversial. Where we may question the implications of pixel-based systems, following Pias, is in their lack of transparency as a screen-based medium and, more importantly, in the large amounts of data and algorithms they require to generate images. These become the basis of proprietary imaging software on which corporate empires are founded. It is not an overstatement that the pixel-based screen, like point-based writing, centralises meaning and access in corporate powers!

Like the extensible line of Islamic calligraphy, the point or pixel can express infinity because it is capable of producing infinite iterations. This is beautifully illustrated in the classic computer-based work *Every Icon*, 1997, by John F Simon Jr.[35] As deceptively unassuming as the diacritical point under the letter *beh* – from which it is said all other letters arise – *Every Icon* manifests itself as a simple 32 × 32 pixel grid on which the following algorithm is being carried out: 'Given: An icon described by a 32 × 32 grid. Allowed: Any element of the grid to be colored black or white. Shown: Every icon.' Having begun working on 27 January 1997,

34. Simon Yuill, 'Ibn al-Bawwab and the Bastard Codes', 2003, viewed at http://www.lipparosa.org; no longer online.

35. http://www.numeral.com/appletsoftware/eicon.html

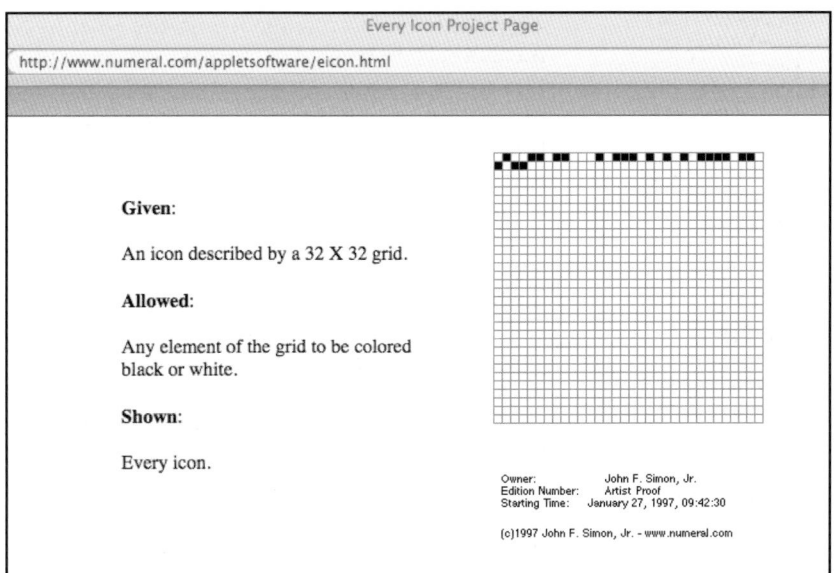

John F Simon Jr, *Every Icon*, 1997, web artwork, courtesy of the artist

at 9.42 in the morning, *Every Icon* is now busily iterating the second line of the grid. One can imagine that as the algorithm grinds away, a great number of icons will make their brief appearance (about 1/100 of a second) on the grid, from the Macintosh logo to the Ayatollah Khomeini, though presently all you see is inchworms.

The catch is that it would take a long time for these icons to appear. Simon calculates that the second line alone will take 5.85 billion years to iterate all its possible variations.[36] In *Every Icon*, an (almost) infinity of forms arises from an algorithm describing the action of 32 × 32 pixels over several hundred trillion years, ie, an unfathomably long time. This modest-seeming artwork brings us into contact with infinity, or at least with a sublimely unimaginable duration that puts the lives of our computers, ourselves and our planet into crushing perspective. *Every Icon* is an absolute *vanitas*; it is a brush with the infinite, minus the promise of salvation.

What gives meaning to an algorithm's tedious journey into the infinite? If anything, it is immanent: the materiality of software, hardware, programmers; the imaginative effort of humans to compare numeric infinity with our own finiteness. *Every Icon* pushes the pixel-based screen to its extensive limit. It subtly relativises the longevity of those images that are durable enough to be recognised in a crude matrix of 1024 pixels, by allowing them to flash onto the screen for only an instant in all eternity. All this shall pass, it says; only transience is real.

To conclude this parallel between the worlds of point-based calligraphy and pixel-based graphics: Both arose as functions of state and corporate power and their need to centralise control; both standardise meaning: form is dictated by the uniformity of templates and software rather than the properties of the point, line and screen. Abbasid regulations subordinated the line's capacity for becoming to the needs of representation; and it is here that Deleuze and Guattari's criticism of state writing applies to Islamic calligraphy. In the pixel-based screen, the indexical truth of the vector is replaced by the boot-faced approximations of pixel graphics. Pixel-based forms can proliferate to infinity on screen, but the 'life' that sprang from the point in vector graphics is subjected to a standardised form. Yet both systems turn out to be means not only of control but of invention, as artists pursue the infinite variations of the standard form. Beginning from an indivisible point, they unfold an extensive universe. And who could conceive of anything vaster than the universe?

Might there be an interior infinity? An enfolded universe?

THE INFINITESIMAL

In fact other strains of Islamic calligraphy do explore an intensive infinity, an infinitesimal universe – *within* the point – the implications of which I can only sketch here. We find some of them in the ambiguous, perplexing kinds of writing cultivated by powers competing with the Abbasids. In the Cairo-based Fatimid dynasty (909–1178), Isma'ili Shi'a rulers resisted Sunni powers for almost two centuries. Rather than emphasise the integration of community as does Sunni Islam, Shi'a Islam admits of interpretation, as there exist both exoteric meanings (*zaahir*) of the Qur'an, available to all people of faith, and esoteric meanings

36. John F Simon, *Every Icon*, artist's statement, available at http://www.numeral.com/articles/paraicon/paraicon.html

(*baatin*) to be pursued by a few. Yasser Tabbaa argues that this belief in the interpretability of sacred texts is embodied in a kind of writing associated with Fatimid Shi'a Islam. While the Abbasid caliphate was replacing the awkward, hard-to-read Kufic script with legible *nashki* and *thuluth* (rather like the evolution of WYSIWYG fonts), its Shi'a enemies were cultivating a more elaborate, *less* legible script, floriated Kufic.

The floriated Kufic script that decorates Fatimid buildings such as the Al-Azhar Mosque (begun in 972), as Tabbaa argues, embodies ambiguity in stone.[37] Floriated Kufic seems always to be alive. Its letters seem to have an internal pulsion to grow and mutate. Its *alif* does not repose at its full height but entwines with *lam* in unpredictable ways; other vertical letters sprout leaves that threaten to grow and spread. What I find remarkable about these letters that give rise to plants, and in other contexts even animals,[38] is that they indicate the internal infinite, or infinitesimal. They suggest that the diacritical mark and the noble line that springs from it are the mere exterior forms of an entirely other set of esoteric meanings. This life springing from *within* the minimal part, like a plant from a seed, suggests the coming into being of a world that is unfathomable *on a different order* of unfathomability.

Computer-based parallels to the infinitesimal world of floriated Kufic do exist, despite the inexorability of the digital computer's minimal part; but this is a discussion that will have to wait.

I have noted two properties that contemporary computer-based art shares with Islamic calligraphy, both in terms of the relationship of point to line. In vector graphics, the line springs from the point, like the *alif* from the diacritical mark, pursuing to infinity the possibilities of movement. In pixel-based graphics, the minimal part itself can be the basis of an unimaginably extensive line that will, in time, reveal the contour of every thing, a secular variation on the infinite knowledge of God. And, as I suggested at the end, there is also an internal infinity, enfolded in the point.

My argument is that these historical properties of Islamic art re-emerge in new media art *independently* of the new media artist's intentions. They express a sort of Islamic *Kunstwollen* (will to art, Aloïs Riegl's term for the life inherent in plastic form itself) immanent to computer-based media. Nevertheless, let me note that several new media artists, Muslim or not, wilfully cultivate Islamic sympathies in their work. John F Simon Jr writes algorithms inspired by the geometric and arabesque forms of the Alhambra. Moroccan video artist Mounir Fatmi plays wittily with the performativity of calligraphy and with Islamic aniconism in several works, including *L'alphabet rouge* (1994), *Arabesque, hommage à Jackson Pollock* (1997), *Manipulation* (2004). An aniconic video by Iraqi-American artist Usama Alshaibi, provocatively titled *Allahu Akbar* (2003), animates Islamic geometric motifs to thumping Arabic-techno dance music. Some designers are specifically adapting Arabic writing for the live-action medium of the computer screen: Lebanese font designer Tarek Atrissi playfully animates the rules of Ibn Muqla's proportioned script.[39]

New media make manifest the latent movement of Islamic calligraphy, both its vector-like becoming and its playful ways with the minimal part. They do this not for divine purposes but, in the best cases, in an engagement with extension and intension, creation and life, in the

37. Tabbaa, op cit, pp 55–7

38. There are numerous examples, mostly in secular artworks and especially in Afghanistan, of *naskhi* letters with animal or human heads.

39. See http://www.arabictypography.com.

context of deeply enfolded human history. I am hoping that the example of Islamic art will inspire us to imagine an *immanent Infinite* in contemporary society, and that contemporary computer-based artworks will continue to be beguiled by the infinite.

I am deeply grateful to the many readers and listeners who offered comments on embarrassingly rough drafts of this article. First among them is historian of Islamic architecture David Simonowitz, who encouraged me in this project and gently and generously pointed out the more egregious of my errors. A shorter and earlier version of this article appears in the Vancouver-region journal *The Capilano Review*, whose editor, Andrew Klobucar, made helpful suggestions. I have yet to take up most of Keith Sanborn's profound comments. And finally, I am most appreciative of the thoughtful and thorough critique from the editors of this special issue of *Third Text*.

Pou Rewa
The Liquid Post, Maori Go Digital?

Maree Mills

Tena koutou, tena koutou, nga mihi nui kia koutou
Ko Tongariro te maunga
Ko Taupo nui a tia te moana
Ko Tuwharetoa te iwi
Ko te Heuheu te tangata
Ko Ngati Hine taku hapu, Korohe te marae
Ko Maree Mills taku ingoa

This formal greeting in the Maori language refers to landmarks associated with my tribe. An affiliation with the *whenua* (land) locates my Maori ancestry and provides me with a place to speak from. I am from the Ngati Tuwharetoa peoples of the Lake Taupo district, Aotearoa, New Zealand, and my name is Maree Mills. I am a curator, video artist and Director of the Hastings City Art Gallery in Hawke's Bay, Aotearoa New Zealand, where I am currently undertaking research on multimedia approaches to communicating the female element within Maori philosophy for the 21st century.

Art that uses non-traditional media and emerging technologies, specifically the electronic or digital, has the potential to create and nurture a distinctive 'public space' for the articulation of alternative Maori world-views. Although a growing number of publications focus on contemporary Maori art practice, no specific attention has yet been given to the swelling numbers of Maori practitioners operating in the field of digital media. This essay contextualises my research in the wider framework of Maori digital art and seeks to explain a Maori creative practice.

At the dawn of a new millennium the Maori welcomed the sun as it first illuminated Mount Hikurangi in Aotearoa, New Zealand. Contemporary Maori artists picked up technology and moved into the light with *Hiko! New Energies in Maori Art* (1999) at the Robert McDougall Art Annex. The nationwide interest in Maori 'new media art' was largely spearheaded by the prolific Lisa Reihana (Nga Puhi, Ngati Hine, Ngai Tu) who quickly developed an international reputation. Reihana emerged from Ilam art school in Canterbury around the time of the birth of video. She was one of a group that happily left the tube camera in the flare of its own path and bounded into a magic digital world. The moving camera initially framed work both aesthetically and conceptually. *Native portraits n.19897*, commissioned in 1998 by our national museum Te Papa Tongarewa in Wellington, located the still photograph in a physical time, confronting the viewer with an alternative reading of the image, and established Reihana nationally. It aligned her with our indigenous neighbours as Aboriginal artists like Tracey Moffatt (with whom she has since exhibited regularly) were also exploring the representation of the indigenous from a colonised gaze, or as Barry Barclay said, 'from the camera of the ship's deck'.[1]

Metaphors for the process of colonisation are also evident in Eugene Hansen (Ngati Maniapoto, Ngati Mahuta) and Nathan Pohio's (Ngai Tahu) early work. Both artists playfully sample footage and sound from George Lucas's *Star Wars*. Pohio isolates the character of Chewbacca as indigenous other in *Untitled, Wookie Shuffle*, (2003) while Hansen uses sound with *Rex's Cybernautic Dreamscape Release Candidate 10* (2002). Like Aboriginal artist Gordon Bennett who created the alter ego John Citizen in order to avoid the essentialism of racial labels, Hansen now exhibits multimedia work under the name V J Rex. Later works like *Outer Nebular Drifter* (2004) provide immersive mixed audio and visual environments that reference a postcolonial game parlour. David Cross says of Hansen, 'he is the Maori Sheriff with the toyshop badge shooting at the bad guys'.[2]

There are other pop culture vultures taking pot shots. Wayne Youle (Nga Puhi, Ngati Whakaeke) and Lawrence Pook (Ngati Tuwharetoa), whose design education gifts them with a slick multimedia approach to colonial narratives, are examples. Often deconstructing this aesthetic but still very much a pop man is the renowned Peter Robinson (Ngai Tahu) who has shown with Gordon Bennett throughout Australia.

The confidence to exploit digital technology in communicating indigenous constructs and its relationship to new media is also evident in the work of female Maori artists. Maureen Lander's (Nga Puhi) *String Games* (1998–2000) is an ongoing body of work that takes traditional string pattern structures into a parallel digital world of coded language. Keri Whaitiri (Ngati Kahungunu, Ngai Tahu) uses aural language in her installation *Hohoko* (1999) to communicate with the talking walls of a *whare* (Maori meeting house), and later, when teamed up with Rachael Rakena (Ngai Tahu, Nga Puhi) for the Christchurch art biennial SCAPE04, moves new age to stone age quite literally with the extraordinary *mauri* (life force) stone *Ahakoa he iti* (2004).

These women, along with sculptor Lonnie Hutchinson (Ngai Tahu, Samoan) and weaver Donna Campbell (Nga Puhi and Ngati Ruanui), have adapted new media to their art practice in order to communicate an essence of what it means to be Maori.

What it might mean to be an indigenous artist in the twenty-first century had been fodder for theorists and practitioners who gathered for the 2003 'Cultural Provocation' conference held in Manukau, Auckland. The year 2003 was a productive one, as the Aotearoa Digital Arts List (ADA) was launched and created a much appreciated national network for digital artists. ADA has since played a major role in promoting our

1. Barry Barclay, 'Celebrating Fourth Cinema', *Illusions Magazine*, New Zealand, July 2003, p 8
2. David Cross, 'V J Rex: Outer Nebular Drifter', *un Magazine*, no 2, 2004, p 59. Available at http://www.unmagazine.org/un2.html (accessed 19 February 2007)

art nationally and internationally, many participants attending the later symposium 'Cultural Futures' (2005) also in Auckland. These *hui* (meetings) indicated a period of growing up for new media arts in Aotearoa New Zealand, particularly as the site for both symposia appropriately included the *wharenui* (now ubiquitously referred to as *marae*), a traditional Maori meeting house. Many *wharenui* held images of *tipuna* (ancestors) on the internal walls, and in a sense these embodied spirits still take part in the goings-on. The well travelled *Digital Marae* (2001) by Lisa Reihana creates a virtual *wharenui* that suggests a shifting meeting place for Maori. She digitally represents impressive female ancestor forms, both in life-sized portraits and animated, in a video work called *Let there be light*. The digital magic of Reihana's work was echoed in the technical virtuosity of *Te Ika a Maui* (2000) by Rongotai Lomas (Tainui). Another Ilam art school graduate, Lomas awed viewers with his 3D animation of the demigod Maui. The work was projected at the 'Techno Maori, Maori Art in the digital age' (2001) exhibition shown concurrently at the City Gallery in Wellington and Pataka Porirua Museum of Arts and Culture. This show was co-curated by Jonathan Mane Wheoki (Nga Puhi) the current Director of Arts and visual culture at Te Papa, and Dr Deidre Brown (Ngai Tahu) senior lecturer at the Auckland University School of Architecture. These two have both been strong supporters of contemporary Maori digital art, placing emerging artists alongside the established names of Michael Parekowhai (Nga-Ariki, Te Aitanga-a-Mahaki, Rongowhakaata) and Robert Jahnke (Te Whanau A Rakairoa, Ngati Porou). In a continued expression of *whanaungatanga* (the spirit of family), Brown showcased emerging Maori digital artists with *Whare* (2002) where she provided artists with the physical architectural framing of the Marae. The *wharenui* structure supported projection surfaces of digital *heke* (roof rafter) and *poupou* (structural side post). Most of the artists from this group have gone on to establish reputations, their names appearing in international shows of Pacific art, including the high-profile 'Pasifika Styles' in 2006–2007 at the Cambridge Museum of Archeology.

While this summary is not nearly exhaustive, I am also mindful to mention that many Maori artists not previously known for new media practice have successfully introduced it into new bodies of work. Charles Koroneho (Nga Puhi), with a background in sculpture, has elevated dance and performance with the inclusion of new media to cross time and space in his collaborative work *arero stone* (2006). Chris Heaphy (Ngai Tahu) has taken his sublime painting aesthetic to the moving image in the untitled work for *Te Puawai o Ngai Tahu: Twelve Contemporary Ngai Tahu Artists* (2003). It is a single channel work of projected moving water that conveys migration, navigation and spirituality. Natalie Robertson (Ngati Porou), known for her photographic work signposting land and journey, has introduced the dynamic element of sound and moving image. In her work *Kati ra e hika* (2004) the coastal land is spiritually lapped and mapped with *waiata* (song) according to traditional custom.

The unifying element of water or navigating of space as digital art concepts is not unexpected in our island nation. The traversing of cyberspace outside the limitations of time is also metaphoric of the soul's journey to *Hawaiiki* (our homeland) or to the realms of *Rangi* (our sky father) where the departed may rest and sparkle as stars. Polynesian metaphors were further noticed at 'Cultural Futures' by Tessa Laird: 'For these Maori new media artists, it is no accident that navigation – that most Polynesian of arts – and surfing – a Polynesian invention – have become the lingua franca of the Internet.'[3]

Trying to summarise indigenous digital practice in Aotearoa makes one think that Barry Barclay's concept of Fourth Cinema has arrived. It is in the form of new media art that Maori artists have embraced ancient core values and are communicating them. My work of thinking and making takes place in this wider context, extending the trajectory of the practice and locating it in a national and international framework of indigenous researchers and practitioners.

While Maori culture is rich in visual metaphor and its mythology has been visually articulated in the traditional arts of carving and weaving, Maori digital artists have confirmed that video and digital media have also enabled indigenous artists to engage with Maori philosophy. Video installation in particular has the potential to enable artists to engage with and express inseparable aspects of Maori philosophy and cosmology. It can be used to explore non-linear time, physical space, emotion, spirituality and symbolism concurrently or in specific relationships. An example of this conceptual suitability can be seen in the Maori paradigm of *mauri* (life force of all living things), a view that regards the social, natural, sexual and spiritual as parts of an interrelated whole. This is why I contend that the process of creating *taonga* (treasure), specific to Maori cosmology, cosmogeny and philosophy, in this medium, is a pathway in the continued quest for the celebration and understanding of Maori Culture.

The reclamation of the female element, particularly our *atua wahine* (Maori goddesses), in *tikanga Maori* (culture and belief systems) has been a focus of research by notable Maori academics Dr Aroha Yates Smith and Dr Rangimarie Turuki Rose Pere, among others.[4]

They have addressed the impact of colonisation in terms of the patriarchal re-telling of mythology and cosmology in writing. My own journey towards comprehending the place of Maori women included a moment of realisation that the prolific concept of *tapu* (sacred or restricted) can be remedied with the help of woman's *noa* (common or profane) status. It was a duality or balance that is conceptually ubiquitous in the Maori world. It is also a concept largely lost under colonisation. The consequences of this lost knowledge distanced me from my own Maori culture and led me to believe *Te Ao Maori* (the Maori world) was patriarchal and not for me. This then is motivation for the content of my artwork. As a Maori artist and a woman, I am drawn towards contributing to this discourse by bringing to life these Maori female elements using technology that might articulate concepts not experienced before. New media technology has brought form to the ethereal. As Mark Hanson argues, 'for the first time, if something can be imagined it can become a film'.[5]

MAORI AND VIDEO ART

In *State Of The Maori Nation*, Robert Jahnke refers to non-customary art that has a conceptual alignment with a Maori world-view, but he

3. Tessa Laird, 'Ngatahi – Know the Links: Cultural Futures Symposium', review essay in *Graduate Journal of Asia-Pacific Studies*, 4:1, 2006, pp 92–9

4. Aroha Yates-Smith, 'Hine! E Hine!: Rediscovering the feminine in Maori spirituality', University of Waikato, 1998, unpublished doctoral thesis

5. Matt Hanson, *The End Of Celluloid: Film Futures in the Digital Age*, RotoVision, Mies, Hove, 2004, p 9

does not reference as historical models the products made during *Te Huringa*, 1800 to the present. *Te Huringa* is the style of the period of 'turning' associated with the arrival of *Pakeha* (Europeans) in Aotearoa, and is often referred to by emerging artists of Maori cultural descent embracing new media technology.

> It is a generation for whom cultural identity is a transient notion made malleable by mixed heritage and an accessible dual artistic tradition. It is a generation for whom the laptop, the Internet, and digital and moving images provide the visual data from which cultural discourse is constructed.[6]

It is not surprising that young Maori have embraced digital technology to create a new visual language, any more than it is surprising that Hirini Melbourne, known for revivifying the traditional instruments of Maori music from pre-colonisation, should also have been adept in the use of electronic sound studios and contemporary technology. Maori have always explored new material technology. It could be suggested that a strategy of resistance to cultural reductionism has prompted the uptake of new visual technologies. By 'cultural reductionism' I mean a retreat from the tools and techniques introduced by *Pakeha* (Europeans) to New Zealand, towards a purist return to traditions that in the process risk becoming museum pieces, preserved against their natural evolution.

On a less serious note I have also often wondered if the romance with electronic media wasn't born in my early teens when we Maori flocked around the 'spacies' (video games) at the local hamburger bar. The gaming industry is another digital arts arena where Maori concepts and design have impacted. In 2006 Ignite studios released its first bro'Town mobile game, *Handle the Jandal*, for the Vodafone network and Sidhe Interactive consulted Ngati Toa elders to ensure the haka was appropriately performed for their *Rugby League2* video game for Xbox.

While we were still playing early video games, the birth of video art coincided with a Western explosion of interest in identity politics: of race, class and gender. During the 1970s this was particularly evident in Canada, where video artists and art writers explored the material suitability of video to express these paradigms. Janine Marchessault stated that the new technology 'challenged and extended not only the parameters of cultural production but the very meanings of resistance in the era of global television'.[7]

Indigenous cultural reductionism can take the form of a refusal to use non-traditional media as a mode of resistance to colonisation. But the meaning of the 'traditional' art that results arises specifically from the way it appears as the binary opposite of Western modernity. In this sense, resistance is dependent on what it resists. Marchessault's argument about video is that it has enabled a different kind of cultural activism, opening up tools for speaking and picturing experiences otherwise exiled to the margins of modernity. Video media allow users to go beyond resistance, towards making new alternatives to colonial modernism, rooted in the past but capable of an autonomous evolution into an autonomous future. It is a liberating space of slippage for contemporary Maori artists.

I wish to continue this contextual tradition associated with the video medium by communicating the Maori female element. The ability of moving images to speak in terms of metaphor without the intervention

6. Robert Jahnke, 'Maori Art Towards The Millenium', in *State Of The Maori Nation: Twenty-first Century Issues in Aotearoa*, ed Malcolm Mulholland, Reed Publishing, Auckland, 2006, p 49

7. Janine Marchessault, ed, *Mirror Machine: Video and Identity*, YYZ and Centre for Research on Canadian Cultural Industries and Institutions, Toronto, 1995, p 8

of compositing or other special effects can be seen in Shirin Neshat's work. A strong influence on my recent practice, in terms of aesthetic and thematic content, Neshat has reinvigorated the rituals and traditions of Islamic culture. Her allegorical installations immerse the viewer in a world that references gender and the theme of freedom versus censorship embedded in both Western and Eastern culture. Her approach to video art making also exposes the contemporary debate between the language of cinema and that of the high art world where her recent methods imitate feature film production. In the foreword to Catherine Elwes's book on video art, Neshat states:

> Finally, one of the greatest impacts on the moving image in visual arts has been to encourage artists to be more ambitious – by abandoning 'studio art', by stepping into the world, by blurring boundaries between mediums and by working collaboratively.[8]

This collaborative practice inherent in film production is extended into the artworld and encourages a cross-pollination with other creative practitioners who may work in other media. Combining elements of sound, image, space, site and object has not only resulted in making an emotionally immersive environment for the viewer (installation art), but also creates new structures for artists to work together. They can employ their various skills to achieve a united conceptual outcome. The recent collaboration between sculptor Brett Graham (Ngati Koroki Kahukura) and video artist Rachael Rakena (Ngai Tahu, Nga Puhi) at Te Manawa Gallery in Palmerston North, New Zealand, is a good example. *Aniwaniwa* (2006) references the birthplace of Graham's father, a place now submerged by the damming of the mighty Waikato River. The metaphor of cultural loss is communicated through the drowning of the land visualised in captured vessels that are also suggestive of islands, perhaps our own Pacific islands threatened by the rising tides. It is an evocative work that celebrates each artist's material virtuosity and resonates meaning on many levels. A creative research project funded by *Nga Pae o te Maramatanga* (Centre for Maori Research Excellence) that recognises the significance of collaboration between these Maori artists, *Aniwaniwa* illustrates art's place in communicating both Maori paradigms and Maori practice.

MAORI CREATIVE RESEARCH METHODS

This interweaving and sharing of skills and knowledge sits well in my own practice, as it is a *kaupapa* (principled) Maori approach and conceptually inherent in Maori philosophy. It is characteristic of *kaupapa Maori* to combine thinking with doing and making, and to consider from the start who the knowledge or the art you make is for. In my practice, this means analysing the use and practice of new media technology and participatory methodologies, including *kaupapa Maori* methodology, in contemporary Maori art practice to date. To do so, it is first necessary to examine the political, cultural and practical issues associated with indigenous creative practice. For example, it is unsurprising that most of the artists mentioned in this essay are also teachers at institutions that provide the technology required to make the artwork. It is

8. Catherine Elwes, *Video Art: A Guided Tour*, I B Tauris, London, 2005, p 8

therefore important to pay attention to debates about relations of power and knowledge, the representation of indigenous peoples and ideas, as well as my own area of interest, the visual construction of cosmological/philosophical concepts pertaining to the feminine. Like most indigenous cultures, Maori require participatory and place-based methodologies in both the creation and documentation of video installation in Aotearoa, New Zealand. One purpose of undertaking this work is to discuss the future of research by creative practice and the construction of Maori knowledge communicated through new media. A second purpose will be to elucidate the relationship between the ontological and epistemological assumptions of the artist/researcher in context. The contribution to knowledge about contemporary Maori art practice and its embrace of digital culture will be best realised through appropriate media forms, but some of it needs to be expressed in words, if only to explain the transition from cultural reductionism to the tradition of innovation and invention of new forms.

A way to articulate my creative/critical research practice within a *kaupapa Maori* framework is to illustrate the process through a case study. In 2003, I became interested in Hine Ahu One, the first woman in Māori mythology. I read about her and I talked to a lot of *kaumatua*

Maree Mills, *Hine Ahu One*, 2004, cardboard paper frame, compost, seedpods, video projection from head of life-size figure, two minutes DVD, ArtsPost Gallery, Hamilton, New Zealand, photo: Maree Mills

(Maori elders). I then approached a number of Maori women artists with an invitation to casually workshop our knowledge and discuss our different *iwi* perspectives regarding the female element (with the outcome of collaborative artwork in mind). During this time I was invited to a Maori women's *wananga* (enclosed school) at Rongomaraeroa marae in Porangahau, aptly named Hine Ahu One.

The *wananga*, which aimed to empower Maori women using ancient knowledge, gave fellow artist Anahera Kingi (Ngati Kahu, Ngati Kuri) and me what we needed to collaborate. Over the next six months we worked together and in isolation, interweaving our ideas and exploring the concept of Hine. I decided to make Hine's human form out of compost so that all parts of her would return to the earth after the exhibition was over. I wanted the viewer to smell earth and engage in a visceral way, providing a feeling that they had been transported in time to the native bush before European contact. The soundtrack was a layered cacophony of native bird sounds, many from species now extinct.

The moving imagery projected from her seeded head became a manifestation of her *mauri* (life force) as she takes a first breath and flies from the forest floor, elevating herself beyond the canopy up to Ranginui, the sky father. At this stage of production a number of other women had become involved. A big idea made possible through a collective vision.

Fourteen days before the exhibition opened, Anahera and I made sure we prepared the way spiritually. The installation space was cleansed and we did much *karakia* (prayer) and *waiata* (song) as the group built her at the gallery space. At the formal opening, the exhibition was blessed by our Maori elders, and viewers were asked to engage in the *kaupapa* by conducting a purification ritual before viewing the work. The public response from Maori and Pakeha was more than we could have hoped for. The knowledge of Hine Ahu One was resurrected and those who saw her felt moved to engage with their relationship with the *whenua*, with *Papatuanuku* (Mother Earth).

Friendship, trust and exchange are profound Maori and artistic values difficult to square with the individualistic ethos of Western research. Finding solutions to these challenges and building a *kaupapa Maori* creative research practice are goals of this work, not merely its methods.

The context for this kind of research was confirmed at the 7th World Indigenous People's Conference on Education (WIPCE) hosted by Te Wananga o Aotearoa and held on the University of Waikato campus in November 2005. One of the three themes for the conference was 'New Horizons of Knowledge' and many presentations were given by indigenous academics and educators who are conducting research and development in the area of indigenous epistemology and its place and function within contemporary society. The keynote speaker for this session, Dr Manulani Aluli Meyer, spoke on Native Hawai'ian epistemology and the specifics of universality. On a local level Maori are also introducing our paradigms to the world as an alternative way of thinking about globalisation. Makere Stewart-Harawira says:

> Far from irrelevant in the modern world, traditional indigenous social, political and cosmological ontologies are profoundly important to the

Maree Mills, Tania Mills, Twin sisters installing Hine Ahu One at the Artspost gallery, 2004, photo:Anahera Kingi

development of transformative alternative frameworks for global order and new ways of being.⁹

My latest work, a single-channel diptych *Pourewa*, illustrates my journey towards the place in which I stand as a Maori woman. *Pourewa* suggests balance between the complementary roles of male and female. It weaves together sacred chants and iconic landscapes, using the tools of digital non-linear video editing as a new form of textile. Like the weaving used in traditional architecture, the two-screen installation binds together places and people separated by geography and time, but whose collective memory of the crossing of water and settling of land create a new kind of space. This is a meeting place for the present constructed from the convergence of the ancient and modern understanding of how we have come to be where we are, not male and female but human, separated yet joined. Inspired by the *waka taua* (canoe of warriors) massed at Turangawaewae Marae for the annual Ngaruawahia Regatta, the vessel stresses continuities expressed in the ceremonies celebrating life. The waka is *whare tangata* (vagina) and its navigation by man is the act of procreation made manifest by the endless flowing of the river.

9. Makere Stewart-Harawira, *The New Imperial Order: Indigenous Responses to Globalization*, Zed Books and Huia Books, London and Wellington, 2005, p 101

Maree Mills, *Pourewa: The Quest for Balance*, 2006, video still from single-channel split-screen projection, mini DV 3 minute Loop, EA Gallery, Auckland, New Zealand

The visualisation and public exhibition of these concepts is intended to facilitate public interest in Maori philosophy and knowledge prior to European contact. It also seeks to contribute to the empowerment of Maori women who have been marginalised in the ethnocentric and patriarchal re-telling of their origins. This work has been shown here in Aotearoa and to indigenous tribes of the American Northwest. It has made me realise that my research practice has implications for other indigenous cultures that are also embracing experiential and digital media in an effort to communicate their own cosmogeny, cosmology and philosophy to others.

Agents for Change
The Contemporary Art Centres of the Soros Foundation and C³

Nina Czegledy and Andrea Szekeres

INTRODUCTION

In 1983 when George Soros first spoke of his Budapest-based Foundation plans practically nobody believed him. Why? Since the end of the Second World War in 1945, the very idea of an autonomous Foundation had been an alien concept in Hungary and by extension the entire Soviet Bloc. The creation of an independent non-profit organisation in the mid-1980s – even with the 'softening' political atmosphere – seemed out of the question.

George Soros, the successful American investor of Hungarian origin, has been an active philanthropist since the 1970s. In 1979 he established the Open Society Fund in New York, an organisation that supports activities in more than fifty countries worldwide. The aim of this initiative was to promote the 'open societies' concept originally proposed by the philosopher Karl Popper. Adopting Popper's theories, the Society's mandate states:

> While there is no set definition of what an open society is, among the key elements are: reliance on the rule of law, the existence of a democratically-elected government, a market economy, a strong civil society, respect for minorities and tolerance of divergent opinion.[1]

In the following years, when the Soros Foundation and the network of the Soros Centers for Contemporary Arts (SCCA) became a reality, lavish praise as well as harsh criticism was regularly heaped on the organisation and the people associated with George Soros. This might be partly explained by the fact that the atypical methods employed by the SCCA in various circumstances seemed strange and unfamiliar to Central Europe, strange – bordering on the alien.

Subtleties in communication methods, integration issues within the local community, as well as other matters, have caused misconceptions and misunderstandings resulting in allegations of partiality and even

1. Open Society Foundation, http://www.osi-az.org/faq.shtml

nepotism. Nonetheless the innovative cultural incentives greatly contributed to stimulating positive effects.

The unique beginnings and the subsequent operation of the SCCA network including the Center for Culture and Communication (C³) cannot be fully appreciated without considering the regional sociocultural context. So, working in this controversial territory and within the scope of this brief commentary, it is our difficult task to present the essence and the influence of SCCA initiatives and support. What follows is not intended as a critical evaluation of the SCCA network and C³, Budapest. Such a study would require in-depth research into decades of relevant cultural history. Instead we present a cultural narrative in the context of documented evidence and our own experience.

THE FIRST STEPS

In 1984, after lengthy negotiations with the authorities, a compromise was reached and the Soros Foundation was established in close collaboration with the Hungarian Academy of Sciences. In the beginning the Academy and some of the authorities had what amounted to the power of veto in operational decisions. The stated goal of Soros (and his Budapest-based advisory board) was to support fresh contemporary intellectual deliberations and initiatives linked to developing autonomy. The Foundation aimed from the start to bring a new working morality, a new informal style, creativity and, most importantly, transparency into the sociopolitical landscape, thus introducing a tool of pluralism unknown in the previous forty years. These decisions reflected the operational methods of Soros who has been described as 'the Champion of Change' – thus the Foundation and later the Contemporary Art Centers followed an elastic agenda, always on stand-by and ready to adapt. Several books, articles and interviews have been published on Soros, and especially on the connection between the person and his role in the operation of the Foundation. It is beyond the scope of this article to analyse these sources, although we would like to mention that Soros commented that he found it surprising how his 'public role-play' grew into a practically independent 'personality'.[2]

While the Soros Foundation's support of culture and, by extension, contemporary arts, is widely known, it is important to draw attention to the significant aid provided to many other worthwhile causes such as health (including hospital equipment), the oral history programme, English-language education, libraries (including a library for the visually impaired), postgraduate education, manager education, student exchange programmes, the 'milk' programme for elementary schools, publishing, and environmental and ethnic minority causes including the Roma. It is crucial to note that no pre-existing plans or precedents were available at that time. The entire funding structure and all its details were developed out of necessity. To elucidate some of these programmes we would like to mention one of the first initiatives: the Xerox programme. For those who live in developed industrial countries it might be difficult to believe how the gradual distribution of one

2. Béla Nóvé, *Tény/Soros*, Balassi Publishing, Budapest, 1999, p 33

thousand copying machines to libraries, schools, health centres, churches and research institutes changed the informational environment in the country. Just imagine the practically overnight development of a public communication and information service in a state where previously every typewriter had to be registered, copying was strictly monitored and copy machines were locked up overnight due to fear of subversion during the security-conscious Socialist period.

The list of projects supported by the Soros Foundation is long and complex, and includes the establishment of the Central European University in 1995.[3] Over the last ten years CEU graduates have played significant professional roles in a regional and international context. Today the CEU Alumni Association has a membership of 6000 residing in eighty countries.[4]

Over the years, funding support has been widespread, contributing to numerous disciplines in many countries, yet the Foundation has never granted support for political parties in Hungary,[5] or organised dissent,[6] and despite pressure Soros never invested in other business initiatives during the fifteen years of his intense non-profit based support in this country.[7]

1985–1991 SOROS FOUNDATION FINE ARTS DOCUMENTATION CENTER

From early on the Foundation's activities included major support for the arts, especially for innovative or experimental art projects. The significance of this is made clear when one considers that experimental or alternative art practice was practically prohibited in the Socialist era. It is hard to imagine today why an abstract painting was such a fearful symbol of dissidence for the authorities in Hungary and the entire Socialist Bloc region. For decades, all attempts to promote unofficial forms of visual art were discouraged; this explains the importance of establishing a platform for producing and showcasing contemporary art forms.

In May 1985, an agreement was reached between the Soros Foundation and Katalin Neray, Director of the Műcsarnok (Kunsthalle, Budapest) to establish the Soros Foundation Fine Arts Documentation Center. Under the direction of an International Advisory Board, the resource centre provided information on contemporary Hungarian artists to students, scholars, collectors and dealers from within Hungary and abroad. The first year of the new institution was dedicated to drawing up artist profiles, including English translations and some grant support. This activity was invaluable at a time when centralised art administration was breaking down, but there was as yet no sign of what was to replace it. Furthermore the methodical organisation of portfolios offered enormous assistance to artists seeking international integration. Portfolio development and project administration were unfamiliar practices to Hungarian artists in the 1980s. Of course for seeking commercial outlets abroad or for the promotion of artworks in the international exhibition network it was absolutely essential to submit professional portfolios. The assistance provided by the Center might seem insignificant in a developed country, but it

3. Central European University, Budapest, Hungary, http://www.ceu.hu/

4. Central European University, Alumni Association, http://www.ceu.hu/alumni/index.html

5. Nóvé, op cit, p 195

6. Ibid, p 193

7. Ibid, p 26

represented a major reinforcement for artists with international ambitions in Hungary.

In 1991, the Documentation Center expanded its activities under the name Soros Center for Contemporary Arts (SCCA), Budapest, with the aim of better supporting contemporary Hungarian culture. Continuing its comprehensive documentation, SCCA also organised different art projects, managed a grants programme for contemporary Hungarian artists and arts institutions and contributed to the printing of catalogues. Throughout its history SCCA aimed to introduce the latest, most up-to-date concepts in the shape of progressive and innovative projects, which eventually led to the founding of the Center for Culture and Communication, C^3.

1992–1999 THE NETWORK OF THE SOROS CENTERS FOR CONTEMPORARY ART

The Budapest-based SCCA served as a model for opening similar hubs in countries where the Soros Foundation was already present. The notion of this expansion came from George Soros himself. Between 1992 and 1999, twenty Centers were established in seventeen countries with a mission to support the development and international exposure of contemporary art in Eastern and Central Europe, the countries of the former Soviet Union and Central Eurasia as a vital element of an open society. In the initial years the centres were developed and operated by an exacting 'code of Soros rules', nicknamed by insiders the 'Bible'. While this adherence to 'McDonaldian'-style methods was criticised, it might also explain why in a region where cultural environments differ from country to country, these organisations collaborated successfully with each other, as well as with other arts organisations. The string of SCCA's annual exhibitions of local contemporary art both documented the work of local artists and offered grants programmes. A critical constituent of the network's operation was its educational programme, including the organisation of seminars, conferences and lectures. It was expected that after a few years these various centres would gain their own identity.

The role of the art centres was vital at a stage when Western interest was focused on the opening up of Eastern Bloc societies. The art centres provided information on the local art scene, organised studio visits and exhibitions, and supported their artists. One of the first large events organised and supported by the SCCA network, featuring Eastern European participation, took place at the São Paulo Biennale in 1994. Perhaps the last major manifestation of the SCCA mission was the 1999 exhibition 'After the Wall – Art and Culture in Post-Communist Europe' organised by Moderna Museet in Stockholm, but whose curators were assisted by the work the art centres had already done in selecting exhibition material. A subsequent example of collaboration is evident among the editors and contributors to *Praesens*, the Central European Contemporary Art Review, who were initially participants of the network and offered advice on further contributors. Despite the numerous projects organised in many countries, the legacy of the SCCA network remains difficult to gauge at this time, but it suffices to note that its activities revived the tradition of alternative concepts and inspired artists, curators, writers and musicians for years to come.

1991–1996 SOROS CENTER FOR CONTEMPORARY ARTS BUDAPEST

From its beginnings SCCA Budapest initiated and organised a series of exhibitions and events on themes seldom (if ever) before presented in Hungary. These included 'Sub Voce' (1991) the first show of video installations, 'Polyphony' (1993) the first forum for issue based art, 'V = A · Ω', a novel exhibition of electronic art installations in 1994, and the 'More than ten' (1994) exhibition of Hungarian Contemporary Art, marking the first decade of the Soros Foundation's cultural activities in Hungary.[8] Some of these exhibition projects, especially the subsequent exhibition 'The Butterfly Effect', merit further description.

In 1991 'Sub Voce', the first large-scale exhibition of Hungarian video installations at the Műcsarnok (Kunsthalle), included an open-call procedure for the selection of works to be exhibited, and also provided financial support for productions. This procedural shift illustrated an unusually transparent process for Hungary at that time. Simultaneously with this show, a Dutch touring exhibition of video installations, 'Imago: *Fin de siècle* in Dutch Contemporary Art', was exhibited in the same venue.[9] The work in this high-tech exhibition clearly demonstrated the contrast between the established scene in the Netherlands and the Hungarian situation, providing a strong impetus for future Hungarian video art production.

The 'Polyphony' exhibition of site-specific works, installations and a symposium was presented in 1993 on the initiative of Suzanne Mészöly (then director of SCCA). The exhibited artworks engaged with social issues or so-called 'issue-based art'. This was not only a novelty but also occurred barely four years after the fall of the Wall; it took political risks by publicly endorsing provocative works. The installations were shown on the streets, buses, telephone booths, the banks of the Danube, the parks of Budapest and even beyond the city limits. Not surprisingly this innovative project was controversial and received a mixed press. In the end the completed thirty projects provided an inventory of the complexities surrounding 'political art' in post-Communist societies, as Susan Snodgrass reported in *Art America*.[10]

Of all these projects, 'The Butterfly effect', an exhibition of media works and a series of events by Hungarian and international artists in 1996, had the most far-reaching outcome. The catchphrase for 'Butterfly', 'the coordinates of the moment before discovery', caught the attention of artists and the general public alike. Promoting the phenomenon of 'sensitive independence on initial conditions', the 'Butterfly Effect' web pages provided the following information:

> We have no way of knowing what effect technological media will have on the future of contemporary art. Today's situation is just as unpredictable as that of the last century, prior to the new discovery of film, television, holography and the computer. If, while examining the routes to our present we realize what the original idea or invention meant (or could have meant) at the time, keeping in mind even aspects which were later

8. Soros Centers for Contemporary Arts, http://www.C³.hu/scca/index.html
9. Imago, http://www.experimentaltvcenter.org/history
10. Susan Snodgrass, 'Report from Budapest: in a Free State', *Art America*, 1 October 1998. It includes information on the art scene outside the capital.

forgotten, then we may be able to 'see into the future'. Applying this method, we can perceive the new in the old, recognizing the original richness of that which later became tradition. We can see the old in the new, too, with its transience and the boredom of its fashionability.[11]

The extensive Butterfly project – the first large-scale media art event in Hungary – included a historical exhibition of Central and Eastern European technological and experimental inventions, an exhibition of contemporary media artworks by Hungarian and international artists, an international retrospective of video, film and animation works, multimedia performances and symposia on media theories and practice and technological discoveries in the field of media art. This programme reflected the high ambitions and standards of the Center and prepared the ground for future projects. The incredible public successes of 'The Butterfly Effect' eventually led to the establishment of the Center for Culture and Communication (C^3) Budapest.[12]

1996 C^3 CENTER FOR CULTURE AND COMMUNICATION BUDAPEST

C^3 opened in June 1996. One of the primary reasons for establishing this centre was to develop a large-scale facility for Internet access including schools, NGOs and private individuals. The popularity of 'first time public Internet access' during the Butterfly Effect events prompted the Foundation to extend SCCA's function into a wider public sphere. As a result, C^3 was launched as a three-year pilot project by a cooperative effort between the Soros Foundation, Silicon Graphics Hungary and MATÁV: the Hungarian Telecom corporation. In addition to public access C^3 also offered educational tools such as ongoing courses for Internet use. Within the emerging C^3 it was feared that unless a commitment to the expected public role were fulfilled the artistic aims of the institution would be thwarted. When it became clear that the key expectation of some of the supporters was the opportunity to showcase their products a contentious situation arose in the non-profit-motivated environment.

Of course C^3's mandate went much further then public Internet access. Media art educational concerns featured strongly among C^3 goals. In the history of Hungarian media art one of the first steps taken was the establishment of the Intermedia Department in 1990 under the direction of Miklós Peternak at the Hungarian Academy of Fine Arts.[13] Peternák became the director of C^3 in 1997 and he prioritised an educational outreach programme at C^3 linked to educational institutions.

From the late 1990s C^3 maintained an extensive artist residency programme.[14] Among the beneficiaries of this programme were many outstanding international artists. One of its main goals was to expose Hungarian artists to an international exchange of ideas and media art practice. International participants included Masaki Fujihata, Olia Lialina, Bill Seaman, Bjørn Melhus, George Legrady, Matthew Barney, Alexei Shulgin, Etoy and JoDi. Many important installations, showcased worldwide, resulted from this process and the projects created during these residencies also influenced and involved many local media artists.

11. The Butterfly Effect, http://www.c3.hu/scca/butterfly
12. Center for Culture and Communication, C^3, http://www.c3.hu
13. Intermedia Department, Hungarian Academy of Fine Arts, http://www.intermedia.c3.hu
14. C3 Artist residency programme, http://www.c3.hu/collection/index_en.php?t=2

Among the annual exhibitions developed by C³ and presented at Műcsarnok, notable examples included 'Perspective' (1999), an international media art and history exhibition presenting the historical transformations of the image based on the discovery of perspective.[15] The 'Vision' project (2002) focused on the connections between the neurosciences and visual arts. The project was initiated by discussions between neuroscientists and Miklós Peternák, director of C³, and represented a pioneering arts and science project in Hungary. 'Vision' included a discussions platform on the neurobiology of perception and neuronal, behavioural and theoretical approaches to brain research. The symposium ran augmented by a major exhibition at the Műcsarnok.[16]

'Kempelen: His Life and Era' (2007) represents the latest exhibition initiated and developed by C³ in collaboration with ZKM, Karlsruhe, Germany, and the Műcsarnok. The project traced the history of automata in an extensive exhibition of models and originals of historical works, as well as contemporary examples of artworks related to the theme. Documents and portraits of the era provided an excellent contextualisation of Kempelen's life and times.[17]

A considerable proportion of C³'s operation consisted of providing in the mid-1990s intensive software and internet-use courses on offer at C³ and mainly for artists who had little or no previous knowledge in these fields. The changing circumstances in Hungary, with the advent of Internet cafes and liberalised Internet access, rendered these public aspects no longer essential. As a result C³ changed its focus from public access to defined art projects for target audiences. The phasing out of these projects narrowed the local visibility of C³. Additionally while the large exhibitions conceptualised and developed at the centre proved popularly successful, much of the credit went to the venues instead of C³.

1999 –

Since 1999, C³ has operated as a non-profit independent Foundation with the aim of developing collaborations between art, science and communications, and educational and cultural programmes such as the international exchange platform. It maintains, *ex-index*, an online cultural journal, a free-mail service (a Hungarian interface for internet users), domain registration and a video archive as well as international connections and special projects.

The flexibility of the mandate and the organisational structure of C³ has often allowed prompt reaction to unexpected events. A good example of this happened in 1999 when at short notice an international meeting was called in response to the bombings in Serbia, which were affecting artists and cultural workers. This meeting was originally planned for Belgrade but due to the difficult circumstances was moved to Budapest. A number of international residencies and exchange projects resulted from this meeting.

Long-term sustainability of media centres (especially in large cities where public funding is spread among many institutions) is fraught with ongoing difficulties and remains a global problem. In the changed Hungarian economic climate, C³'s situation is no exception. The loss of

15. 'Perspective' exhibition, http://www.c3.hu/events/index.html?99
16. 'Vision' project, http://www.c3.hu/events/index.html?2002
17. 'Kempelen', http://www.kempelen.hu/index_en.html

major funding from the Soros Foundation, the Hungarian Telecom Corporation and the constant need for technical upgrades all contributed to a new definition of aims and mandate. Moreover some artists who were not accepted for residencies, and some of the public, regard the centre as an ivory tower. Considering the precarious situation, one might ask how the founders envisaged ensuring the long-term survival of such a centre.

THE PHASING OUT OF THE SOROS NETWORK

In 1999 and 2000, following the restructuring of the Soros foundations, all Soros Centers for Contemporary Arts gradually became independent and either transformed into organisations under the membership of the new association ICAN (International Contemporary Art Network) based in Amsterdam – or ceased to exist.[18] As a related activity, the Open Society Cultural Link programme[19] promoted arts and culture events involving the participation of artists from countries in Central and Eastern Europe, Central Asia and Mongolia. Its primary goal was to encourage and facilitate artistic collaboration and networking in the region.

Since 1993, Arts Link, an Open Society Institute initiative,[20] has supported exchanges between artists and art organisations in the US, Central Europe, Russia and Eurasia. At the beginning of 2000 Cultural Link changed its mission following the introduction of a new programme strategy. Due to the re-structuring of the organisations, keeping track of the former SCCA Centers became a complex task. Although the ICAN network seems to have stopped its official networking activities, most of the centres are active in their local environments, and maintain networks with their geographically and historically 'natural' partners within the region and beyond. One may criticise the network for not achieving far more 'spectacular' results, such as staging large-scale art events on the international art scene; nevertheless, the established formal and informal connections throughout the region have remained active to this very day.

To give an example the SCCA Center for Contemporary Arts–Ljubljana presents active projects,[21] circulating a regular update of its activities such as the 'Laboratorium in the Gallery' (23–29 June 2007) and LabSUs, an open platform for curators, artists, writers and theoreticians. The Center maintains important segments of the support system for contemporary arts and culture and civic society.

In Chisinau, Moldova: the KSAK – Center for Contemporary Arts organises workshops and theoretical courses in the field of media art,[22] and its most recent project has been the Found Footage Workshop for participants from Moldova, Romania, Bulgaria, Macedonia, Bosnia and Herzegovina, Kosovo, Serbia and Montenegro, Croatia and Slovenia. In Almaty, Kazakhstan, the Soros Center for Contemporary Arts supports local contemporary art and its integration into the world's artistic processes.[23] As a unique cultural institution in the Central Asian region, SCCA–Almaty is involved with several types of cultural activity. The most recent project is 'Destination Asia: Non-strict Correspondence', an exhibition by Indian and Pakistani artists.

18. ICAN (International Contemporary Art Network), http://www.ican.artnet.org/ican/

19. Open Society Arts Link, http://www.osa.ceu.hu/

20. Artslink, http://www.cecartslink.org/

21. SCA Ljubljana Press Release No. 11/2007, Ljubljana, 20 June 2007, LabSUs, http://www.worldofart.org/current/archives/41

22. KSAK, Chisinau, Moldova, http://www.art.md/

23. Almaty, Kazakhstan, SCCA, http://www.scca.kz/

Some other centres still operate, promoting and supporting contemporary art across the region. They are to be found in the Czech Republic;[24] Romania;[25] Slovakia;[26] the Ukraine;[27] Russia;[28] Latvia;[29] Bosnia and Herzegovina;[30] Macedonia;[31] Lithuania;[32] Warsaw, Poland;[33] and Zagreb, Croatia.[34]

CONCLUSION

Generous support by George Soros has attracted considerable envy, causing local and regional difficulties and drawing undue media attention. In addition some Centers found themselves in a difficult position when defending their funding choices within the Open Society Network. The autonomous structures of SCCA, independent of state bureaucracy, however, allowed for flexibility in addressing topical issues and promoting new initiatives. Nonetheless the original aims of funding and presenting the most up-to-date projects were latterly often restricted by limited budgets.

So although it is difficult to evaluate how efficiently the Centers operated, nevertheless their work provided an initial point of reference to the entire region. This can be said in relation to all forms of contemporary art and especially the emerging media art scene. Media art requires a major investment and without SCCA support there would have been considerable delay in the development of electronic and media art in Central and Eastern Europe. Fortunately, there are new media labs emerging all the time; for example, the recently opened Kitchen Budapest which provides practice-based educational and production facilities for a new generation of Hungarians.[35]

The initial goal of re-integrating Central and Eastern European artists to the rest of the world had been more or less accomplished by 2000. The next stage in this process is now up to the individual countries, according to George Soros. While there have been numerous political and personal objections expressed against the cultural policies and funding by Soros – conspiracy theories included – the positive results are undeniable and unprecedented. One day, when an unbiased observer comes to review the major contemporary artists from this region, he or she will find numerous references to concepts and artworks supported by the Soros Network.

24. Center and Foundation for Contemporary Arts, Prague, http://fca.fcca.cz/
25. International Center for Contemporary Art, Bucharest, Romania, http://www.icca.ro/home_en.htm
26. Center for Contemporary Arts Foundation, Bratislava, Slovakia, http://www.ncsu.sk/
27. Kiev, CCA Center for Contemporary Art, http://www.cca.kiev.ua/newsite/en/
28. PRO ARTE Institute, St Petersburg, http://www.proarte.ru/us/about/
29. The Latvian Centre for Contemporary Art (LCCA), Riga, http://www.lcca.lv/
30. Sarajevo Center for Contemporary Art, Bosnia and Herzegovina, http://www.scca.ba/
31. Contemporary Art Center Skopje, Macedonia, http://www.scca.org.mk/
32. Contemporary Art Information Center (CAIC), Lithuanian Art Museum, http://www.ldm.lt/
33. Arts and its Time, Warsaw, Poland, http://www.sztukaiwspolczesnosc.art.pl/index_e.html
34. Institute for Contemporary Art, Zagreb, Croatia, http://www.scca.hr/
35. Kitchen Budapest, http://www.kitchenbudapest.hu/en/

Photographies

EDITORS:
David Bate, *University of Westminster, UK*
Sarah Kember, *Goldsmiths, University of London, UK*
Martin Lister, *University of the West of England, Bristol, UK*
Liz Wells, *University of Plymouth, UK*

Photographies seeks to construct a new agenda for theorising photography as a heterogeneous medium that is changing in an ever more dynamic relation to all aspects of contemporary culture. ***Photographies*** aims to further develop the history and theory of photography, considering new frameworks for thinking and addressing questions arising from the present context of technological, economic, political and cultural change. ***Photographies*** will investigate the contemporary condition and currency of the photographic within local and global contexts. The editors seek research papers and innovative visual essays, shorter papers engaging new debates, review essays evaluating publications, cultural events, key developments, exhibitions and conferences.

CALL FOR PAPERS

The Editors of ***Photographies*** are now inviting the following kinds of submissions:

- Research papers and innovative visual essays (6000–8000 words)
- Shorter papers engaging new debates (circa 4000 words)
- Reflective review essays evaluating publications, cultural events, key developments, exhibitions and conferences.

Papers and proposals should be sent to: photographies@plymouth.ac.uk

---

To sign up for tables of contents, new publications and citation alerting services visit **www.informaworld.com/alerting**

Register your email address at **www.tandf.co.uk/journals/eupdates.asp** to receive information on books, journals and other news within your areas of interest.

For further information, please contact Customer Services at either of the following:
T&F Informa UK Ltd, Sheepen Place, Colchester, Essex, CO3 3LP, UK
Tel: +44 (0) 20 7017 5544 Fax: 44 (0) 20 7017 5198
Email: subscriptions@tandf.co.uk
Taylor & Francis Inc, 325 Chestnut Street, Philadelphia, PA 19106, USA
Tel: +1 800 354 1420 (toll-free calls from within the US)
or +1 215 625 8900 (calls from overseas) Fax: +1 215 625 2940
Email: customerservice@taylorandfrancis.com

View an online sample issue at:
www.tandf.co.uk/journals/rpho

Old Contexts for New Media Cultures (in Russia)

Olga Goriunova

The primary aim of this article is to look at the development and perception of new media art, cultures and theory in Russia today, as informed by its particular political history and cultural context. Here I would like to put forward a rather simplistic claim that may have some explanatory power in this case. Numerous speculative devices and frameworks have been developed to grasp the sociality of art forms (Valerian Pereverzev,[1] Mikhail Bakhtin and the Marxist sociology of art), to map the field of art as a social system and to balance the relative autonomy of cultural production versus economic order (Niklas Luhmann and Pierre Bourdieu), to express the social value of cultural phenomena or understand the symbolic value of social processes (the whole history of British Cultural Studies), to identify the political potential of art (Jacques Rancière), and to explain creativity through the demands of late capitalism (Autonomist Marxism and its developers). This text starts from my comprehension as a participant faced with personal dilemmas related to professional development; it is based on a lively and particular experience whose formalisation is suggested below. As such, it serves as an account of a mixed set of principles, bastardised paradigms and abandoned concepts manifested in a mishmash and dismal plane of perspectives and informing principles to be found in the clutch of historical, geographical, linguistic, political and other forces manufacturing what has come to be known as contemporary Russia. Such principles are not tonic enough to stimulate any totalising embrace or causal determinism, but rather the opposite: they are slack and stagnant and contaminate practices, structures and networks with a special kind of lethargy.

It is my understanding that the dynamics with which digital media fields (such as organisations, networks of charged concepts and practices, and 'electric' fields of thoughts and work) unfold and manage themselves at a certain level of sustainability is dependent on their intricate and opaque co-constitutive relationships with art, education and production sectors. Ultimately, all are related to the general capacity of their value to be produced, translated, misinterpreted and appreciated, as rooted in the history of a language-based semiosphere (Vernadsky and

---

1. Valerian Pereverzev was a highly original thinker who developed an impressive analysis of literature by focusing on the complexity of its connections to social reality. He contributed to the form–content debate of the beginning of the century, and his account at some moments comes close to Mikhail Bakhtin's critique of formalism in *The Formal Method in Literary Scholarship: Critical Introduction to Sociological Poetics*, John Hopkins University Press, Baltimore and London, 1991. Pereverzev started writing before Bakhtin, and his first book, *The Work of Dostoevsky*, originally published in 1912, presents an amazing analysis of Dostoevsky's dramas through the staging of its sociopolitical vectors without ever falling into direct determinism. In this book he analyses female characters from positions that gender studies only developed decades later, for example through their conceptualisation of love informed by their (lack of) agency, or their construction of the prostitute/saint model of sacrifice. Pereverzev created an influential school of analysis that boomed in the 1920s,

drawing on the works of Karl Marx and Georgy Plekhanov, a current interrupted by Stalinist repression and one still not widely known or popularised even within Russian academe. Imprisoned in 1938, and rehabilitated in 1956, Pereverzev remains, in my opinion, one of the most exciting among the tragic and forgotten theorists of the twentieth century. The works of Valerian Pereverzev are available only in Russian. See: V F Pereverzev, *Tvorchestvo Dostoevskogo* [*The Work of Dostoevsky*], Sovremennye Problemy, Moscow, 1912; V F Pereverzev *U istokov russkogo realisticheskogo romana* [*Tracing the Origins of the Russian Realist Novel*], Khudozhestvennaja literatura, Moscow, 1965. There is an extensive list of literature that accompanied and to a degree documented the 'campaign' against Professor Pereverzev and his school from the late 1920s and early 1930s. See: *Protiv men'shevisma v literaturovedeniji. O teorijakh prof. Pereverseva i ego shkoly*. Sbornik statei [*Against Menshevism in Literary Theory. On the Theories of Prof. Pereversev and his School*. A collection of articles], OGIZ RSFSR 'Moskovskij rabochij', Moscow, 1931; S Malakhov, *Pereverzevsshina na praktike. Kritika teorii i praktiki.* [*Pereverzev-ism in Practice. A Critique of Theory and Practice*], Gos Izd Khud Lit, Moscow and Leningrad, 1931; S Didamov, *Prof. Pereversev i ego partijnyje 'druzija'* [*Prof. Pereversev and his Party 'Friends'*], Gos Izd Khud Lit, Moscow and Leningrad, 1931.

2. The concept of the semiosphere was initially proposed in the 1920s by Vladimir Vernadsky, a geochemist and a mineralogist, under the

Lotman[2]), a history of thinking and understanding in media. I do not aim to suggest a new sociology of art here, neither would I like to propose a narrow determinist view of economic dependencies or formulate utopian laws of autonomy for new media. What I would like to do is to use these concepts (those of the art field, education, production, market, semiosphere), as pragmatically as possible, and to explain why one country, Russia, has proved fertile ground for the birth of a number of brilliant ideas and works, but is a desert for any long-term self-sustaining development of these essential related areas.

Contemporary Russian culture is structured by gaps. In this it is not unlike the global landscape,[3] but Russia demonstrates a closer, more direct confrontation between poles, pushed towards each other by the boundaries of a cultural world united by language, state and history. Digital cultures in Russia, especially if conceptualised in terms of the 'participatory web', are a rich field active in the development of colourful and potent aesthetic phenomena. However, there is a lack of understanding of these forms as culturally significant, whether by analysts seeking to position them in a theoretical tradition, or by practitioners themselves whose canons of cultural value remain closer to traditional sacred forms of art and distanced from their own life. An example of such a dichotomy taken from a different field is gender inequality, structured through a gap between the conditioning of women through traditional cultural images and their real social positions and lived experience in contemporary society, experiences which do not find any relevant symbolic expression. Such gaps are formed in part by processes Russia underwent during the 1990s when, due to the rapid collapse of a massive set of political, social and economic systems, and the resulting instability, shifts, drop in the quality of life and ethnic conflicts among other factors, an abyss cracked open in areas that had formerly progressed relatively smoothly under the management of the state ideological apparatuses and policies, such as, for instance, higher education or ethnic tolerance.

New media cultures, as informed by digital folklore, grass-roots activities, everyday creative practices and various kinds of subcultural creativity, form an important element of Russian cultural life below the radar of any formal recognition or conceptualisation. As part of the same process, new media art, as a practice that demands a higher level of self-conceptualisation, is radically lacking in context. Such a context, or the necessary means, material and fuel for development and sustainability can be described through a geometric figure of relationships between three elements – art, education and production/market. The choice of graphics signifying the positioning of the elements in relation to each other with different degrees of dependency and autonomy is a matter of school and ideology.

The field of art engaged with digital media technology exists in the context of affinities and tensions produced in the relationships between art, education and the production sector. New media, as artistic practice, speculative endeavour and field of experimentation, aspects readily translated to other registers, exhibit a certain pace and sustain a certain level of visibility and value in countries with developed new media production sectors that work beyond local needs. Educational institutions provide the workforce for new media production sectors; they bridge the gaps between philosophical and cultural histories of technology, contemporary aesthetics and conceptual accounts of the potentialities of media. They may also serve as bodies of legitimisation and valorisation within the dynamics of the artworlds. Both educational programmes and production/market need new media art as an alternative, disinterested, autonomous 'Other' to balance out the 'pragmatism' of capitalist production, to construct the relative autonomy of culture, to produce difference.

Unlike some contemporary artists, new media artists' means of survival are often connected either to education systems or to production/market (or to state support), but by and large not to any 'commercial' spectre of the artworld. New media thus present a field that is both quite traditionally structured but also more closely (if indirectly) related to late capitalism. It may seem a paradox that new media art practices, as essentially avant-garde, rooted in the anti-institutional ethic of the early World Wide Web,[4] related to the histories of open source and the rise of anti-globalisation movements, exhibit such clear linkages to the production sector and educational systems. But as we learn, it is in the 'nature' of late capitalism, based on the capitalisation of creativity, both to empower people (or indeed the 'multitude') and to monetise their effort, a process that can never be exhaustively concluded.[5] New media arts and cultures present a specific field indeed, an experiment that unpacks its fullest potential in countries that demonstrate clearer forms of both the advances of late capitalism, a successful history of public debate and a more or less 'autonomous' academe. Such 'clear' forms, curiously enough, allow for more hybridity and heterogeneity in the playing out of interests, energies and objects than the memory blocks and lacunae that obtain within societies with histories structured by rapid changes and annihilating voids.

The simple geometries above do not attempt to explain the genesis of ideas or influences in new media, most of which today work internationally, involving actors originating from countries absent in media production and markets and low in media education resources, and from countries with low degrees of 'individual freedom'. But it seems that any combination of the three elements, regardless of the ideologies behind the relative positioning of art, education and the production sector, is capable of explaining the sustainability and continuance, the production mechanics – or lack thereof – of new media discourse in the large sense of the word. Without any one of the three elements, the spheres of interest of new media find themselves not dead, but deserted.

To clarify with a simple example, let us look at the net.art scene in Russia. There were a number of influential actors in the international current of net.art who originated from Russia in the mid-1990s: the most internationally acknowledged include Alexei Shulgin and Olia Lialina, but the list could be continued with Andrei Velikanov, Dasha Struchkova, Sergei Teterin and many more. Institutionally, net.art and net culture in Moscow was supported by institutions such as Moscow MediaArtLab, which was actively involved in organising festivals and conferences at the end of the 1990s. Once net.art's international climax was over, and MediaArtLab slowed down its activities due to the closure of the Moscow Soros Centre, one of its main financial sources (see Czegledy and Szekeres in this issue of *Third Text*), the context for

name of a noosphere (in *The Biosphere*, published in Russian in 1926, English translation: *The Biosphere*, Springer-Verlag New York, New York, 1998), a concept to be later developed by Yuri Lotman and the Tartu–Moscow semiotic school. See Yuri Lotman, *Universe of the Mind: A Semiotic Theory of Culture*, I B Tauris and Co, 2000.

3. One of the arguments Rosi Braidotti focuses on in her *Transpositions: On Nomadic Ethics*, Polity Press, Cambridge, 2006.

4. See, for instance, Julian Stallabrass, *Internet Art: The Online Clash of Culture and Commerce*, London, Tate Publishing, 2003.

5. Nick Dyer-Witheford, 'Cognitive Capital Contested', *Multitudes*, 2002, available at http://multitudes.samizdat.net/Cognitive-Capital-Contested.html. 'Autonomist Marxism and the Information Society', *Multitudes*, 2004, available at http://multitudes.samizdat.net/Autonomist-Marxism-and-the.html

net.art – and the larger cultural discourses about networks – literally dissolved in Russia. More acknowledged artists (such as Olia Lialina) gained teaching jobs in Europe. The less well known had to radically change their field of work, withdrawing entirely from the new media field. Since there were no cultural institutions that could reproduce that discourse, a vacuum replaced a previously vivid space.[6] It was disturbed once again with the first Readme software art festival organised in Moscow in 2002.[7] Software art as a global field was going through a phase of rapid growth in 2001 and 2002. Transmediale, the Berlin-based festival, had just launched a category for artistic software and the new festival was born to address this exciting field of practice.[8] Readme became financially possible as the Russian State Centre for Museums and Institutions acquired an ambitious new directorship that wished to leave a mark on the cultural landscape. Once they had quickly moved on to the management of more established arenas, such as the national pavilion in the Venice Biennale, Readme ceased to exist. Given that such a withdrawal did not 'kill' the event, which subsequently travelled around Europe to be held three more times in Helsinki (Finland), Aarhus (Denmark) and Dortmund (Germany), and that the contingency of Moscow-based support had been expected from the beginning, some of the consequences appeared striking to me as an organiser. The Readme festival was well attended, was covered in the media and was even selected as one of the best art events of the year by *Afisha* magazine (analogous to *Time Out*). However, it did not leave any trace in the 'cultural memory'. In fact, Readme never happened in Moscow in the way it happened in other places. There were not enough forces, materials, bodies, programmes or institutions that could have been affected by such a festival to help digest its significance and continue the accumulation of meanings it sought to introduce. Readme 2002 rests like a wrecked ship at the bottom of a well to be rediscovered as exotica by local radicals.

This proposition should not be taken as homologous to a change of paradigms in theory or art, or as a disruption of individual pathways. It is a rather 'general' situation, in countries lacking in the kind of stable context maintained elsewhere by educational institutions and the production sector or market. When an art current goes down in a country or culture with a 'context', the 'context' remains. When an art current goes down in a country or culture without a 'context', nothing remains.

In Russia, a general cultural understanding of technology that could potentially challenge the existing state of things is nearly non-existent due to a particular history of erasure. Educational institutions wounded by the same history cannot fill this gap, due to their conservatism, and due to the absence of a demand that could originate from the non-existent market or wider context of new media production. Individual efforts take place without leaving any traces of significance.

How did Russian academe and art arrive at this present state where institutional rigidity leads to an incapacity to deal with new media technology culturally, philosophically or artistically? What is the source of the general reluctance to think more widely and culturally of technology in Russian culture? In order to compose some kind of answer to this question, it is useful to trace a path through the history of the condition

6. Here I do not intend to propagate a 'fall of the Wall' explanation. A common aside in critical texts on net.art, this thesis suggests that the collapse of the Soviet Union permitted Western cultural interest in post-Soviet countries, which in turn was responsible for a renaissance of art and culture. The rise of Russian net.art and related practices of the 1990s can be interpreted through this largely political effect; however, I cannot pinpoint any analysis that provides sufficient grounding for such a viewpoint.

7. The Readme software art festivals website archives are available at http://readme.runme.org

8. For an account of the development of Readme, and its political implications for the field of software art, see introductory articles in the Readme catalogues, especially Olga Goriunova and Alexei Shulgin, eds, *Read_me 2.3 Reader: About Software Art*, NIFCA publication, no 25, Helsinki, 2003; Olga Goriunova and Alexei Shulgin, eds, *Read_me: Software Art and Cultures*, University of Aarhus, Digital Aesthetics Research Center, Aarhus, 2004; Olga Goriunova, ed, *Readme 100: Temporary Software Art Factory*, Hartware MedienKunstVerein, Dortmund, Germany, 2005.

of ideas in this national territory, taking the history of available theorisations of media and technology as a resource.

Bourdieu argues for the relative autonomy of the field of cultural production as its main characteristic ('the economic world reversed'), one that is productive of influential avant-garde and intellectual positions (for example in analysing French literary production of the end of the nineteenth century or calling for the support of the endangered autonomy of academe in the present day). In the political regime of the USSR such issues certainly could not be raised. The dictatorship of the proletariat was aimed radically at changing not only social systems, but human (= class) consciousness itself. The vast battle for a new human being was fought at every level of social, political, cultural, psychological and biological structures, making any 'autonomy' unthinkable. Censorship was exercised in the field of cultural production not only through its institutions, but at much subtler, non-formalised and brutal levels.

Control over newspapers or film production as a massive and central means of ideological domination did not distract the Communist Party's attention from more marginal theoretical thinking on media technology. Marx's interpretation of the capitalist production system laid the ground for thinking about media in the USSR, where it was never allowed to grow beyond the Father's original ideas, as interpreted by Lenin, Stalin and a number of other 'approved' theorists. For Soviet researchers, any medium carries, first of all, an ideologically charged message. A number of academics of this period suggested adding a sixth element, 'aim', 'condition' or 'intent' of the message, to Claude Shannon's five-term mathematical theory of communication with its source, transmitter, channel, receiver and destination elements.[9] As early as the 1940s, when information theory started off and cybernetics adopted Shannon's model to conceptualise the organisation and homeostasis of complex structures, a few participants in the Macy conferences in the USA (as core venues in the formation of 'first-order' cybernetics) objected to the disembodiment of information integral to Shannon's formalisation. Donald MacKay suggested a theory of information that took meaning into account, putting forward a distinction between the 'selective information' that concerned Shannon, and, in his account, a 'structural' aspect of information that would indicate ways to produce meaning out of selective information.[10]

In the parallel Soviet system of thought, the 'ideological' or content/form context potential of the media message was directly linked not only to ownership over its means of production and distribution, but to ownership, class structure and principles of production in the society at large. As is well known, it is not a simple, technocratic dependency, but a complex system of conditioning in which all subsystems of society are born from a particular historic mode of production, one that is contemporarily capitalistic. Thus, for Soviet researchers reflecting on media in capitalist and Socialist (Communist in Western terminologies) societies, any media message could only be interpreted as a carrier and a potential propagator of the capitalist ideology due to the very material conditions of its production, encoding and decoding, and the channel used. On the other hand, in the Soviet bloc, supposedly conditioned by a different system of material production, media represented and served the interests of the people who were believed to have become the ruling class itself.

9. G Davidiuk and V Bobrovskij, *Problemy 'massovoj kultury' i 'massovykh kommunikazij'* [*Problems of 'Mass Culture' and 'Mass Media'*], Nauka i tekhnika, Minsk, 1972, p 127; Vladimir Borev, *Fotografija v structure massovoj kommunikazii* [*Photography in the Structure of Mass Communication*], Mintis, Vilnius, 1986, pp 64–5

10. For an attentive and passionate account of cybernetics, see Katherine N Hayles, *How We Became Posthuman: Virtual Bodies in Cybernetics, Literature and Informatics*, University of Chicago Press, Chicago, 1999. See also Donald M MacKay, 'The Nomenclature of Information Theory', in *Cybernetics, Circular Causal and Feedback Mechanisms in Biological and Social Systems, Transactions of the Eighth Conference*, ed Heinz von Foerster, Josiah Macy Jr Foundation, New York, 1951.

Soviet academics could not come close to any analysis capable of unpacking the intricate and complex set of interdependencies conditioning media in relation to their owners in the manner of Noam Chomsky and Edward Herman's *Manufacturing Consent: The Political Economy of the Mass Media*. Nor could they accept the studies of perception, representation, interpretation or audience reception advanced by non-Soviet media or cultural studies. Soviet accounts of media can be summed up by the general claim that capitalist media ensure the domination of the ruling class by serving to fill up workers' leisure time with activity that manipulates and degrades them (again without adding on or explicitly referring to the Frankfurt School's 'culture industry'). Soviet media on the other hand work to educate workers and mould them by bringing them up culturally and thus 'spiritually'.

In a quite integral but deeply schizophrenic way, Soviet academics had to regard media in a materialist Marxist-Leninist fashion as conditioned by the overall mode of material production, and at the same time from an exclusively idealistic standpoint, as serving 'spiritual' growth, educating society by appealing to classical culture and traditional values. Dialectical materialism forced academics to claim primacy for socio-technical relations of production over ideological systems. But when moving from general claims to practical analysis, they could only focus on ideological content, ignoring the materiality of the medium, as its analysis would have demonstrated the mechanisms of Soviet propaganda.

To take one example, formalist critics who engaged with the novel and fairytales aimed to describe the dynamics of mutual generation running back and forth between content and form.[11] As we might expect, literary form is the materiality which actualises literary content. Such materiality could be studied aesthetically, politically or historically. But the Party ran public abolition processes against those enquiries, banning them for 'simplification', because, in Communist opinion, they prioritised questions of literary form and systems over social conditions resulting from the mode of production. Supposedly, if the material conditions of production in a society change in a country where the Revolution has been won, literary form and content should change accordingly. As is well known, ten years after 1917 Soviet culture turned to traditionalist and classicist aesthetics, closing off and physically crushing avant-garde movements in all areas of practice. Soviet traditionalist aesthetics, charged with ideological content, had fully replaced the radical aesthetics and theoretical approaches of the 1920s by the mid-1930s. Formalism as a school of thought, along with the sociology of literature initiated by Valerian Pereverzev, was banned. Enquiries into the particular forms of Soviet literature, for instance, could not have demonstrated its freedom, its promotion of alternatives, of change, or its achievement of the initial Marxist goals, but only the materiality of dictatorship. Thus, academics were obliged to focus exclusively on content in the most simplified and vulgar sense of the term, divorced from form, as a direct and clear representation of the proletariat and its 'interests' as subject and hero, while constantly having to reassert the primacy of the material they were constrained to ignore.

For media theory this meant, for instance, banning Marshall McLuhan, charging him simultaneously with 'subjective idealism' and 'formalism' and attempting to prove that focusing on the 'moulding' instead of 'manipulative' effect of media (that is, emphasising the education and 'spiritual

---

11. Many works of Formalist literary scholars, especially those by the best known authors, are available in English. See: Viktor Shklovsky, *Energy of Delusion: A Book on Plot*, trans Shushan Aragyan, Dalkey Archive Press, London, 2007; Viktor Shklovsky, *Theory of Prose*, Dalkey Archive Press, Elmwood Park, 1991; Yuri Tynianov, *The Problem of Verse Language*, eds and trans Michael Sosa and Brent Harvey, Ann Arbor, Ardis, 1981; Lee T Lemon and Marion J Reis, *Russian Formalist Criticism: Four Essays*, University of Nebraska Press, Lincoln, 1965, includes essays by Boris Eichenbaum, Viktor Tomashevsky and Viktor Shklovsky.

improvement' of the audience through the content over the agency of the materiality of the media) makes the message independent of the medium (the message is not the medium).[12] Similarly, Soviet television had to differ radically from capitalist television since all the socio-technical conditions were based on the non-capitalist, Soviet mode of production, thus only ever disseminating not propagandist but humanist messages. Such a theoretical complex, unable to detail and update itself, froze many lines of thinking that might otherwise have been able to arrive at results demonstrating more complex sets of dependencies, more development of intricate systems of thinking and stimulation of theoretical apparatuses.

In fact, early twentieth-century Russia saw a rise of interest in technology from the philosophical viewpoint. Philosophy of technology at that time was a term not widely used outside Germany, with the notable exception of a Russian of German origin, Piotr Engelmeier (1855–1942), who analysed the role of technology as a cultural factor. Engelmeier lectured at technical schools and published some hundred articles and books. In the late 1920s he led a correspondence study group within the Polytechnic Society of the All-Union Association of Engineers (AAE). In 1929 he survived a political campaign against the philosophy of technology and withdrew from his philosophical career. The AAE was liquidated. Engelmeier sought both to define technology ontologically and to understand human beings and society through technology as a new ecology.[13] He tried to formulate a theory of technical creativity and invention, but received the death-threatening label of 'idealist-utopian' from B Markov in the January 1929 issue of *Engineer Labour* magazine, as a part of the campaign against his philosophy of technology. Today a large part of his writings could be interpreted as technocratic, a quality which did not save his work from banishment by technocratic Soviet ideology.

A parallel story can be told about artistic enquiries into technological potential. The tradition established by Aleksandr Rodchenko, Alexandr Skriabin, Sergei Eisenstein, Dziga Vertov, Lev Termen (Léon Theremin) and others, though interrupted in the 1930s, was occasionally upheld in the twentieth century by the isolated efforts of Eduard Artemiev, Bulat Galeev, the 'Movement' group, by the first synthesiser of Evgenij Murzin – experiments that could not enter the body of culture and had to remain marginal. Even photography was not regarded as a form of art in Soviet times, while at the same time it was tightly controlled and directed through the all-union network of 'amateur' photo clubs. The magazine *Soviet Photo* suggested only two models of photography: amateur ('sunset' photography) and professional reportage (newspaper photography). If individuals were capable of producing interesting work, it had to remain marginal in the cultural context.

The absence of an uninterrupted, lived tradition of critical inquiry into and artistic engagement with technology led to the spread of a certain ideology regarding media or digital media which can be characterised as deterministic, instrumental and essentialist. Technology is still usually regarded today as a black-box phenomenon beyond the culture of humans, mostly neutral, not capable of playing significant roles in original creation or cultural life at large, or as vicious, something destructive to civilisation at large. Contemporary Russian culture is unprepared to accept technological forms of art or even think of technology culturally

12. Davidiuk and Bobrovskij, op cit, pp 130–40, Borev, op cit, pp 86–9. See also: U Voronzov, *Massovyje kommunikazii v napravlennom formirovanii obsshestvennogo mnenija v burdguaznykh stranakh*, [*Directed Formation of Public Opinion by Mass Media in Capitalist Countries*], Moscow, 1968.

13. Engelmeier was a prolific writer. Some of his books include *Filosofija tekhniki. Volume 2. Sovremennaja filosofija* [*Philosophy of Technology. Second Edition. Contemporary Philosophy*], Moscow, 1912; *Filosofija tekhniki. Volume 3* [*Philosophy of Technology. Third Edition*], Nasha zhizn', Moscow, 1912; *Filosofija tekhniki. Volume 4. Technizism* [*Philosophy of Technology. Fourth Edition. Technicism*], Moscow, 1913. For an account of Engelmeier's work, see Olga Goriunova, 'Vitalist Technocultural Thinking in Revolutionary Russia (on Piotr Engelmeier)', in *Place Studies in Art, Media, Science and Technology. Historical Investigations on the Sites and the Migration of Knowledge*, eds Andreas Broeckmann and Gunalan Nadarajan, Verlag und Datenbank für Geisteswissenschaften, VDG, Weimar, 2008.

as informing our times. In Russia, until 2000 and for broad layers of society, the most current critical inquiry into technology remained Heidegger's article 'The Question Concerning Technology' and the avant-garde in technological art was still video art. Only a very few specifically individual and isolated positions are available in the end for new media artistic and cultural practices.

Electronic Image
Identities and the Experience of Globalisation in the International Festival of Electronic Art – *Videobrasil*

Eduardo de Jesus

FIRST MOVEMENTS

We live amidst images in a complex and fast-moving circuit, in which media and mediations cross over in different narrative forms. Daily life, in its multiple facets and unfolding developments, feeds the media circuits in several ways. In our age, images circulate on several screens and devices, prompting us somehow to know and experiment with distinct facets of the real, even if they are at a distance. Images constituted by media systems, configured around diverse interests, circulate alongside images home-produced in new media circuits such as YouTube, Vimeo and other image circulation websites.

Consequently one's memory accumulates not only directly lived experiences, but also a multitude of fragments absorbed from these images that we see all the time. Our life daily is encrusted with images from the most diverse circuits and this results in new directives to our experiences.

It is in this dynamic system that Brazilian audiovisual production is situated. Television is still an important territory of production for local social life. Little by little, other circuits are starting to infiltrate social life, displacing the effects caused by this asymmetric mode of communication. Often, the images do not correspond to real experience, but forge world-views that are taken to be the absolute truth, when in fact they barely conceal the interests of those groups who are in power.

Perhaps it is enough to approach video art production in Brazil – and specifically that video art related to the context of the main electronic art festival, Videobrasil – as informing the perspective of a small circuit infiltrated within a wider system, operating as a form of resistance, and in this way generating possibilities of new gazes. Initially the path diverges from the circuit towards the creation of another image repertoire, favouring the peripheral vision of in-transit subjectivities, rather than the gaze already configured by the dominant media.

In retrospect, when video production began in Brazil, it embodied, albeit tenuously, two veins which today have been mixed up and mutually contaminate each other. However, in the beginning, the difference between them left a mark on local production. On the one hand, we have, as is the case with video history internationally, the approximation of artists from the most diverse tendencies who sought a new tool of investigation in video. A few of them worked continuously and productively with amateur cinema formats and gauges, such as super-8 or 16 mm,[1] or in the production of so-called audiovisuals – sound-synchronised slide projections – developed by several Brazilian artists. On the other hand, a second generation emerged who saw an anti-television utopia in video but who also needed exhibition circuits in order to sustain and legitimise themselves. This second generation emerged at the beginning of the 1980s almost simultaneously with Videobrasil.

ANTECEDENTS AND PIONEERS

The first electronic image-recording devices arrived in Brazil right at the end of the 1960s, but the production of video art effectively began in the middle of the 1970s by way of an invitation for Brazilian artists to participate in a show in the USA. According to Walter Zanini – one of the most important promoters of video activity at its inception in Brazil – '1974 was a key year for video art in the country'. In that year, Zanini, then director of MAC/USP (São Paulo University Contemporary Art Museum), received:

> ... an invitation from the Institute of Contemporary Art of Pennsylvania University, in Philadelphia, to coordinate a Brazilian representation at the 'Video Art' international exhibition. Several artists who had held multimedia events and exhibitions in the museum prepared projects, facing, however, the greatest difficulties for the continuation of the work in fruitless efforts with universities and other institutions.[2]

In 1975, the São Paulo Biennale brought together several video art pieces, putting Brazilian audiences in touch with American productions, and amongst these Nam June Paik's *TV Garden*. This enterprise, despite the public's unfamiliarity with video art, certainly fomented and opened up possibilities for Brazilian artists to find out about more recent productions.

The Brazilian drive for the production of video art in Rio de Janeiro took the shape of a group of artists who used the equipment of local artist Jom Tob Azulay for the creation of their first videos. Anna Bella Geiger, Fernando Cocchiarale, Ivens Machado and Sônia Andrade, among others, participated in these first experiences. In 1976, Zanini bought equipment through MAC/USP and offered it for use to a group of artists in São Paulo.[3] Of the works produced by this group *Marca Registrada* by Letícia Parente is noteworthy. In this video, Parente sews the words 'Made in Brazil' into the sole of her foot, a clear gesture of the quest for identity and recognition by reference to the description printed on commercial goods and often in English. However, as Arlindo

---

1. For more information about the audiovisual productions, 16 mm and super-8, see the text 'Algumas Idéias em Torno à Expo-projeção 73' ('A Few Ideas Around the Expo-Projeção 73'), by Aracy Amaral, for the show that screened films produced by artists, in *Crítica de Arte no Brasil: Temáticas Contemporâneas*, ed Glória Ferreira, Rio de Janeiro, FUNARTE, 2006. In the same book, texts by Walter Zanini and Frederico Morais point to other aspects of this fertile period of Brazilian new media art.

2. On the emergence of video art in Brazil, see Walter Zanini, 'Primeiros Tempos da Arte/Tecnologia no Brasil', in *A Arte no Século XXI – a Humanização das Tecnologias*, ed Diana Domingues, EDUSP, São Paulo, 1997; for further reading on the subject see 'Itaú Cultural', in *Made in Brasil – Três Décadas do Vídeo Brasileiro*, ed Arlindo Machado, Itaú Cultural, São Paulo, 2003

3. Walter Zanini, 'Videoarte: uma Poética Aberta', in Arlindo Machado, op cit, p 53

Machado remarks,[4] this gesture places the work in tune with the production of American artists such as Vito Acconci and Joan Jonas. These first experiments, despite being fundamental for the construction of a Brazilian 'videographic image', were not sufficiently abundant; there were few artists who took up video as a working tool and means of expression. This situation changed at the end of the 1990s with a clear turn in Brazilian artistic production that placed video and the electronic image within the central circuits of art.

Returning to the history of Videobrasil, it first took place in August 1983 when Brazil was in political upheaval. A few months before, a movement demanding the return of direct elections for the presidency, known as *Diretas Já* (Direct Elections Now), had just begun. The movement gained national impetus between January and April of 1984, with huge demonstrations in the main Brazilian cities. The year 1984 saw an end to the military dictatorship, one of the darkest periods of Brazilian history. Video art expanded in the 1980s and groups of artists emerged who followed in the steps of pioneering researchers, but from a perspective of expansion and support of the visual arts generally, as well as the renewal of production modes geared towards television. Despite their origins in the end of the dictatorship period, the videos entered in the festival competition did not directly mirror the Brazilian political moment. Many of the works reflected the opening up of politics, above all through their freedom in dealing with issues that up to then had not been part of Brazilian culture, or that could not be aired in the period of intense censorship and repression.

It is important to stress that, although the Festival was staged after the dictatorship, structures of control and censorship continued. According to Solange Farkas, director and curator of the Festival, in the early years of the competition films that were to be screened had to be sent to a censorship body for approval. These structures were increasingly dismantled, but they persisted in the first years of democracy in Brazil. The generation that grew up under the imposed silence of the dictatorship later had the opportunity to show aspects of Brazilian daily life without the shackles of censorship.

A few video-makers emerged in the first Festival, who, from that moment on, would begin the second phase of video history in Brazil. We can highlight TVDO, an independent company founded at the end of the 1980s by television students of the Arts and Communication School at São Paulo University (ECA-USP). The group was initially formed by Tadeu Jungle, Walter Silveira, Ney Marcondes, Paulo Priolli and Pedro Vieira, and produced several pieces shown in the first Videobrasil festival.

Although the group's production did not directly address the social and political issues of the Brazil of that period, it did question the monopoly of television broadcasting companies which kept the doors closed to revitalising language renovation and the new generation's experiments. In this sense, TVDO's action was political and expressed the desire of these young artists to renew the language of television and thus occupy a visible space in Brazilian culture.[5] The television debut of film director Glauber Rocha (1939–1981) at the end of the 1970s, in his programme *Abertura*, echoed in some ways the productions of the 1980s developed by TVDO. Rocha, who was the driving force behind the emergence of the 'Cinema Novo' movement in cinematographic

4. For an overview of art and technology in Brazil on the Itaú Cultural site: http://www.itaucultural.org.br

5. Ibid, Itaú Cultural, coordinated by Arlindo Machado, 'Panorama de arte e tecnologia do Brasil'

language, its renewal through influences from Italian neo-realism and the French *nouvelle vague*, participated in one of the *Abertura* sketches, one of the most important programmes of Brazilian television, broadcast between 1979 and 1980, at precisely the moment of the democratic turn in politics.

Brazilian television, which had always been conservative in content, approach and language, at this moment seemed to break the pattern with Glauber who went on to influence other artists in search of renewal. Two streams were now effectively configured in Brazilian videographic production, one leading towards a kind of appropriation and renovation of television, and the other flowing from the first experiments linked to the visual arts scene. These two trends peculiar to the history of video in Brazil still reverberate today, but now seek other configurations within an even more complex circuit.

Back in the 1970s, and in parallel to this trend towards video, another movement began, associating artistic production with the technological universe. Waldemar Cordeiro put on the 'Arteônica' exhibition and conference at Fundacão Armando Álvares Penteado (FAAP) (São Paulo) in 1971 which showed images created through the use of information technology. In the following year, at the recently created Arteônica Centre of the Arts Institute at Unicamp, the state university in the city of Campinas, he developed a series of works fundamental to the development of media art in Brazil. The production of images using information technologies, initiated by Cordeiro, would incorporate video only in the 1980s in another technological context, driven mainly by the emergence of micro-informatics.

This double link between electronic image recording, typical of video, and data processing and IT experiences seems to have been resolved in the course of time. Today, we have both young and established creators trying out increasingly radical experiments in the use of both means, always with a strong tendency to subversion. Lucas Bambozzi illustrates this trajectory that starts in video and little by little opens up to experiments in other technological means, with or without the use of images. In curating projects such as arte.mov (2006) or in works such as *O tempo não recuperado* ('Non-recovered time') (2004) (DVD-ROM and installation), Bambozzi creates extremely productive tensions within the technological field.

Immediately after their first experiments in the visual arts, the generation of independent producers – represented mainly by TVDO – sought more than an entry into the art scene. Their work in the television broadcasting circuit has profoundly marked the second generation of Brazilian video-makers. This is clear in the catalogues from the first years of Videobrasil, as well as in the choice of professionals who sat on the jury, the lecture cycles and even some of the works submitted, which placed themselves at the forefront of innovation as an option within televisual language. This fact has contributed to the specificity of video history in Brazil which was first formed around community televisions, encouraging the dream of another kind of communication contrary to video production in other countries (such as the USA). In other words, instead of establishing alternative television circuits, Brazilian production sought insertion into an already configured televisual media, in a strategy of infiltration.

The Olhar Eletrônico production company of São Paulo, which emerged at the beginning of the 1980s, circulated a repertoire of creative video possibilities in tune with the aim of infiltrating Brazilian television and creating work fundamental to Brazilian videography. Olhar Eletrônico seems to have achieved a more productive approximation between video art and commercial television. Besides gaining Videobrasil Festival awards, it has generated participation in highly experimental television programmes broadcast by commercial channels, such as *23ªhora*, on TV Gazeta, as well as *Crig-Rá* and *Olho Mágico* for Abril Vídeo.[6]

Other forms of thinking video were being carried out, albeit less intensely, in the course of the 1980s festivals. These first experiments have succeeded in showing that the nature of the electronic image was really fluid, a thinking-state of the images prior to, and after, the emergence of video. As Philippe Dubois remarks: 'Video is not an object, it is a state. A state of the image. A form that thinks. Video thinks what the images (all and any) are, make or create.'[7]

The eighth Videobrasil festival in 1990 went international. It promoted the circulation of productions that would establish dialogues, exchanges and hybridity, as indeed it had also inevitably circulated artists, curators, theoreticians and ideas that widened our perceptual horizon on the world. What role has Videobrasil's internationalisation played in Brazilian video circuits? How have the identities situated in that circuit, at the time hardly globalised, shown us different approaches and world-views? How did we relate to the global and the local in view of the formation of subjectivities and identities by means of the video image?

GLOBALISATION AND IDENTITIES: THE TENSION BETWEEN THE LOCAL AND THE GLOBAL

In the press release for Videobrasil 7 in 1989, the Festival's director and curator, Solange Farkas, emphasised an international circulation of the work that aimed beyond the desire to widen its market possibilities:

> We are aware that festivals serve as a stimulus to creation, but unfortunately they have not been sufficiently efficient as market stimulators. We are also aware that this stimulus will be given as the diffusion and diversification of the work is increased, with the creation of an image diffusion and reproduction network geared towards the public as a whole… I believe we are beginning an important process of international diffusion of the work, with the presence and participation of personalities from other European countries and Brazil, linked to the creation, production, distribution and diffusion of this still in gestation art.[8]

This seventh festival hosted a series of informative international shows, as well as inviting curators and theoreticians. The effort set out in Solange's text did generate an initial and productive exchange between Brazilian artists and international production from countries such as France, Britain and the Netherlands, amongst others, and a series of informative screenings brought important work to Brazilian audiences. However, the festival competition was still limited to Brazilian artists.

6. On the production relations between video and television, see Yvana Fechine, 'O Video Como Projeto Utópico da Televisão' (Video as Television's Utopian Project), in Arlindo Machado, op cit

7. Free translation of: O vídeo não é um objeto, ele é um estado. Um estado da imagem. Uma forma que pensa. O vídeo pensa o que as imagens (todas e quaisquer) são, fazem ou criam.

8. Philippe Dubois, *Cinema, Vídeo, Godard*, Cosac Naify, São Paulo, 2004, p 116

Market protectionism, specificity of models and production modes, lack of dialogue with international production – such issues were countless when productions from Brazil and abroad began to make regular and institutionalised contact. Thomas Farkas, documentarist and renowned photographer, president of Fotoptica, Videobrasil's main sponsor that lends its name to the Festival Fotoptica Videobrasil, indicated in his introduction to the catalogue a process of internationalisation aimed at imprinting video with a world language:

> To advertise and to promote the production of national videos in the country has been an unceasing task of the Festival Fotoptica Videobrasil's producers... At this particular moment, when we are taking an important step as the show is internationalised – bringing in professionals from abroad and providing our participants with a closer contact with the world outside. I believe that this healthy exchange will become productive and yield good fruits. Especially as we internationalise video, we give it a unique world, language.[9]

At that moment, there were still clear borders between formats, VHS and Umatic, and between genres – fiction, documentary, musical, video art and a special prize for the best video. These demarcations became increasingly fluid, as did the work itself and its exhibition circuits. Certainly the porosity of the borders between genres and formats, which now dominates the audiovisual environment, is due to the very way in which productions are engendered in diverse circuits. Besides, the passages between the work's production, exhibition and modes of circulation promoted in themselves an easing of frontiers to the benefit of total hybridism. This was evident in the seventh festival which showed videos from countries such as Australia and Mozambique and from South American countries such as Argentina, Uruguay and Chile with which Videobrasil has kept up intense and productive exchanges of various natures ever since.

The internationalisation process initiated at this festival culminated with the entry of foreigners to the eighth Festival competition in 1990, and continued into the ninth, but with a change in yearly to biennial which afforded more time for research and dialogues with other festivals, media centres, museums and institutions of diverse countries. A geographic division was adopted as a reference for the selection of foreign submissions to the competition show, which now encompassed the southern hemisphere. If, at first, this selection privileged the countries of the region, with the passing of time it was increasingly devised around another map, less geographical and more political, cultural and social, geared towards the geopolitical situation of the diverse countries. So, in the course of time, several countries of the geographical North, such as Mexico, or even from the Middle East, came to participate in the competition. This rendered Videobrasil a space for the convergence of videographies and audiovisual experiments in this expanded and geopolitical Southern axis, openly privileging emergent videographies, allowing for intense exchanges between institutions, curators, artists, theoreticians and the public at large.

The choice of the Southern hemisphere as the region encompassed by Videobrasil's competitive entries was a political position taken in the face of the globalisation that began to take shape in the early 1990s. The

9. Solange Farkas, Catalogue of the 7th Fotoptica Festival Videobrasil, São Paulo, 1989, p 3

decision was to maintain a dialogue with countries that in some way were similar to Brazil, especially regarding their political and economic situations. This proposition seems to have been intensified over time, as indicated by the by Solange Farkas's text in the catalogue. In her text for the eighth, then still called Festival Fotoptica de Vídeo, 'North and South: Desires and Limits', Farkas points out that widening the scope of the competition show to the Southern hemisphere would:

> ... render viable the exchange between the Southern and Northern hemispheres, by means of the organisation of meetings between people hailing from diverse places, with agendas about the desires and limits of this relationship [between North and South].

Contrary to the idea of infiltration previously used by TVDO and Olhar Eletrônico, the view widened in favour of dialogue and collaborations between independent producers and commercial broadcasting companies. Thus, in the 'Television and Independent Production' debate, companies such as Channel 4 (United Kingdom), Canal Plus (France), MTV (Brazil), RTBF (Belgium) and Nueva Imagen (Chile) were brought face to face with the aim of thinking and instigating production modes and alternative strategies for the exhibition of independent productions. In the same field another debate around 'Creation and the Alternative Market' addressed the market issues and the experiences of more configured markets, such as the United Kingdom, USA, Germany and France in addition to those of Brazilian producers.

The festival hosted artists such as Marcel Odenbach who exhibited the video installation *As If Memories Could Deceive Me*, and Dominik Barbier and Cathy Vogan who showed *The No Way Buster Project*. The most definitive step towards internationalisation of its programme was taken by promoting both an intense exchange of experiences and a search for Brazilian identity which seemed to reconfigure itself in the ninth festival, two years later, in September 1992.

In the introduction to the tenth catalogue, Solange Farkas placed Videobrasil as a centre 'to which a good part of the dispersed creative energy, both in Brazil and all over the world, converges', emphasising Videobrasil as an agglutinating centre for experiences around the Southern axis electronic image which would further gel in the festivals to follow. One could already perceive in the ninth a productive tension between local and global identities which might generate 'processes of singularisation, of existential creation, moved by the wind of happenings'.[10]

In at least two pieces, *Parabolic People* (1991) by Sandra Kogut, and *Essa coisa nervosa* (*This nervous thing*, 1991) by Eder Santos, it is possible to see this widening focus and the opening to new agencies resulting from cultural exchanges, travels and contacts. Kogut, in the eighth festival, showed two pieces that pointed to this process of identity recognition. In *What Do You Think People Think Brazil Is?* (1990), the artist assembled a vertiginous sound and image collage, edited with the overlapping of texts, images and animations, dealing essentially with identity issues in Brazil but from the point of view of foreigners, as the video synopsis indicates: 'Foreign tourists voice opinions about Brazil. In their clichés, they associate the country with sex, beautiful women, corruption, poverty, Carnival, overpopulation, football, monkeys and bananas.' Kogut made use of a device – the Video Cabin – that she developed in

10. Ibid, p 5

order to collect statements. This 'device-procedure' was also used in the production of *Videocabines São Caixas Pretas* (*Video Cabins Are Black Boxes*, 1990). Her participation in Videobrasil's eighth festival enabled Kogut to produce Video Cabins in other countries with the support of CICV, Centre International de Création Vidéo Montbéliard Belford, at the time coordinated by Pierre Bongiovanni, the curator who screened it at the same festival, which also led to the production of *Parabolic People*, exhibited in the ninth competition.

Despite developing Video Cabins in foreign countries, Kogut did not abandon the critical vein present in her first video works. The artist used CICV's good technological structure to produce a kaleidoscope of images, stereotypes, identities, urban images and musical rhythms in short sequences broadcast during French television commercial breaks. With editing that seemed to rebuild cities and scenes, Kogut re-creates the world by means of the tenuous relationships between people, their testimonials and the images from the several countries which she had visited with her Video Cabins. We see the same questioning gaze on Brazilian identity in *What Do You Think...*, but now directed to how identities are perceived in the present world by means of media and the processes of globalisation.

The passage to a more internationalised context has also echoed in the work of Santos, who always approached issues linked to local culture in his work, as in *Uakti* (1987) and *Mentiras e humilhações* (*Lies and humiliations*, 1988). In the first piece, we see a series of video clips of a band of the same name interpreting Ravel's famous *Bolero* with instruments created with water vessels and PVC tubes. Santos fills the screen with overlapping images from Brazilian and clearly African elements edited to the rhythm of the melody. Close encounters with the universe of Brazilian culture also appear in the delicate video *Mentiras e humilhações*, based on the poem *Liquidação* by Carlos Drummond de Andrade, one of Brazil's most important poets, born, like Santos, in Minas Gerais State. In this work, the sale of a house discloses images from the past, produced by the overlapping of old super-8 footage.

In the eighth festival, Santos, who had been awarded prizes in the third, fifth and sixth festivals, showed the enigmatic work *Não Vou à África Porque Tenho Plantão* (*I don't go to Africa Because I Am On Duty*, 1990) that, alongside Kogut's pieces for the same festival, pointed towards globalised phenomena. In the case of Santos, the video, spoken in English, deals both with ecological issues and the volume and speed of information production. Santos was awarded the Montbéliard prize for this video, and Kogut the best video art prize for *What Do You Think*. Pieces by these two artists show that identity negotiations can generate extremely productive tensions between local and global identities. Instead of claiming that local identities are imprisoned or succumb to pulverisation from abroad, perhaps the more propitious thing to do, as Kogut and Santos have done, is not to domesticate the force that comes from these encounters. Suley Rolnik comments on this clash between local and global identities:

> Two processes take place in subjectivities today, corresponding to opposed destinies arising from this insistence on identity in the midst of an earthquake that is transforming irreversibly the subjective landscape:

the hardening of local identities and the threat of total pulverisation of any and every identity... These strategies, both those that aim for a return to local identity and those that aim to support global identities, hold a common goal: the domestication of forces. In all of them, such attempts necessarily fail. But the damage is done: the continuous tension between figure and forces is neutralised, de-potentialising the disruptive and creative power of this tension, processes of subjectification are halted. When this happens, the resistance to the contemporary wins.[11]

Subsequent festivals were dedicated to the consolidation of these first movements initiated in the eighth and ninth, causing the festival to become increasingly open to exchanges but without losing sight of specificities of the Southern axis. Latin America's circuits began increasingly to draw together, especially those of Chile and Argentina, through the participation of artists in the competition or as part of specific and curated shows, such as the one organised by Jorge La Ferla, featuring a panorama of the audiovisual poetry produced in various countries, including Latin America. La Ferla, the main promoter of video in Argentina, became a frequent collaborator in and distributor for the festival in his country, and had participated with a considerable amount of artwork since the eighth.

The Southern axis notion expands in the later festivals, encompassing other countries and thus providing visibility to new video production. One of the more recent and most memorable festivals was the fourteenth, held in the aftermath of the World Trade Center outrage in New York. The production profile had changed with the development of editing platforms, digital recording, CD-ROM and Internet work that was now included. This festival took place only eight days after 9/11, at a moment of confusion. The festival team, shaken by the event and its consequences, had to work around a series of abstentions caused by the attacks. The proximity of the event and the heat of discussions that followed, both during the festival and after, gave rise to the theme of the following year – *Deslocamentos/Displacements*. This was developed, with the active participation of Brazilian poet Waly Salomão, together with curators Akram Zaatari and Christine Tohme, in a large exhibition focused on artistic production in Lebanon. Video projections, video installations, performances and lectures by philosophers were part of the 'Possible Narratives' in the show. This moment, perhaps one of the most productive and rich in Videobrasil's history, brought the festival into the whole discussion around the political context of images, in the search for specific issues typical of a Southern bias – a vocation that was consolidated in the course of Videobrasil's successive festivals.

OTHER UNFOLDING DEVELOPMENTS

The festival in 1991 was organised by the Associação Cultural Videobrasil, 'a public interest organisation dedicated to the encouragement, diffusion and the mapping of electronic art in the Southern circuit'. Also created in 1991, it is 'the international reference and exchange centre for artists, curators and thinkers'.[12] The Associação Cultural Videobrasil's events and productions have always relied on local partners, such as SESC-SP (Serviço Social do Comércio de São Paulo) which has supported them, providing a venue and co-producing the festival since 1992. The festival also relies

11. Suely Rolnik, 'Toxicômanos de Identidade: Subjetividade em Tempo de Globalização', in *Cadernos de Subjetividade*, ed Daniel Lins, Papirus, Campinas, 1997, p 3

12. Solange Farkas, catalogue of the exhibition 'The Pan African Exhibition of Contemporary Art', São Paulo, 2005

on sponsors and international collaborators such as the Prince Claus Fund for Culture and Development which has sponsored several of its events and productions.

The path to internationalisation has led the Associação cultural to reaffirm and widen its goal of being a meeting point for artists, curators, theoreticians and the public linked in some way to the Southern geopolitical axis and of allowing dialogue with and affiliation to other centres geared towards the same region.

In this perspective we can highlight two contemporary art shows mounted by the Associação Cultural Videobrasil. The 'Pan African Exhibition of Contemporary Art' was held in 2000, at SESC Pompéia in São Paulo, bringing into the country a selection of artwork by some of the major contemporary African artists. William Kentridge's *Screensaver* (2000) was commissioned for the exhibition. Produced specially for the 'Pan African Exhibition of Contemporary Art', the installation, as stated in the catalogue, 'is an apparently simple idea, but of great visual impact'. In it, a projection system inside a car transforms the vehicle's windows unexpectedly into a fishbowl where fish of diverse colours swim about. The car thus loses its original function and becomes an object of contemplation. The image, says Kentridge, creates an ambiguous situation: what is being seen, after all? Is it the water, or is it a virtual background as in a screensaver? Solange Farkas and South African critic Clive Kellner curated the exhibition, which included debates and lectures, with the clear aim of bringing Brazil closer to its African origins and exposing Brazilian audiences to contemporary art produced in Africa.

A few years later, in 2005, the Associação Cultural Videobrasil promoted the second show focused on Africa, this time at the Bahia Museum of Modern Art, in the city of Salvador, the Solar do Unhão, one of the places where African slaves arrived in Brazil. The 'Pan African Exhibition of Contemporary Art' promoted the meeting between Brazilian and African artists brought together by the sea, across which the slave trade routes between Africa and the Americas were set up, as the text by Solange Farkas informs us:

> Nearly 5 years have passed since the São Paulo show and, now, we can say that the sea was the starting point for the curatorial work. The sea physically divides the Americas and Africa, and was, for centuries, the great transport and trade pathway. A trade that served the interests of the colonial matrices, in which Man was at once merchant and merchandise. In the triangular logic of the trade between Africa, the Americas and Europe, slave labour was an important trade item. The enslaved person was a tradable commodity.[13]

In this show, African, Cuban and Brazilian artists showed their film and work and also participated, alongside theoreticians, researchers and curators, in the debates, lectures and panels that highlighted contemporary issues of identity, prejudice and the ties that unite black cultures on several continents.

Associação Cultural Videobrasil's second important activity in facilitating relations between work, artists and contents, within the perspective of the Southern axis, was the creation of the archive Videobrasil Authors' Collection. The collection is completely focused on contemporary art

13. Extracted from the Associação Cultural Videobrasil site, http://www.videobrasil.org.br

production of the Southern axis and was launched in 2000 with the documentary *Certain Doubts of William Kentridge*. Two more titles followed: *Rafael França, Obra Como Testamento* (*Work as Testament*, 2001) and Mau Wal's *Encontros Traduzidos* (*Translated Encounters*, 2002). The first documents the itinerary of Rafael França (1957–1991), one of the most important Brazilian video artists. França's oeuvre oscillates between the investigation of narratives in single-channel pieces and, in his installations, a reflection on the nature of electronic media, especially television sets. In his short life, the artist moved between events in the urban milieu, with the group 3nós3, as well as print-making and photocopies before exploring the medium of video. The second title features the duo Maurício Dias and Walter Riedweg and their work which is often inserted in the cityscape or confronts the real in the situations in which they place their work. *A Gaze on the Gazes of Akram Zaatari* (2004) featured the work of the Lebanese artist and the contemporary art scene in Lebanon.

Coco Fusco, an American artist of Cuban origin, was the focus of the documentary *Coco Fusco: I like girls in uniform*. Taking as a starting point the vivid performance, *Bare Life Study # 1*, presented in the American Consulate in São Paulo in the context of the fifteenth festival, the documentary features Coco's artistic itinerary in several performances, installation and video work.

Videobrasil International Electronic Art Festival and Associação Cultural Videobrasil focus on identities and subjectivities in a globalised context and how these are assimilated in different ways and rendered viable so as to create a space of exchange and multiplicity. It is typical of video to appropriate dissonant gazes, non-conventional views and discourses that privilege the subjective. This twin process of internationalisation has taken place productively in such a way as to open possibilities for audiences to understand video production and its complex agencies in today's world.

The artworks exhibited at the Festival and the Associação's activities in several countries of the Southern axis allow us to observe trends towards adopting alternative viewpoints to the political interests and economies that dominate the more consolidated audiovisual circles.

We might say that the Southern focus was a process of 'internalisation' gradually being structured, and which attended to the wider possibilities of dialogues, of visibilities and productive exchanges of artistic production, but that in the end points back to the political, social, economic and subjective issues typical of the Southern bias.

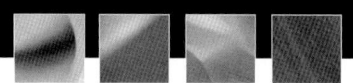

Text and Performance Quarterly

Published on behalf of the National Communication Association

INCREASE IN CONTENT IN 2009

EDITOR:
Bruce Henderson, *Ithaca College, USA*

INCOMING EDITOR FOR 2010:
Heidi Rose, *Villanova University, USA*

Text and Performance Quarterly (***TPQ***) publishes scholarship that explores and advances the study of performance as a social, communicative practice; as a technology of representation and expression; and as a hermeneutic. Articles address performance and the performative from a wide range of perspectives and methodologies, and they investigate all sites of performance from the classical stage to popular culture to the practices of everyday life.

TPQ also features a 'Performance in Review' section that provides a scholarly forum to document performances and to situate and critique them within enduring and emergent issues in performance studies praxis. Projects about artists working outside the academy are featured, however, work is also encouraged from or about academic scholar-artists who use performance as a method of inquiry.

In addition to standard monographs, ***TPQ*** also publishes papers that examine and analyze performance in other scholarly modes, including experimental critical essays, photo essays, interviews, and performance texts/scripts.

NATIONAL COMMUNICATION ASSOCIATION

To sign up for tables of contents, new publications and citation alerting services visit **www.informaworld.com/alerting**

Register your email address at **www.tandf.co.uk/journals/eupdates.asp** to receive information on books, journals and other news within your areas of interest.

For further information, please contact Customer Services at either of the following:
T&F Informa UK Ltd, Sheepen Place, Colchester, Essex, CO3 3LP, UK
Tel: +44 (0) 20 7017 5544 Fax: 44 (0) 20 7017 5198
Email: subscriptions@tandf.co.uk

Taylor & Francis Inc, 325 Chestnut Street, Philadelphia, PA 19106, USA
Tel: +1 800 354 1420 (toll-free calls from within the US)
or +1 215 625 8900 (calls from overseas) Fax: +1 215 625 2940
Email: customerservice@taylorandfrancis.com

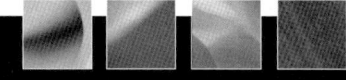

View an online sample issue at:
www.tandf.co.uk/journals/tpq

New Technologies in Central American Contemporary Art
A Partial Archaeology and Some Critical Appreciations from the Institutional Realm

Ernesto Calvo and María José Monge

To narrate processes, above all very recent ones, has great advantages but also some disadvantages. When you refer to first-hand facts, data can be richer, broader and more complex; but at the same time, in order to appreciate these processes up close, one risks losing a vital 'critical distance'[1] in relation to the object of study.

Despite this risk we will attempt a brief tour through some of the main characteristics, as much institutional as artistic, of video creation and new technologies in Central America. For this we will refer to two Foucauldian root terms that we consider key to a good part of these reflections: in the first place the term 'archaeology' that explores the less recognised, marginal and hidden facts; and second the concept of 'institution', precisely the point from which we are trying to make an impact on the consolidation of these languages and processes in Central America.[2]

FIRST STEPS

In Costa Rica, the relationship of art and new technologies has had some casual and isolated encounters since the 1980s;[3] in the case of Central America – although this is an investigation still needing to be undertaken – its presence, as far as we know, barely registered until the end of the 1990s. Some of the causes of this lack of artistic exploration of new technologies can be explained by the severely limited access to few platforms in training, production, diffusion and circulation, as well as the unstable and conflictive sociopolitical situations in the Central American isthmus until the 1990s; all of which restricted in a decisive way the development of these links between art and technology.

---

1. The term 'critical distance' plays on the polysemy of the term. If for Kant the 'critique' should have an ineluctable component to take the thought and analysis of the object under study 'further', but at the same time establish a certain 'distance' or 'objectivity' with respect to it, then there is a dual and ambiguous character at work that can make of the 'critique' a polyvalent exercise: at once objective, scientific, balanced, but at the same time subjective, semi-literary and even arbitrary. To recognise the ambivalent character of the concept and exercise of the 'critique' at a methodological level, we consider it pertinent to use the category 'dialogical critique' proposed by T Todorov in *Crítica de la Crítica*, Monte Avila, Venezuela, 1983, and the term 'dialogism', which M Bakhtin emphasises as the exercise of the critique as a constant interactive activity: objectivity with subjectivity, closeness with distance in relation to the object of study.

2. Michel Foucault discusses these two key concepts in his historical, theoretical reflections in *The Archaeology of Knowledge*, [1969], Routledge, 1972.

3. Two of the first artists in Costa Rica to work with video art and video installation were Otto Apuy and Manuel Zumbado whose projects, however, did not have the longevity or impact to foster any tendency or contextual movement in this direction. In the case of MADC, before 2000 there was some video creation and use of new technologies in some of its exhibitions, but a systematic and sustained engagement had yet to occur.

4. The show was undertaken on the invitation of Lidia Blanco, the then director of the institution, and was curated by Ernesto Calvo and artist Priscilla Monge. The participants were Brooke Alfaro (Panama), Andrés Carranza (Costa Rica), Marco Chía (Costa Rica), Darío Escobar (Guatemala), Jonathan Harker (Panama), José Alberto Hernández (Costa Rica), Priscilla Monge (Costa Rica), Alejandro Ramírez (Costa Rica), Joaquín Rodríguez del Paso (Costa Rica), Karla Solano (Costa Rica), Jaime David Tischler (Costa Rica), Ana de Vicente (Costa Rica–Spain), Patricia Villalobos (Nicaragua–USA), Manuel Zumbado (Costa Rica).

5. The Costa Rican Museum of Contemporary Art and Design emerged in 1994 as part of an institutional renovation that also created the National Centre for Culture (CENAC), on the mid-nineteenth-century heritage site of the National Liquor Factory in the centre of San José. From its birth this institution became a centre for the major presentations and legitimisation of new

One could say that it was not until the second half of the 1990s that research into the diverse realms of new technologies started to achieve a certain degree of development and systematisation in art in the Central American region, thanks to the increased availability of these new technological means, greater access to information, and the incipient 'democratisation' of its use, at least between artists and professionals in related and complementary fields, such as design, architecture and the audiovisual.

Despite this, when we devised a show about video creation in Central America in 2001, which came about as a result of an invitation from the Spanish Cultural Centre in Costa Rica, the prospect did not seem encouraging at all; it was difficult to assemble the fourteen artists who finally took part. Maybe for this reason, the writer who reviewed the exhibition included in the title both a question and a hopeful response: 'Video Art in Central America?: It breathes.'[4]

RESTLESS IMAGE: VISUALISING FROM THE INSTITUTIONAL

Seeking to remedy this lack, the Costa Rican Museum of Contemporary Art and Design (MADC)[5] took the initiative in mid-2002 of mounting the exhibition 'Contaminated: (Ex) Tensions of the Audiovisual', the first international video creation and digital art show in Central America. In this exhibition renowned international artists, together with young Central American artists, participated with works that mixed video and audiovisuals with photography, cinema, painting, graffiti, architecture, sculpture, installation, performance, and interactive and internet works that emphasised the multidisciplinary condition of the project.[6] Parallel to this important show MADC called for entries to the First Central American Video Creation Contest 'Restless Image' ('Inquieta Imagen'), an initiative that during its first round received forty-three applications from which ten were selected by a jury composed of Ken Feingold (USA), Nora Fish (Argentina) and Felipe Taborda (Brasil), all specialists in the fields of video creation, audiovisuals and new technologies.[7]

Despite the variable quality of the works presented in this first incarnation of 'Restless Image', as a whole they bore significant witness, without distinction of age, nationality or artistic trajectory, to the nascent exploration of new technologies that was to broaden the horizons of the Central American visual arts. Subsequent rounds of this annual contest, which continued until 2005, confirmed this fact. The participation figures show an increase from forty-three entries in the first competition in 2002, to eighty-four in 2003, a drop to seventy in 2004, and then an increase to 102 in 2005.[8] Even if this numerical increase does not necessarily signal a rise in the quality of the works presented, nevertheless in that short period of time there had been substantial improvement in the technical quality, formal concerns and theoretical intentions of the works of the participating artists. As a reflection of this, we need only consider how the proposals presented at the four instalments of the contest have acquired a certain identity in terms of the experimental use of new technologies. These diverse proposals and their general thematic, aesthetic and visual approaches ranged widely from exercises close to documentary work or animation to pieces more directly affiliated to investigations of a strictly technological and digital mould.

With a view to nurturing these growing transformations, MADC modified and extended the conditions and profile of the event and thus responded to the demands of the local as well as international contexts. The initial emphasis on video creation was later amplified to include all types of digital works and their infinite possibilities, and the hierarchical prize-giving format was also modified to produce a show with a selection of distinguished works.

In this process of readjustment – and as part of our essential commitment to preserve the institutional legitimacy and the context of this event – the show in 2007 was presented as the Iberoamerican Biennial. With this change and without sacrificing the specific role of visualising Central American production with respect to new technologies, it claimed to further encourage interaction and links with similar environments on an Iberoamerican and international level. In connection with this event, and in general as part of the efforts of MADC, there has been another very significant result: encouraging relationships between art, new technology and the growing interactions established between institutions, artists and cultural managers. These include elements that have expanded collaboration and brought possibilities of feedback to local artistic production on an international level.

One of the most important aspects of these links is that 'Restless Image' has encouraged the presence in Costa Rica of prestigious artists, curators, cultural managers and researchers who have participated as jurors. For example, to name but a few, Andrea di Castro (Italy–Mexico), pioneer in the use of new technologies and interactive works in Mexico and Latin America; young but distinguished promoters such as José-Carlos Mariátegui (Peru–England); young but significant artists, such as Karin Schneider (Brazil–USA) and Nicolas Guagnini (Argentina–USA); or researchers of the calibre of Laura Baigorri (Spain), Gilles Charalambos (France–Colombia) and Gabriela Rangel (Venezuela–USA), curator of the visual arts of the Americas Society. These specialists have set up talks and workshops as offshoots of the event, giving it a broader artistic context. This has proved an important contribution for the artists themselves and the general public.[9]

Each year at MADC, and running parallel to the 'Restless Image' exhibition, the programme 'Spaces for Experimentation' presents an international selection of experimental audiovisual works. During this event important shows have been scheduled, such as 'L A Freewaves: Latin American Video Art' (put together by the Los Angeles Museum of Contemporary Art and coordinated by Juan Devis), the shows of the 'Salón y Coloquio Internacional de Arte Digital del Centro Pablo de la Torriente Brau' (Cuba), the International Development Bank's 'Latin American Video Art' contest, and multidisciplinary and interactive projects such as 'E-TESTER' (sponsored by the Fundación Rodríguez and the Fundación Arteleku from the Basque Country), as well as selections from international and Iberoamerican institutions such as the Gate Foundation ('History of Video Art in Holland') and Peruvian Andean High Technology ('Via Satellite: Panorama of Contemporary Peruvian

---

projects and visual languages being explored by artists of the Central American region. Previously they had had no museum or other institutional space dedicated to the contemporary visual arts. For the history of MADC consult its web page, 'What is MADC?', 'Previous Exhibitions' and 'Publications': http://www.madc.ac.cr

6. The participants of 'Contaminated. (EX) Tensions of the Audiovisual' were Fabián Marccacio (Argentina), Guillermo Gómez Peña (Mexico–USA), Karin Schneider and Nicolas Guagnini (Brazil–Argentina), Santiago Echeverri (Colombia), Andrés Tapia (Chile), Fernando Llanos (Mexico), Txuspo Poyo (Spain), Takehito Kogenazawa (Japan–Germany), Ken Feingold (USA), Regina Galindo (Guatemala). The curators were Rolando Barahona and Ernesto Calvo.

7. In this first round of 'Restless Image' the following works received awards: the video projection *Wind, Water, Stone* (2000), by Joaquín Rodríguez del Paso; the video installation *Autoopsis* (2002), by the young Costa Rican artist José Alberto Hernández; and the video *Aria* by Brooke Alfaro, the Panamanian artist who gave a new twist to audiovisual experimentation.

8. The winning artists of the second round were Lucía Madriz (Costa Rica), Edgar León (Costa Rica–Mexico) and Ernesto Salmerón (Nicaragua–Colombia). The jury awarded them with prizes of equal value; and again in the third, Enrique Castro (Panama), Alan Omar Mairena (Honduras) and Sandra Monterroso (Guatemala). Prize winners in the fourth round were Hugo Ochoa (Honduras–

Photography and Video') and Fundació La Caixa de Barcelona ('Panorama of Spanish Video Art').[10]

These events have also instigated the production of curatorial bodies of works that MADC has exhibited in museums and alternative art spaces in various countries in the Central and Latin American region, the USA and Europe. These curatorial proposals have included: 'The Dinosaur Was Still There: Video Creation Beyond and Within Central America' (invited in 2002 to the event L A Freewaves in Los Angeles and later taken to different countries); 'Hybris: Space, Body, Politics and Aesthetics in Central American Video Art' (invited in 2005 to the 'Salón Internacional de Arte Digital del Centro Pablo de la Torriente Brau' [Cuba]); 'Video Creation in Central America? It Breathes' (curatorial body of works presented in 2007 in the Laboratorio Centro de Arte Alameda, Mexico, DF).

MADC has also received invitations to participate as jury members and lecturers in Central American and Iberoamerican events related to the artistic implementation of new technologies with the emphasis on video art. Equally, Central American artists have won prizes (First Prize for Brooke Alfaro in the International Development Bank American Biennial), and have been invited to important regional and international video creation exhibitions, with videos *BrasII* (Jorge Albán), and to develop curatorial projects such as 'Invisible Videographies'.[11]

BECOMING VISIBLE ON THE INTERNET

In 1998, in response to this decisive link to new technologies and in the context of the incipient mass use of the internet, MADC created its web page.[12]

This site made it possible to provide immediate and up-to-date information on the institution to a wider network within and outside the Central American region. The web page positioned the museum as a barometer evaluating institutional work from the perspective of the users, and allowing for more fluid interlocution between artists, institutions and the public at a regional and international scale.

One of the key tools of the web page is the Directory of Central American Artists, which helps to strengthen the links between contemporary artists in the Central American region and substantially increase knowledge of the national contexts of each country in the area. In addition, it permits the growing interaction between artists and institutions, as well as creating the possibility of expanding these connections to include other artists and institutions from other latitudes.

To achieve these objectives, the MADC web page has continually overhauled the visual presentation of its contents in order to increase the possibilities of dialogue with the different users that visit it.

For instance, during the last few years, it has changed from a static structure to a dynamic site directly administrated by the museum. Open technologies have also allowed it to increase content by creating new sections and options for accessing information. Equally the page has been improved by the incorporation of videos documenting the principal exhibitions through youtube.com, including interviews with the main artists and curators from MADC shows and, with the use of loudblog,

Costa Rica), Ramsés Giovanni (Panama), Ana Luisa Sánchez (Panama–Costa Rica), Sandra Trejos (Costa Rica) and Patricia Belli (Nicaragua).

9. For information on the jury, talks and workshops offered at this event, see *Memoria Audiovisual 2002–2004* and *Memoria Audiovisual 2005* in addition to other details on the MADC web page under the link 'Publicaciones' and in 'Actividades Paralelas. Actividades relacionadas con tecnología'.

10. The MADC web page link 'Actividades Paralelas. Actividades relacionadas con tecnología' provides information about the programmes and those from other experimental art spaces, related shows, workshops and events.

11. Invitations to talks, conferences with screenings, curatorial projects and jury-led events were undertaken at MOCA (Los Angeles, USA), the Americas Society (New York, USA), Casa de América (Madrid, Spain), ARCO (Madrid, Spain), Zaragoza Latin Festival (Zaragoza, Spain), Laboratorio Centro de Arte Alameda (Mexico D F, Mexico), Fundación Telefónica y Centro Cultural de España (Lima, Peru), Centro Pablo de la Torriente Brau (La Habana, Cuba), Centro de Arte León (Dominican Republic), and Centro Cultural de España y Fundación Clic (El Salvador) among others.

12. This web page was created thanks to the support of the HIVOS Foundation, Holland. Its first designer was Luis Fernando Quirós (1998–2000), then later Henry Vargas (2000–2005) and Carlos Murillo (2006–2008). http://www.madc.ac.cr

the more varied inputs and possibilities on the web page have increased the number of site users.

We should highlight the support for new technologies by other institutions in Central America that, despite space limitations and budgets and precarious access to technological resources, have made a great efforts to provide workshops, programmes and other events during the last few years. An example of this in El Salvador is the Fundación Clic[13] that was born as a portal for the arts and has so far held three digital art contests (2004, 2005 and 2006). The last round of this contest was taken beyond the national level to become the First International Festival of Digital Arts, an event that, among its novelties and its successes, introduced a Diploma in Digital Art.

In addition, in El Salvador and Guatemala, universities and other media education institutions have also begun to give importance to training in new technologies, with an emphasis on the internet and its relationship to design, photography and/or video. Other spaces, like Mujeres en las Artes (Women in the Arts)[14] in Honduras have organised shows and workshops, inviting artists and specialised cultural managers to work with themes linked to video creation and digital art. Along the same lines the projects EVIL[15] and Espira, Espora (Espora-la Espora),[16] both in Nicaragua, have also put on exhibitions and workshops with a strong emphasis on training in new technologies.

In Costa Rica, the University of Veritas,[17] although it focuses on animation, cinema and television rather than video creation or interactive art, has become the first university with training possibilities – in the latter at a Central American level. Another space that has given relative importance to these technologies is the Teoré/Tica Foundation,[18] which has mounted exhibitions of video art, new technologies and individual artists such as the Colombian Oscar Muñoz. All these spaces and projects have a fluid relationship with MADC through the exchange of materials, experiences and collaborations for the diffusion of information.[19]

ARTISTS WHO EXPLORE VIDEO CREATION AND NEW TECHNOLOGIES: PROPOSALS, THEMES AND SEARCHES

We would now like to move on from institutional practices to artistic creation itself, introducing a brief panorama of the main artists in the Central American area who have adopted video art and new technologies in general. This will reveal some thematic and conceptual affinities among those working in this area.

An artist like Brooke Alfaro (Panama), after some years of success as a painter, started to link video art to his work at the end of the 1990s, focusing his investigations on the marginal people with whom he has maintained close relations. From *Click, click, toc, toc* (2000), moving to *Cortes* (2001), through to the exquisite *Aria* (2001) or the powerful video performance *Nine* (2003), Alfaro has demonstrated that he is one of the most solid and consistent artists of Central America.

From another perspective, Joaquín Rodríguez del Paso (Costa Rica), an artist who has recurrently explored different languages – from painting and drawing to installation and video art – has been making audiovisual works with the choreographer María Amalia Pendones since the

13. http://www.clic.org.sv
14. http://www.muaartes.org
15. http://www.marcaacme.com
16. http://www.laespora.org
17. http://www.uveritas.ac.cr
18. http://www.teoretica.org
19. The web page links to all of these institutions can be found on the MADC site. In many of these institutions the exhibits from 'Restless Image' have been presented and an exchange of programmes in the form of talks, discussions and the reciprocal diffusion of events has taken place.

Brooke Alfaro, *Aria*, 2001, video, 3 minutes 20 seconds, collection of the Museum of Contemporary Art and Design, Costa Rica, photo: Museum of Contemporary Art and Design, Costa Rica

end of the 1990s, with themes concerned with the relation 'centre–periphery' (*Exotica–the Ultimate Other*, 1997) poetry and television (*Water, Wind, Stone*, 2000), or the habitual everyday in *Last Round for Friday* (2003).

In a different vein, and through starkly formal exercises, the renowned artist Priscilla Monge (Costa Rica), has presented an ironic series of 'lessons' – a trilogy on the theme of violence exercised over women (*Make up lesson, How to (un) dress, How to die of love*, 1998–2000). Also working with the problematic of the feminine, the artist Lucía Madriz (Costa Rica) has produced simple, though very precise videos related to violence and manipulation – symbolic or real – to which women are subjected through intimate and social relationships, in videos such as *Tell me when to smile* (2002), and *Headache* (2003). More recently this artist has explored ecological and food production issues, through animation and video installation, targeting the problems of genetic manipulation of crops and conflicts over oil.

Another artist, Donna Conlon, an American living in Panama, has produced subtle audiovisual exercises whose main theme has almost always been ecological and through which she has reflected on the – negative – impact of humanity on nature (*Single solitary*, 2002; *Coexistence*, 2003; *Unleashed*, 2003).

By documenting their own performances, other artists like the Guatemalan Sandra Monterroso (*The essence of life*, 2002; *Your tortillas my love*, 2004) and Regina Galindo (*Auto cannibalism*, 2002; *Lips*, 2003; *Who Can Rub Out the Footprints*, 2005) take a metaphorical, although at the same time cruel and even visceral approach to political themes

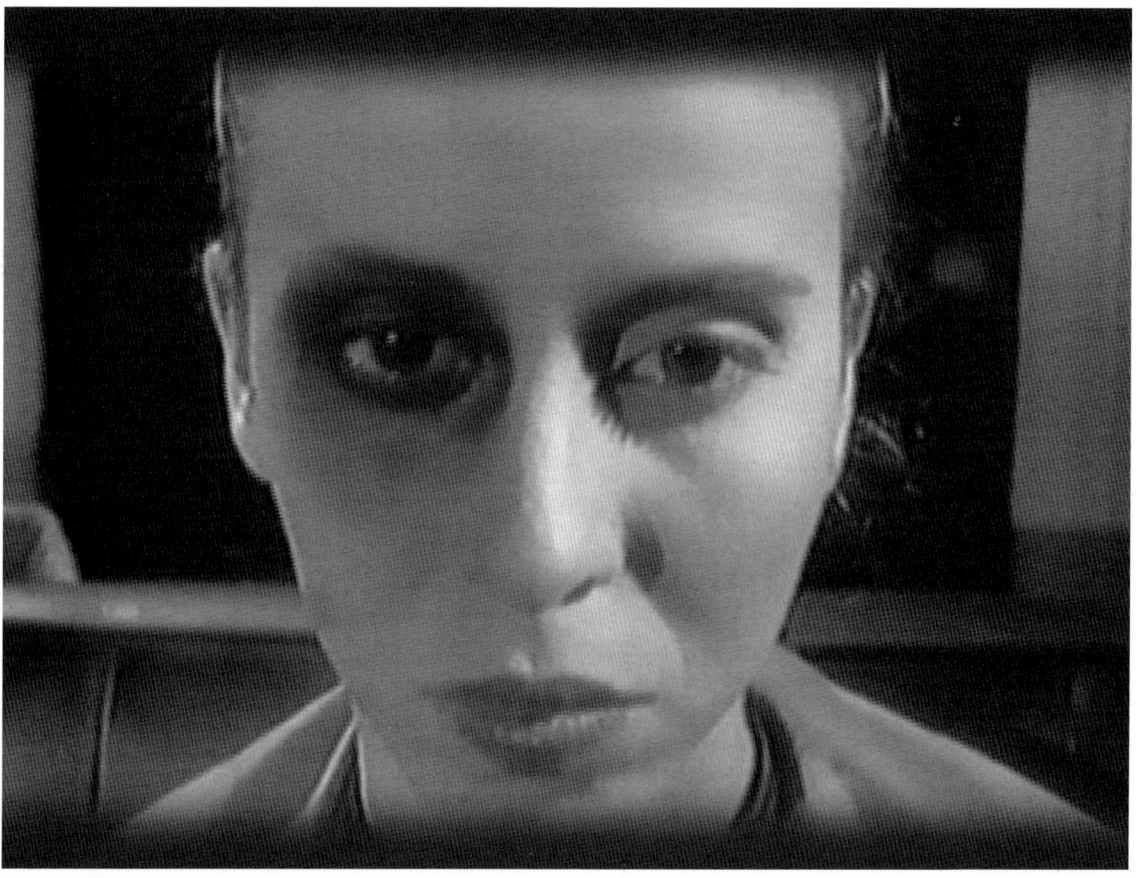

Priscilla Monge, *Make-up lesson*, 1998–2000, video, 2 minutes 30 seconds, collection of the Museum of Contemporary Art and Design, Costa Rica, photo: Museum of Contemporary Art and Design, Costa Rica

such as the limited area assigned to women by the patriarchal tradition in Central American societies.

Another artist who has worked with the feminine subject, though from a more intimate and personalised perspective, is Karla Solano with works such as *Canvas*, (2001) and *Stitches* (2004), where aesthetic performances are carried out using her own body. On the other hand, the New York-based Costa Rican artist Natacha Pachano has explored the feminine image in a playful manner (*Labial*, 2001), together with other themes linked to identity dislocations or appropriations of the cinematographic (*Un Chien Appropriated*, 2003).

Through a more formalist and conceptualist approach, Ana de Vicente, a Spanish artist living in Costa Rica, has dealt with anthropological and natural themes (*The Planted*, 2001; *Dis Continuity*, 2004) or more aesthetic and social themes (*The Light*, 2003; *Popular Mechanic*, 2003; *Paint Trains*, 2005). And midway between conceptual reflection and political or aesthetic reference, one can find the video installations of Edgar León (*Memories of the Why*, 2003; *1, 2, 3*, 2004).

Conceptual and formal purity is evident in the video installations of Cynthia Soto, a Costa Rican resident in Switzerland, in *A Flower is not a*

Flower, Neptune, Llo-ver (2003), where the artist plays within the diffuse frontiers between reality and representation. Another artist exploring the links between representation and reality is the Nicaraguan Patricia Belli with her video installation *The Equilibrist* (2005), which in a subtly personal way relates a fixed image in movement.

In the field of animation, notable for their technical quality and suggestively resonant character are the works of the Honduran, Alan Omar Mairena (*Gravity*, 2004, the ingenious *Dolls* 2002), the Guatemalan, Álvaro Sanchez, the lucid and fresh *Using John* by the Costa Rican artist Paulina Velásquez, or the more intimate and surreal *Sofia* from the El Salvadorian, Danilo Girón. Other works explore the theme of homosexuality; for example, Ramsés Giovanni of Panama has created poetic exercises that play with simple animated drawings and real-life symbolic elements (*Fear of the sea*, 2005).

Working midway between animation and metaphysics, the Honduran Hugo Ochoa has produced *Tales of Honduras and blindness* (2002) and has established links between anthropology, documentary, literature and photography (*What is the Name of the Piece*, 2004; *Allegory of the Fourth World, Kung Fu*, 2005).

Hugo Ochoa, *Tales of Honduras and Blindness*, 2002, video, 8 minutes, collection of the artist, photo: Museum of Contemporary Art and Design, Costa Rica

Regina Galindo, *Auto Cannibalism*, 2002, video, 3 minutes, collection of the Museum of Contemporary Art and Design, Costa Rica, photo: Museum of Contemporary Art and Design, Costa Rica

The photographer and designer José Alberto Hernández from Costa Rica has produced powerful reflections on sickness, birth, life and death in video installations that adopt a documentary and anthropological style and *Auto-opsis* (2002), and *280 days or 40 weeks* (2003).

Projects suggestive of public interventions into social and identity debates have been produced by the artist Alejandro Ramírez. His work ironically explores the paradoxes of 'tranquillity and passivity' in his native Costa Rica (*The Patriotic*, 2001; *Lullaby*, 2002), ridiculing the position taken towards the Iraq war (*My Beloved Ambiguous People*, 2003) and manipulating the links between graffiti, painting and traditional patriotic songs (*Vandalising Action in my Pretty Costa Rica*, 2003).

Jonathan Harker, who appropriates the city of Panama, has produced interesting audiovisual exercises with urban and playful implications (*Metropoly*, 2001), transiting it in an almost Dadaist way (*The Plumber*, 2002) and parodying political and traditional social elements (*Take distance*, 2004). From a more experimental development in animation, the Costa Rican Clea Eppelin and the Panamanian Ana Luisa Sánchez have created attractive visual narrative exercises in works such as *A fourth of a short* (2002), *Zona Pasaje* (2002) or *German Tale in*

Red (2003). Their latest work included interactive pieces of a political character, such as *Angie Against the World* (2005). Also making a political critique, but this time from the perspective of the memory, expressed by mixing videographics and cinematography together with historical documentation and intimate reflection, the Panamanian Enrique Castro produced exceptional work in *Memories of the Son of the Old Man* (2003).

In this polemical field of political criticism, various artists have made strong statements about the chronic mediocrities of power and repressions. In this vein, *Nos Vale Verga/We Couldn't Care Less* (2002) is a sarcastic animation documentary created by Regina Aguilar and 'The artists of the people' and one of the sharpest political works of recent years.

Another artist who has worked closely with political documentation is Guillermo Vargas/Habacuc in works such as *Police Intervening in a Work That Talks About an Abuse of Authority* (2005). His work also reflects on the links between photography, video, still image and movement, representation and reality. The Nicaraguan Ernesto Salmerón has been developing a series of excellent appropriations of found footage (*Document 1/2/3/29*) through which he recovers and re-signifies Nicaraguan history through his use of audiovisual archive material. In addition, Salmerón has also looked critically at contemporary documentation in ironic works about infancy, such as *True False* (2006) and *They Are Not Poor* (2006).

Other works in the sphere of performances, documentation or works with political and social-anthropological scope have been produced by the Hondurans Adán Vallecillo, Leonardo González, Gabriel Galeano, the Nicaraguans Wilbert Carmona and Rodrigo Pacheles, and also the Guatemalans Aníbal Lopez, Alejandro Paz and José Osorio y Rodolfo Washi, this last one dealing with the theme of gangs in *My Crazy Life* (2001).

Another recurrent theme in some Central American video art is that of migration. Patricia Villalobos, a Nicaraguan residing in the USA, has dealt with the vital fissures in migrant life (*Snow*, 1999; *Shortcut*, 2000)

Ernesto Salmerón and Mauricio Prieto, *Document 1/29*, video, 3 minutes 47 seconds, collection of the Museum of Contemporary Art and Design, Costa Rica, photo: Museum of Contemporary Art and Design, Costa Rica

with video installations that mix painting, audiovisual material and performance. The Costa Rican Christian Bermúdez (*Dear Neighbour*, 2006) and Naufus Ramírez, a Honduran residing in Canada, have produced playful but at the same time absurdist performances (*Skin Changer*, 2002; *Original Banana Republic*, 2002; *Doing Other People's Cleaning*, 2003). The Panamanian resident in England, Humberto Vélez (*El Guachimán/The Cartaker*, 2001) also refers to the traumas and the oddities of migration.

Finally, in the sphere of internet and interactive work, the photographer Jorge Albán (Costa Rica) has exhibited works with direct political and social implications, such as *Kennedy and Cia* (2004), *Bambuzal en la Catedral* and *TLC: Todos los Chiapas* (2005). He has also carried out curatorial work for shows such as 'Plots before the Spectacle in Central America',[20] which includes photography, video and blogs from various artists: Mayra Barraza, Hugo Ochoa, Víctor Rodríguez, Ileana Arauz, and reflects works that explore different conflicting themes in the Central American context, sometimes taking the internet and other interactive modes as the basis for their enquiries.

SOME FINAL REFLECTIONS

A variety of themes and formal strategies have been developed by the Central American artists who have incorporated video and new technologies into their projects. In recent years there has been a relatively steep increase in the use of these media and an ever greater sophistication in the artistic proposals behind projects, both on a discursive level and in the exploration of these languages in terms of technique and concept.

There exists today a field of Central American production, above all linked to video, which has earned the title 'Restless Image'. Taking into account the palpable results obtained and the exchanges that have been created and consolidated at a regional and international level, we consider that MADC's role in supporting and making accessible the new technologies has contributed significantly to the development of these tendencies, in a context that, until only a few years ago, was characterised by the absence of institutional platforms, training and diffusion of material, and as a result lacked a referential tradition.

Despite all these positive aspects it is possible to point out significant lacunae in the use of new technologies in contemporary Central American art. Among these we can pinpoint the crucial aspect of training. Although training in this field has existed through incipient opportunities in some of the private and public universities or from institutional or alternative spaces, there is still a lack of permanent training opportunities that can maximise the use of these ever-changing and developing tools. With this deficit in training and provision of technological tools, the responsibility has been left in the hands and to the efforts of individual artists.

Another important limitation – perhaps linked to the preceding one – is that the bulk of Central American new technology production tends to rely on framing a protagonist as a strong visual component of the work to the detriment of other related expressive possibilities such as those of sound, touch and other sensorial dimensions. Along these lines, we

20. http://www.artenemo.org

should point out that projects of an interactive character and those related to the internet are also still very limited.

Finally another important lack, this time in the institutional environment, is the limited availability of finance for artistic events that emphasise new technologies. The initiatives dedicated to the encouragement of this kind of project and exhibition are nearly always dependent on sponsors and strategic alliances that can support the funding requirements of these often very complex technological demands. In the specific case of MADC, its work has been made possible thanks to the constant support of organisations such as HIVOS, the Spanish and French cooperation, and through the collaboration of a network of alliances at a Central American and Iberoamerican level.

The most pressing need in the current situation is to establish strategies, programmes and renewable alliances with a view to strengthening and amplifying the existing platforms, enabling them to have an impact on the processes of training, professionalisation and the projection of artistic works along these lines.

It is with this need in mind that a network of collaboration and exchange at the Central and Ibero America has been developing. It is vital to build on this work with the aim of opening up new opportunities and possibilities for Central American artistic production linked to new technologies.

Electronic Art in Peru
The Discovery of an Invisible Territory in the Country of the Incas

Mauricio Delfín and Miguel Zegarra

THE CONSTANT REINVENTION OF THE PAST

If there is any characteristic that defines Peru in a local and global context, it is the permanence of its pre-Columbian past. The country is viewed as a cultural archaeological territory, distant from any process of modernity, tied to its exotic image as the 'country of the Incas' that has persisted throughout its history.

The patrimonialist vision of the territory, configured by the cultural idiosyncrasy of social elites and political powers, defines the country as a permanent *huaca*.[1] The origin of this discourse can be found in the narratives of Spanish chroniclers during the colonial period, later adopted as the official discourse of the state and the republican elites of the nineteenth century. It is still in force today under the notion of 'cultural heritage'.

From this perspective, the state favours the development of all traditional manifestations of culture (mainly related to folklore) that have the capacity to generate income through the commercial exploitation of tourism.

This growing industry privileged by the state influences the construction of what is contemporary in Peru, instrumentalising and capitalising the past and its constant reinvention, while leaving aside the promotion of contemporary products.

A central element that defines the official discourse on cultural identity in Peru is the constant renovation of an indigenist[2] and nationalist imaginary, coinciding with the permanent need to refer to an ancestral-mythical history and past.[3] This discourse on what is national conditions the present cultural development, establishing directions that get fixed in the collective imaginary as the only paths towards local legitimisation and international recognition.

The strength of these perspectives on Peruvian culture has contributed to generating a resistance artistic exploration associated with the use of new technologies. The disconnection between technology and

---

1. From the quechua language 'waqa', which means sacred. It designates both the divinity and the place in which it was venerated. Today the notion extends to any archaeological site of pre-Hispanic origin.

2. *Indigenismo* was an intellectual movement of artistic and political dimensions that appeared at the end of the nineteenth century in the ex-Spanish colonies of Latin America with a cultural past in complex pre-Hispanic civilisations. In the case of Mexico and Peru – the central axis of the movement – a literary, artistic and political ideology with Pan-American ambitions was developed. The starting point was the cultural and social affirmation of the indigenous people and the configuration of a national identity different from that of the colonial Spanish heritage. The most important Peruvian intellectuals who took this approach as an analytical perspective for cultural and

culture in the official imaginary has consolidated this reaction. In this panorama, the initiatives of artists who use new media from an *outsider* history is marked by independent and discontinuous experiences.

NO-LATIN PARTY

If we consider the international art scenario, it becomes evident that the centres show increasingly less interest in artistic production in Latin America, considering it an *old-fashioned* and irrelevant cultural territory as compared with other cultural peripheries – strategic enclaves under a geopolitical and economic map of global capital expansion – such as Eastern Europe, Africa and the Middle East. The art of Latin America is usually associated with social preoccupations and cultural identity themes, from a perspective constructed in the 1970s of a 'politically engaged' art in a context marked by political insurrections against military dictatorships and authoritarian regimes. The continuous referral of the art centres towards this heritage limits new discursive possibilities that might arise from a contemporary social scenario in the countries of Latin America.[4]

In a text on globalisation and cultural difference, the Cuban critic Gerardo Mosquera compares the global art scene to a big cake that needs to be sliced, not only with a variety of knives but also by a variety of hands, and then handed out accordingly.[5] Stemming from this image (graphic in terms of the global scheme of inequalities repeating itself in the artworld), the Peruvian artist Diego Lama produced the video *No-Latin Party* (2003) of an altered scene from Francis Ford Coppola's *The Godfather II* in which the heads of the Mafia hand out pieces of a cake. In this cake, Lama places the device of the Venice Biennale, which in its scheme of pavilions ignores the presence of the majority of Latin American countries.

In recent years we have observed that economically strong Latin-American countries like Argentina, Brazil and Mexico have been able to promote the production of contemporary media art with the support of private corporations and the state. This advantage has helped to generate funds and institutional platforms to promote artistic production, education, research and the creation of an official memory of the history of art and new media in their societies.[6] Artists from these countries have gained greater participation on the international scene, a situation that contrasts in the remaining Latin American countries.

TECHNO-HUACA

In Peru we can distinguish two tendencies in the production of electronic arts. One is the increase in global aspirations related to digital paradigms of production and the professional use of media technology, and the second relates to local critical research on recent memory and the participation of information and media in society.

The first scenario has its origins at the end of the 1990s with the confluence of two initiatives that introduced those working on the local scene to international work using video and other technologies. One was

---

social reality were Manuel González Prada, José Carlos Mariátegui and José María Arguedas.

3. The use of myth for the construction of the present and the elaboration of contemporary products is a paradoxical sign that allows us to understand Peru's antagonisms. This is the case of reinvented traditions that border on kitsch, like the feast of Incan origin called 'Inti Raimi' (Feast of the Sun) in the city of Cuzco; millenarianist guerrilla movements like the MRTA (Tupac Amaru Revolutionary Movement), or the messianic sect with syncretic-Andean traits called 'Israelites of the New Universal Pact'. For more information see Juan José García Miranda, 'Myth and violence in Peru', in *Perú Contemporáneo: El Espejo de las Identidades*, eds Ricardo Melgar Bao and María Teresa Bosque Lastra, UNAM, Mexico, 1993.

4. Artists from this territory who choose to emigrate to Europe or America find greater possibilities to insert their work in global contexts, although the ghost of social and political commitment remains implicit, as does the recurrent theme of revindication of cultural difference against the centres.

5. Gerardo Mosquera, *Notes of Globalisation, Art and Cultural Difference*, Rijksakademie van Beeldende Kunsten, Amsterdam, 2001

6. This is the case with platforms like the Videobrasil Cultural Association, the CENART (Centro Nacional de las Artes) Multimedia Centre in Mexico, or the Espacio Fundación Telefónica in Buenos Aires.

Rolando Sánchez, *Matari 69200*, 2004, Atari game, five games designed and programmed by the artist, collection of the artist

7. Some observers of the Biennales of Lima phenomenon have outlined the coincidence in interests between the expansion of large transnational corporations (specifically the Bellsouth and Telefónica telephone companies) and the interests of an oligarchy in power searching desperately for national

the National Biennale of Lima (later named the Iberoamerican Biennale) which coincided with the municipal government's efforts to make highly visible to the country and the region as a whole the recovery of the Historic Centre of the city as a world heritage site. The promotion of Lima as the 'Main Square of Iberoamerican Culture' was the catalyst that helped produce the event, allied with particular economic and political interests.[7]

In the same year, 1997, the International Festivals of Video/Arte/Electrónica began, with the intention of promoting local video and electronic arts, linking them to an international context. The Festival,

José Carlos Martinat, *Inkarri/Stereoreality Environment 3*, 1997, fibreglass sculpture covered with plasticised moss 164 cm high × 135 cm diameter, three thermal printers, algorithm and web searcher, network connection, private collection

Diego Lama, *No-Latin party*, 2003, video, 2 minutes 17 seconds, IVAM Instituto Valenciano de Arte Moderno Collection, Spain

roots and public legitimacy. For more information see Max Hernández and Jorge Villacorta, 'Globalización C O D', in *Franquicias Imaginarias. Las Opciones Estéticas en las Artes Plásticas en el Perú de Fin de Siglo*, Pontificia Universidad Católica del Perú, Lima, 2002.

directed by the organisation Alta Tecnología Andina (ATA), managed to generate a space for the exhibition of national video artworks that were presented at different international events. The confluence of these two events geared the attention of local artists towards their professionalisation, aiming at international recognition and local legitimacy in the use of contemporary electronic media.

Those events also coincided with a neo-liberal economic policy promoted by the state and determined by the entry of transnational capital into the country. Urban homogenisation processes began in different cities of Peru, imitating the development model offered by the capital Lima and initiating a universalisation of consumer patterns across the population. These patterns, when applied to a context of underdevelopments, such as that in Peru, produce simulation phenomena, the precarious imitations of global consumer paradigms. In this way, the ground was laid for a great simulation in a population familiarised with the entertainment media industry and information networks, but unable to cover their basic needs.[8]

Coinciding with this cultural and social context (defined by some critics as the 'zapping and shopping phenomenon'),[9] and with the popularisation of the internet and cable TV, artists came into contact with international tendencies linked to the use of new technologies. The reception of this information triggered a rapid diversification of production formats and the growing presence of media projects in institutional and commercial spaces. New generational paradigms of success arose, aimed at earning a space in the almost non-existent local market and obtaining visibility in the international mainstream.

With the restoration of democracy in 2001, the artists who had dominated the Peruvian scene up to then showed a certain exhaustion. The new scene that flowed from electronic art to the fields of perception emerged simultaneously with a new moment for the nation, through the cultural presence of electronic devices, in the imaginary of the new generations. How many types of digital visuality did this new scene propose? These possibilities came together with a determination to produce not in solitude but through teamwork, something that entailed a planned structure of management sequences. In this way, work on the visual is approached by putting trust in some kind of narrative yet to be explained and a type of production that went beyond the individual. Hence, certain mythological visual models were created through cinematographic quotation but also through a preference for symbols in the narrative.[10] In this context we find Diego Lama's works, ranging from pioneering videos in the Peruvian scene such as *Schizo Uncopyrighted* (2001), which appropriates cinematic images to establish links between the original version of the Hitchcock movie *Psycho* and its remake, to pieces with narrative episodes like *The Death of Eros* (2004). His work applies cinematographic techniques to video, giving rise to a hybrid cinematic-video style.

Another approach adopts a critical view towards the local with an emphasis on parodying the strategies used by mass media and the culture of spectacle. This is the attitude of artists like Roger Atasi, Cristian Alarcón Ismodes and Rolando Sánchez who developed a political stance along the lines of 'guerrilla TV' in the Peruvian context. In 2001, coinciding with the fall of Alberto Fujimori's dictatorial government (1990–2001), Atasi produced the video *Hola y Chao* (2002) that openly criticised the manipulation of television and mass media by the central powers. The artist 'zaps' until he comes to a well-known 'vladivideo',[11] which is then altered and a plate of food is thrown at the Director of the National Intelligence Service as he openly bribes a corrupt politician. From a similar perspective, Rolando Sánchez creates the video game *Matari 69200* (2004) in which different episodes of the armed conflict in Peru, characterised by the massacre of indigenous populations in the southern Andean region by military and subversive groups, are revisited with an Atari joystick.

Cristian Alarcón Ismode's project *Desplazados* (*Displaced*, 2003) documents the years of political violence in Peru (1980–2001) by appropriating archives and modifying them through video and animation. Alarcón is interested in the conflict at the level of memory, and he looks at the relationship between the perpetrators and victims of the violence using a 'gore' aesthetic. In another video-installation work, *Esto no es video-artesanía* (*This is not video-crafts*, 2005), he develops a critical commentary on the disconnection between people from the capital city and the areas affected by the armed conflict, around the notions of responsibility and commitment after the times of violence.

8. Jose-Carlos Mariátegui and Miguel Zegarra, *Vía Satélite: Panorama de la Fotografía y el Video en el Perú Contemporáneo*, Espacio Fundación Telefónica, Buenos Aires, 2005 and Centro Cultural de España, Lima, 2004

9. Augusto del Valle and Jorge Villacorta, 'Las artes visuales de los 90: zapping y deslizamientos', *Cuestión de Estado*, no 24, August 1999

10. 'Incertidumbre y certezas en el arte peruano reciente: Imaginarios de Lima en transformación, 1980–2006', in *Post-Ilusiones/Nuevas Visiones: Arte Crítico en Lima*, Fundación Wiese, Lima, 2007

11. The 'vladivideos' were internal video-recordings by the National Intelligence Service (SIN) of meetings between members of the political and business class, and the presidential adviser Vladimiro Montesinos. These recordings were broadcast on national television and marked the beginning of the fall of Fujimori in 2001.

Diego Lama, *La muerte de Eros* (*The Death of Eros*), 2004, video, 22 minutes, Caixa Forum Collection, Spain

The first- and second-generation video artists, to which Atasi and Lama belong, are located within an evolutionary process that started in the early 1990s and which initially lacked access to sophisticated video equipment. Later the process was carried forward by the appearance of international media and electronic art at the events we have described, which motivated artists to work more closely with new media. In recent years the spread of personal computers has brought young people closer to these technologies and increased the possibility of generating audiovisual materials with their own equipment. This new context that – in theory – should allow for greater creative freedom is accompanied by the absence of educational opportunities in the visual and new media arts, a situation that generates a gap between available references and media, and the quality and results obtained by independent creators.

REALITY

The violence and grief that affected Latin America for a large part of the twentieth century has turned us into enemies of memory.[12] Peruvian art carries its own conflictive charge, emerging as it does from a specific social, political and cultural weft (and trauma) in the Latin-American context. Concepts like crisis, independence and identity have acquired great relevance in sociocultural studies in this area, and globalisation has

12. Jorge Villacorta and José-Carlos Mariátegui, *Videografías Invisibles*, Museo Patio Herreriano, Valladolid, 2006, p 24

become the conceptual framework for these investigations, which allow us to see the fragility of the Latin-American states when dealing with conflicts rooted in the competition for power and control. The 1980s was a decade marked by social and political conflicts that had their origin in the transformations that Peru underwent during previous military regimes and in internal migration.¹³

Recent video-art production in Peru reveals a certain rejection of the memory of violence. Artists refer to the contemporary international art scene, mass communications and entertainment culture – global consumer society referents par excellence. This is a collective artistic erosion – of the experience of violence, an attempt to forget a traumatic past and channel those traumas through globalised strategies that may or not refer to an aesthetic of violence, but are more likely to stem from Japanese manga animation, action cinema and video-games than from Peruvian reality.

This path in new media production is orientated towards a representational horizon of a 'spectacularised reality', towards simulacra that borrow from the reality show.¹⁴ A common strategy is one of humour and parody, smoothing over the harshness of reality and allowing the artist to take a restorative distance from facts, which are embedded in the recognisable codes of media entertainment. Self-referencing is

13. Nancy Rojas, *Hacia un Idealismo de Clase Glamrock*, unpublished text distributed during the exhibition 'Twenty C Boy' by Giancarlo Scaglia, Galería Lucía de la Puente, Lima, 2007.

14. Although spectacular and globalised, this production does not set aside its critical potential which finds common ground in humour and irony. In the international scene we can cite the example of Olaf Breuning's works, and in Latin America, artists such as Héctor Pacheco (Mexico) and Martín Sastre (Uruguay). For more information on the contemporary video art scene in Latin America, see *Videografías Invisibles*, op cit.

Giancarlo Scaglia, *Twenty C Boy*, 2007, video, 3 minutes, 58 seconds, private collection

another common strategy in these works, as well as constant references to an 'addiction to consumer imperialism'.[15]

These references to the media spectacular reveal, nonetheless, a point of encounter and integration for the Latin-American collective imaginary in tune with the rest of the world: news, soap operas, wrestling or independent cinema. Could we then talk about a phenomenon of Latin-American integration through media, of the simultaneous experience of the registration and transmission of edited realities? This will perhaps be a future point of departure for contemporary artistic practices and their representatives at an international level, reformulating the notions of simulation and entertainment.

INTERNATIONAL FESTIVAL OF VIDEO/ARTE/ELECTRÓNICA: A NEW GENERATION

Since 2004 the organisation of the International Festival of Video/Arte/Electrónica (VAE) has been in the hands of a new organisation called Realidad Visual. This transfer responded to the need to promote the evolution of the event, letting new generations develop the project in new directions. Realidad Visual, a collective formed by an interdisciplinary team, aimed to centralise the Festival, producing exhibitions, presentations and concerts in a circuit that included five cities in Peru: Arequipa, Cuzco, Lima, Trujillo and Puerto Maldonado. The new organising team looked to promote the presence of international artists in Lima and extend their visits to other areas in Peru, generating collaborative projects between Peruvian and foreign artists. This is the case of the Ruido al Paso (2004) project in which the Peruvian artists Christian Galarreta and Paruro joined Polish composer Zbigniew Karkowski to present sound interventions in villages and cities of Arequipa and Cuzco.

The same year, during the Festival, Lucas Bambozzi (Brazil) presented some of his works in public spaces in the city of Puerto Maldonado, Christophe Havel (France) gave concerts in Trujillo and Canadian artist Leslie Peters exhibited her videos in Cuzco. Each of these artists presented his work in Lima and then visited another city, establishing links with artists from different locations. In this way a series of VAE Festivals were inaugurated, looking to generate new audiences and reach a public outside the traditional circuit of art promotion and cultural management.

Realidad Visual co-produced *El Paraíso en la Tierra* by French-Peruvian artist Santi Zegarra in 2004, a work aiming to show the reality behind the *castaña* or Brazil-nut economy, a reference to a product that comes from the poorest Amazon region in Peru and is geared to the demand of the most developed countries in the North. This video installation developed a critical discourse on globalisation and was simultaneously presented in Madre de Dios (Amazon region), Lima and Lyon (France). The piece sought to generate a critical view from the peripheries, making visible the interconnections and dependencies between different cultural contexts related economically through globalisation.

The series *Omnívoros* (2005–2006) was developed during the ninth and tenth instalments of the VAE Festival, which intended to promote national productions and especially new creations by locally emerging

---

15. Rojas, op cit

media artists. The title referred to the condition of local creators, who feed from heterogenous sources and survive in a hostile and diverse social context. The works produced revealed an important thematic diversity: the analysis of the effects of the consumer society, the value of difference in the configuration of cultural identities, the appropriation of media images and their use as conceptual devices in different contexts, and the relationship between body and technology.

The VAE10 Festival (2006) celebrated a decade of electronic art promotion in Peru and invited Canadian experimental film-maker Michael Snow to participate. He presented the anthology-based exhibition 'Works of Light and Time' in the Museo de Arte de Lima. The show consisted of a selection of single-channel videos, interactive installations and an anthology of his experimental films. This acted as a point of reference for the festival's other parallel exhibitions and concerts undertaken by national and international artists, and numerous workshops offered to the general public to introduce them to the works of invited artists.

The VAE Festivals have been events of great importance in the promotion of electronic art in Peru, serving as a source of access and international exchange for artists, as well as a platform for the presentation of Peruvian works that have become more complex through time. As a general reflection on these experiences, we would be justified in saying that the VAE Festivals (at the end of the 1990s) took a pioneering and 'heroic' approach, since they were developed in a context that lacked local referents, and in which local artistic institutions reacted adversely towards this category of work. In this way, the first festivals slowly dismantled conventional and established conceptions of the arts. The last three VAE Festivals aimed to decentralise the event and create new audiences, inaugurating a 'utopian' stage in which the organisers set out to reach new spaces independently without the support of the state and insisting on the possibility of generating a broad circuit for artistic promotion. Today, after ten years of uninterrupted work, the VAE Festival is looking to define new horizons for the promotion of art and technology, integrating new arts collectives into the organisation, trying to reach new audiences and consolidate an organic community of national artists who work through new media.

Journal of International and Intercultural Communication

Published on behalf of the National Communication Association

EDITOR:

Thomas Nakayama, Arizona State University, USA

Journal of International and Intercultural Communication publishes scholarship for an international readership on international and intercultural communication from a range of theoretical, conceptual and methodological perspectives. The journal features leading edge inquiry that cuts across academic boundaries to focus on international, intercultural, as well as indigenous communication issues. It invites manuscripts that not only address pressing issues in multiple regions, multilingual communities, social, political, and cultural practices from the standpoint of communication, but it also invites manuscripts that push the boundaries of contemporary work in international and intercultural communication. A nation-state should not necessarily be synonymous with a single culture as nation-states might be more productively viewed as comprising multiple cultures, nor should a culture be thought of as bounded by national boundaries, as cultures may cross the boundaries of multiple nation-states. International and intercultural communication, from interpersonal interaction to mass media, should be considered in the context of contemporary tensions, including globalization, post colonialism, cultural imperialism, and more. Theoretical, historical, experiential, experimental, as well as critical, discursive and textual analyses are welcome.

NATIONAL
COMMUNICATION
ASSOCIATION

To sign up for tables of contents, new publications and citation alerting services visit **www.informaworld.com/alerting**

Register your email address at **www.tandf.co.uk/journals/eupdates.asp** to receive information on books, journals and other news within your areas of interest.

For further information, please contact Customer Services at either of the following:
T&F Informa UK Ltd, Sheepen Place, Colchester, Essex, CO3 3LP, UK
Tel: +44 (0) 20 7017 5544 Fax: 44 (0) 20 7017 5198
Email: subscriptions@tandf.co.uk
Taylor & Francis Inc, 325 Chestnut Street, Philadelphia, PA 19106, USA
Tel: +1 800 354 1420 (toll-free calls from within the US)
or +1 215 625 8900 (calls from overseas) Fax: +1 215 625 2940
Email: customerservice@taylorandfrancis.com

View an online sample issue at:
www.tandf.co.uk/journals/jiic

Chinese Contemporary Video Art

Pi Li

Video art, though an exotic genre in China, does not merely follow in the trail of Western society. The emergence of video art in China or its acceptance by Chinese artists found a happy medium only after certain cultural conditions had fallen into place. Therefore, before we broach the topic of Chinese contemporary video art, I believe it is necessary and meaningful to review the process of how video art appeared in China.

The peculiar fate of the Chinese nation in the last century has forced Chinese society to view art in a utilitarian way (for example, the concept of content determining form and art for the sake of politics). Such thoughts were established at the Yenan Forum on Literature and Art by Mao Tse-tung in 1942 and were then maintained as guidelines for the arts. The emergence of Chinese contemporary art initially challenged that guideline. The work done by Chinese contemporary artists during the 1980s overturned the emphasis on the 'Socialist Realism' of ideological propaganda. Specifically, what they were overturning was not a kind of artistic style; rather it was the cultural authority that this style represented. Therefore, Chinese contemporary artists came close to repeating the overall art history of the West within a decade. During this process, the styles of conceptual art such as installation and performance began to appear. The political events of 1989 caused artists to realise that there was a power within their society that, for the time being, could not be contested, and that they really did not have the ability to implement their own artistic convictions. Thus, a malaise of low morale, cynicism and malaise began to spread.

On the one hand, due to the change in political climate at that time, the style of conceptual art was animadverted as decadent. All the channels that might introduce Western conceptual art were blocked. On the other hand, due to the long existence of and education in Socialist Realism in China, artists began to take advantage of a familiar style of painting to satirise society by reflecting it in a tedious, boring and ridiculous way. They also adopted popular commercial symbols that amused the ruling ideology by creating a genre of cynical realism and political pop. Compared with the 1980s, from both the angle of cultural aspiration and that of artists exploring new directions, the early 1990s was a time of withdrawal. Cynical realism and political pop, though conservative to some degree, underwent a different fate in the 1990s.

The 1990s was a decade that gradually opened the Chinese market to the West. Multinational enterprises set up thousands of representative offices and branches in China. While the opening of China's market appeared rather slow, when judged by the wishes of Western investors, multinational enterprises were still willing to spend large amounts of money to maintain their representative offices in China. People employed by such offices with little work to do, foreign ambassadors residing in Beijing and officious journalists from the foreign media together formed the channel of communication between Chinese contemporary art and its international counterpart. As a result of the Chinese nationalisation process in the last century, there was no economically independent middle class in China, and therefore no chance for art to sustain itself and survive. Art fanciers of this politically indiscriminate type formed the sole connection between Chinese contemporary art and the outside world. China, as the last Socialist country, began to attract the interest of curious art tourists and collectors.

Driven by commercial interests, galleries in the West began to go in search of such channels to introduce and sell Chinese contemporary art to the outside world. These non-professional channels enabled Chinese art, at the time represented by cynicism and political pop, to appear frequently in the West. Chinese contemporary art in that style, first revealed at the 1993 Venice Biennale, brought these artists a serious income and chances of international exhibition. In terms of the West, this style, which reflects non-Western ideology, established the label and standard for Chinese contemporary art, and also initiated the process of cultural understanding and exchange on that foundation. The success of cynical and political art encouraged even more young Chinese artists to embrace the status-giving image of 'political dissidents'.

If, in the past, artists had sensed the danger of art being controlled by politics, now the style of cynical realism and political pop made young artists feel that these easel works, driven by commercial interests, would be imposed on them by Western postcolonialism on the basis of an old-style art medium and creative methodology (realism-utilitarianism). Against this background, Chinese artists began to introduce and experiment with video art. Young artists wished to find a new art medium which would not be commercialised by Western galleries and their world also posed a strong contrast to official art. The medium would not only allow for personalised feelings and languages but also be easy to use, spread and communicate. Under such circumstances, video art became their choice.

Time-based video art offers a deeper sense of audience experience than traditional media. The strength of such experience lies beyond literal description, since video, unlike realist paintings, resists being interpreted in words. It relies on the audience's real-time-based experience, and moreover video installation invites physical involvement during the appreciation process. China held its first exhibition of video art, 'Phenomenon and Image', in 1996, a title translated into English that has more meanings in Chinese. Video means 'reflection' and image indicates 'response'. Hence the reason why young artists chose video as the medium was that it is an art that embodies 'reflection', which is rather deeper and closer to the nature of art than traditional painting. The curator of the exhibition, video artist Qiu Zhijie, wrote in the preface: 'the falsehood of historical determinism is to consider the human being as a simple perceptive object, while man not only perceives and senses, but also imagines and takes actions to practise'.[1] The equation is as follows:

traditional media = reaction = virtual individual = perception = unilateral

video = reflection = real individual = perception, imagination,

action = interactive

A German professor was invited in 1989 to the Chinese Central Academy of Fine Art to give lectures. He brought eight hours of video art which included work by Gary Hill, Bill Viola and Matthew Barney. Works like these spurred second-generation artists Zhang Peili and Qiu Zhijie to access more video art information and realise the possibilities of this medium for themselves. Zhang Peili is known not only as one of the early experimentalists of Chinese contemporary art but also as the first Chinese video artist. He completed his first works in 1989, greatly under the influence of Gary Hill, an orientation particularly visible in his famous work *Uncertain Pleasure*. His aim was to distinguish video art from mass TV programmes by refusing traditional features, sound effects or even TV figuration in his works. Zhang's style influenced many artists, for example Zhu Jia who fixes a video camera to a wheel during shooting; and Han Xuan and Yang Zhenzhong who recycle everyday life. Similar, and yet different from Zhang, is the artist Wang Gongxin who resided in New York for a decade and was greatly influenced by Viola. The magnified intention of the subtleties of daily life resulted in producing unconventional experiences with a strong visual impact. This strength is perhaps due to the different origins of Chinese and foreign video art. The origin of video art in the West came from a rebellion against the system, while in China the art derived from aesthetic concerns with the media.

Video artist Qiu Zhijie has long been concerned with the possibilities of video technology and its aesthetic value. For him, the route that Zhang followed was to worship Western video art pieces as classics, while on the other hand ignoring the possibility that new inexpensive equipment and techniques had brought. For Qiu, the reason why early video art seems insipid is due in part to its anti-system stance and in part to financial and technical restrictions. In the catalogue to the second video art exhibition in 1997, the curator Wu Meichun wrote:

> ... the problem we are facing is not what video art is, but rather what we can do with video. It is still early to define video art. It appears that a standard video art is coming into being but is destined to weary itself during its shaping. Video with its innate media resources is full of challenges, powerful and inexpensive. It is private, easy to duplicate and spread: it is both intuitive and imaginative.[2]

Under the instruction of such thoughts, video art began to develop in new directions: documentary, narrative and interactive.

DOCUMENTARY

In the mid-1990s, the film-making community in China launched a large-scale campaign, the 'New Documentary Movement'. Director Wu Wenguang emphasised the absence of the photographer during shooting, and tried to show the real state of the objective world. The New Documentary Movement is regarded as a form of resistance to the grand narrative of state TV programmes since the founding of the People's Republic of China.

While there was an improvement in documentary language and method, what it created was 'real documentary' rather than 'new documentary'. This movement coincided with the video art being made as a 'new documentary art' beyond documentary. Wang Jianwei is the pioneer in this aspect. In his *Living Elsewhere*, he traced the life of four farmers dwelling in an unfinished villa. In his works, Wang created a very 'non-professional' documentary in which some images remain stationary for as long as eight minutes, something necessary for him because his work is a reflection on phenomena rather than simply a record.

NARRATIVE

Evolving techniques enabled video art to share in the achievements of film aesthetics – as all the measures classically adopted by cinema are now applicable to video. Moreover, the time element in video has more flexibility because the medium is digital; various digital 'stunts' altered relationships to the time dimension and greatly enriched traditional film language. Three-dimensional animation makes every whim possible and gives endless possibilities for younger artists such as Yang Fudong and Jiang Zhi who have been more influenced by film aesthetics than the video art tradition and are seeking opportunities to shoot films.

INTERACTION

Will video art finally be devoured by film aesthetics and an insipid tradition? Will digital technology bring new aesthetic values, as well as better image quality and convenience? In this respect video installation was emphasised by artists as a 'right time, right place' art, because besides video it also includes the peculiarity of the installation and is more than the sum of the two. Multilayer monitors or various reflected images in pre-designed structures give a three-dimensional dramatic effect. Chinese video art has developed into two distinct types of video installation, which focus on interior knowledge of the medium and interior experience of the artist.

Video installations focused on interior knowledge tend to show in a specific scene with the video image bearing semantic connection to the property and meaning of the scene. For example, Gongxin's *Baby Talk* conveys different facial expressions in play with a baby, as the milk flows out of the mouth of the screen image and circulates elsewhere. In his video installation *Screen*, Wang Jianwei explores the cultural relationship of the secret to its disclosure and the truth and it is like a visual version of 'knowledge archaeology'. Both works waver between a vague interiority and clear exteriority. The visual, audio and kinaesthetic experiences sometimes exceed the original intentions of their authors in their complex and profuse imagination. They sometimes trace the audience's physical movement in the interior structure of the installation, as in Qiu Zhijie's *The Present Tense* and Chen Shaoxiong's *Sight Adjustor*. These works are based on 'anthropo-engineering' of audiences approaching from a certain location and route. The audience's bodies are, as it were, pre-designed as a factor influencing the installation composition itself, and where audience visitation evokes the phenomena and could itself be seen as an interior experience rather than exterior knowledge.

Video installation brings interaction to the agenda in video art. But the more you seek interaction, the more it becomes difficult for that video art to provide it. Therefore many artists began to look for other interactive modes beyond video installation in the possibilities provided by new technology. More technical and more interactive multimedia art then appeared. Artists focused on interior knowledge try to combine space and social interaction by mixing the media. Wu Ershan, together with installation artists, jazz singers and modern dancers, created *Evolved Knight* in 1999. Wu Ershan's own involvement was less spontaneous than coincidental, while Wang Jianwei instead adopted a more active approach. He invited a video artist, puppet players and performance artists to complete the play *Screen* that derived from his installation. In this work, the overall 'stage' was a magnificent interactive work of synchronised video, installation and performance.

We can see that a new era is approaching in China through the development of video art. The professionalisation of video art was achieved in the West after 1968 by isolating it from film, TV and photography and bringing it to art galleries. Video art thus was diverted from criticism of informational culture to combine with the social mainstream, which in return brought validity to video art itself.

However, personalised contemporary art cannot substantially enter into a significant dialogue with the commercialised information media nor can it rein it in. Judging by video art practice before 1968, we clearly see that the relationship of video art to mass media is like that of a fly in a fly trap. Chinese artists, like all other artists in the world, began to realise that they could only find their own territories and styles beyond the scope of the mass media. Pursuit of interaction is forever a dream of contemporary art. And, like other artists around the world, some Chinese artists lost confidence in the medium and finally abandoned it and turned to multimedia art, which is more technical and more interactive. I do not object to the emergence and existence of multimedia art. On the contrary, I am confident about the future of multimedia. But Chinese video art makes me ponder: video art turned from criticism of information culture to the social mainstream in order to assure its own validity. Is it time now to connect video art with film, TV, photography and more? For Chinese video art, it may be the time to choose. Do we value video as one kind of media or one kind of culture? Choice will result in evolution and multi-polarity, and two completely different results.

Digital Creativity

EDITOR:
Lone Malmborg, *IT University, Denmark*

ASSISTANT EDITORS:
Tony Books, *Aalborg University, Denmark*
Sue Gollifer, *University of Brighton, UK*

Digital Creativity is a major peer-reviewed journal at the intersection of the creative arts and digital technologies. It carries articles of interest to those involved in the practical task of making or using software for creative purposes. By the term 'creative arts' we include such disciplines as fine art, graphic design, illustration, photography, printmaking, sculpture, 3D design, product design, textile and fashion design, film making, animation, games design, music, dance, drama, creative writing, poetry, interior design, architecture, and urban design. We also address technology-oriented disciplines such as artificial intelligence, computer-supported collaborative work, GPS systems, human-computer interaction, virtual and augmented reality.

To sign up for tables of contents, new publications and citation alerting services visit **www.informaworld.com/alerting**

Register your email address at **www.tandf.co.uk/journals/eupdates.asp** to receive information on books, journals and other news within your areas of interest.

For further information, please contact Customer Services at either of the following:
T&F Informa UK Ltd, Sheepen Place, Colchester, Essex, CO3 3LP, UK
Tel: +44 (0) 20 7017 5544 Fax: 44 (0) 20 7017 5198
Email: subscriptions@tandf.co.uk

Taylor & Francis Inc, 325 Chestnut Street, Philadelphia, PA 19106, USA
Tel: +1 800 354 1420 (toll-free calls from within the US)
or +1 215 625 8900 (calls from overseas) Fax: +1 215 625 2940
Email: customerservice@taylorandfrancis.com

View an online sample issue at:
www.tandf.co.uk/journals/ndcr

Excavating Images on the Border

Hannah Feldman

1. It had been the mid-air collision of a Syrian plane and an Israeli missile a few months previously that had provided Zaatari with this memorable spectacle and the impetus to keep a camera at the ready in order to photograph the subsequent war. For additional analysis, see my 'In This Place on These Days', in *Earth of Endless Secrets*, eds Karl Bassil and Akram Zaatari, Portikus, Frankfurt, and Sfeir Semler, Beirut and Hamburg, 2009.

2. For an expanded discussion of the various terms used to name this region, see Hannah Feldman and Akram Zaatari, 'Mining War: Fragments from a Conversation Already Passed', *Art Journal*, 66:2, Summer 2007, pp 48–67. The present text draws on and incorporates many themes and analyses first presented in this earlier essay, which I wrote based on conversations with Zaatari over the course of a Fulbright-sponsored teaching collaboration in 2006. While many components of these two texts are similar, the current essay has been subject to several significant revisions and is accordingly best understood as the work of a single author. My

On 6 June 1982, Akram Zaatari stood on the balcony of his childhood home in Saida, shooting pictures of the Israeli invasion of southern Lebanon. The event, and in particular the air battles between Syrian and Israeli jets, generated 'the most spectacular' scenes he had ever seen and he was determined to capture their image.[1] Still compelled by these pictures more than twenty years later, he digitally spliced six of them into a single panoramic image that suggests the overwhelming spectacularity of the event. Methodically and systematically, he also filmed these photographs with a non-stationary video camera to create a short piece of looped footage that, coupled with an appropriate-seeming soundtrack, 'documents' what we realise it cannot come close to recreating, ie, the live action of the bombing in all the syncopated plenitude of its actuality. This loop, which also stands as its own independent video, is then stitched into the fabric of *This Day*, 2003, Zaatari's extended video exploration of the meaning of photographic spectacle and its relationship to identity in the Middle East. *This Day* also incorporates three other distinct collections of images into its montage: other photographs taken by the artist and alongside pages from his 1982 diary; an AIF (Arab Image Foundation) collection of 1950s photographs of Bedouins first used to illustrate Jibrail Suhayl Jabbur's massive Orientalist tome, *The Bedouins and the Desert*; and, finally, an array of lo-res digital images that spread across the web and through email as pro-Palestinian propaganda during the first two years of the 2000 al-Aqsa Intifada.

This Day situates the circulation of these three sets of images – metonymies all for the region referred to as 'the Middle East' and the tropes thought to define it – across both place and time as analogous to the circulation of people and ideas across borders.[2] In so doing, the video foregrounds the image's capacity – in both new and old media – to transgress the borders that might otherwise circumscribe both its production and, importantly, its reception. In particular, *This Day* challenges the limitations imposed by the implied 'versus' that separates assessments of fact and fiction in Lebanese conceptual photography since the end of the Civil War in 1990.[3] Indeed, if critics from Lebanon and beyond have consistently noted, if not prescribed, that one of the

Akram Zaatari, *Saida, June 6, 1982*, 2005, composite digital image, 127 × 250 cm, photo: courtesy of the artist and Sfeir-Semler Gallery

gratitude is due Akram Zaatari for the ongoing insights our collaboration has provided and for his continued generosity. Thanks as well to Judith Rodenbeck, Editor-in-Chief of *Art Journal*, for her invaluable editorial and intellectual contributions to the 2007 essay, and to Chad Elias for his research expertise.

3. Some might suggest that the nation was actually not 'postwar' until after the 2000 withdrawal of Israeli military from the ten-mile-wide swathe of Lebanese territory it had occupied as a 'security zone' for nearly two decades, or the 2005 withdrawal of the Syrian military. Similarly, others would prefer the term 'Lebanese Wars' to shift focus away from civil strife and towards the importance of international factors in shaping the conflict.

most prevalent features of what might be defined as a Beirut-based 'school' of contemporary art is its preoccupation with reassessing the role and place of documentary evidence in constructions of historical truth, then *This Day*, along with Zaatari's other works, astutely redirects our attention away from such reassessments and towards an exhaustive evaluation of the photographic image qua image.

Such an evaluation, or, better, a re-evaluation of the image in full recognition of both its spectacular and simulacral qualities is certainly timely in the years 'post 9/11' and following the (photographic) revelation of (photographic) torture at Abu Ghraib. Indeed, these past few years have witnessed a resurgence of thinking about image saturation and mediated numbness in times of war, issues left largely dormant since the flash of missiles across black Kuwaiti skies lit up television screens across the world during the First Gulf War. But our zeal for considering everything made during what some identify as the post 9/11 state of 'permanent war' as implicit to or complicit with that condition should not obscure the other factors that determine photographic meaning. Here, for instance, the specifics of Beirut's art-institutional history beyond or before its devastating civil war are of central importance. Despite a strong Beaux-Arts tradition inherited from the French, post-civil-war Lebanon enjoyed little institutional support for contemporary art, particularly work that aspired to the multi- and new media strategies favoured by international exhibitions and their markets. Following the end of the war, non-profit arts organisations such as Ashkal Alwan (mid-1990s to date) and the Ayloul Festival (1997–2001) – both of which would come to sponsor new and traditional media projects – were originally developed by artists and cultural practitioners alike as ways to circumvent these institutional aporias. In speaking about this circumstance, Zaatari explains that:

> ... in the absence of dedicated art institutions, an artist often finds him/herself focused on the development of structures without being an arts

4. Akram Zaatari, 'Terms Falling: Migrating among artist, curator, and entrepreneur', *Bidoun*, no 6, winter 2006, p 16

5. Tamáss was the first of an ongoing series of exhibitions, symposia, publications and conferences. The exhibition opened at the Fundació Antoni Tàpies, Barcelona in May 2002 before moving to Witte de With in Rotterdam and the BildMuseet in Umeå. *Tamáss 2* concerned work from Cairo/Egypt, opening at the Witte de With in May 2003 and travelling to the Fundació Antoni Tàpies, the Bildmuseet, and the Centro José Guerrero de la Diputación de Granada, Salas del Palacio de los Condes de Gabia. The third exhibition in the series, *The Iraqi Equation*, took place at the KW Institute of Contemporary Art in Berlin in December 2005, before travelling to the Fundación Antoni Tàpies in April 2006 and to the Universidad Internacional de Andalucía-UNIA later that year. Hashem el Madani began his photographic practice in his parents' house in Haret el Keshek in Saida in 1948. In 1953 he opened a professional studio, naming it Studio Shehrazade after a movie theatre in the same building.

6. In another context, David has coined the term 'aesthetic practitioner' to denote the multivalency of these practices, the creative force of which she asserts is one of the lessons the West should 'learn from Beirut'. See 'Learning from Beirut: Contemporary Aesthetic Practices in Lebanon: Stakes and Conditions for Experimental, Cultural, and Aesthetic Practices in Lebanon and Elsewhere', in *Homeworks: A Forum on Cultural Practices in the Region: Egypt, Iran, Iraq, Lebanon, Palestine and Syria*, eds Christine Tohme and Mona Abu Rayyan,

administrator or a curator, interested in histories without being a historian, collecting information without being a journalist. It is indeed distracting to be an artist in such conditions, but it is also an unequivocal privilege to be able to sustain so many positions simultaneously. Such a blurring of positions and roles is neither superior nor inferior to an increasingly clear-cut assignment of roles.[4]

Accordingly, the emphasis on fact-versus-fiction that is often invoked in the same breath as 'Lebanese art' since at least Catherine David's 2002 exhibition 'Tamáss 1: Contemporary Arab Representations Beirut/Lebanon' might be better understood as less the result of the traumatic impact war has had on the possibilities of representation than the result of the same kinds of economic motivations that once fuelled straight photographic practices like that of Hashem el Madani (1928–), whose Saida-based Studio Shehrazade has long been a focus of Zaatari's work.[5] It is without doubt that the hybrid and docufictional works that have marked photography and new media production in Beirut since the 1990s have evolved in specific relationship to the kinds of institutional support available. For the constellation of artists working now in Beirut – and perhaps for those working in places with similar institutional aporias – it is also not without political significance to identify oneself as an art practitioner who works in a variety of media – videos, texts, photographs – and through a variety of analogic strategies – assemblages, appropriation, documentation, creation.[6] In this model, artists are forcibly required to challenge dominant practices and statements, even as these attempt to fix their production in a static form. This challenge often takes the form of what I will call, following cues from Zaatari's work discussed below, an excavation, an excavation which uses the inherent divisions and temporalities of the image to manipulate traditional media such that they perform some of the same flows of simultaneity and boundlessness usually celebrated in relationship to newer, less embodied media.

LOCATING DESIRE: COLLECTING WITHIN THE ARCHIVE

To begin understanding this process, it is first necessary to shift the terms through which we read the docufictional work coming out of Beirut. Instead of reading Zaatari's multi-faceted investigations of both historical photographs and their digital correlates as 'archival' – a phrase worn down not only by its overuse in a decade-plus of 'Archive Fever', but also by its associations with the most bureaucratic and disciplined variety of history – the metaphor of archaeological excavation allows us to focus on the choice, selection and therefore the desire the artist enacts in eschewing comprehensiveness in favour of revelation.[7] More than any kind of hoped-for completeness, the archive represents power, and it is this that Zaatari wants both to examine and to contest. Such indeed is the imperative he gleaned from the allegorical tale told by Roberto Rossellini in his film *La Macchina Ammazzacattivi* (*Machine to Kill Bad People*, 1952). In this film, a saint (eventually revealed to be the devil in disguise) grants a small-town studio photographer (not unlike el Madani, whose projects included the ambition to

Ashkal Alwan, Beirut, 2002, pp 32–9.

7. 'Archive Fever' is the title given to Eric Prenowitz's English translation of Jacques Derrida's *Mal d'archive*, University of Chicago Press, Chicago, 1996; it is also the title of Okwui Enwezor's 2008 exhibition at the ICP in New York, an exhibition which was thought by many to mark the end of the artworld's own 'archive fever'.

8. Rossellini's film is not only about the camera and the powers it might represent, but also about the filmmaker's investigation of imagination and fantasy after his determinedly 'realist' investigations of poverty and destruction. As such, the film must also be seen within a trajectory of Italian postwar cultural production and in relation to the Italian's own long-term project of coming to terms with the legacy of Italy's Fascist past. My thanks to Judith Rodenbeck for having brought my attention to this subtext.

9. Numerous archives were destroyed by natural disasters such as floods and fire, and especially by the ravages of war. For instance, many renowned Jerusalem studios, notably the archives of Krikorian Studio, which date to the late nineteenth century, were destroyed in the 1948 war. In Beirut, most photographic studios, notably those of Gulbenk and Vahe, were concentrated in the downtown area; they were all destroyed during the 1975–1976 war, and the only remnants of their production were the prints collected from Beirut families. Studios across the region had also long since started to recognise the literal value of their negatives, selling them for their embedded silver particles. The process of extracting the silver from

document every resident of Saida) the power to 'kill bad people' by photographing their photographic likenesses, ie, by taking pictures of their pictures, much as Zaatari does in re-shooting his own photographs from the 1982 Israeli invasion. Through the camera's reproductive technology and the potential it represents to create a totalising image of a place and its people in time, the film's protagonist is allowed to assume the simultaneous power and authority of being both judge and executioner.[8] As the film progresses and the photographer decides who he will 'shoot' and who, therefore, will disappear from the picture or be forgotten, the photographer's predilections are revealed as arbitrary, his categorisations increasingly in strict accordance with nothing more than personal prejudice.

Rather famously now, these correlated manifestations of authority – photographic, historic, institutional – have been the subject of a good deal of work produced by Zaatari's Lebanese colleagues, including, for example Lamia Joreige, Joana Hadjithomas, Khalil Joreige, Rabih Mroué, and Walid Raad. Especially well known in this regard is Raad's collective production as the Atlas Group, itself often invoked as the yardstick by which other contemporary Lebanese art is measured. While Raad's production ranges in media from live performance to digitally manipulated or generated images, most often his concerns remain specific to the history and memory of what he refers to as the Lebanese Wars. Taken as a whole, the work of the Atlas Group aims to illuminate the arbitrary (but highly motivated) constructions of the past by experts equipped with power ascribed by such institutional apparatuses with photography and its archives.

While much ink has been spilled describing Raad's very deserving projects as the Atlas Group, much less has been said about his work with Zaatari and with the Arab Image Foundation (AIF), which, at least in part, operates according to a similar ambition. Founded in 1997, or just two years before the Atlas Group, by photographers and aesthetic practitioners Fouad Elkoury, Samer Mohdad and Zaatari, and currently counting Raad, Yto Barrada, Zeina Arida Bassil, Lara Baladi, Nigol Bezjian, Lucien Samaha, Karl Bassil, and Negar Azimi as members, the AIF collects, indexes, studies and exhibits photography in the Middle East and North Africa with an eye to making this history visible. Its mission to acquire and preserve these photographic collections developed after it became clear that many of the documents and archives of commercial studios in Beirut, Saida, Tripoli, Damascus and Aleppo had already been lost.[9] Within those collections that remained, the images, once considered the studio's capital, had come to be considered private documents belonging to clients and therefore of little value. In amassing its collection, the foundation thus intends to function as a traditional photographic archive, providing images for sale and reproduction in publications and so on. But, importantly for this consideration of the photographic image and its circulation, it also stages, or makes itself available to staging, art projects.

In an analysis of Raad's affiliation with the Arab Image Foundation as well as his collaboration with Zaatari on the exhibition and book project *Mapping Sitting*, 2002, Daniel Baird has suggested that while Walid Raad's work as the Atlas Group elides 'the reductive binary between fiction and nonfiction', his collaboration with the Arab Image

the plates, of course, completely erased the image.

10. Daniel Baird, 'Raadical Politics: Walid Raad', *Border Crossings*, 24:2, May 2005, p 40. The title *Mapping Sitting* refers to two related but distinct projects. The project to which Baird refers is the exhibition project by Raad and Zaatari, entitled *Mapping Sitting: On Portraiture and Photography, An Exhibition by Walid Raad and Akram Zaatari, Fondation Arabe pour l'Image*. The exhibition toured Europe, the Middle East and the United States after opening at the Palais des Beaux-Arts, Brussels, in May 2002. The other component of *Mapping Sitting* is the book entitled

Foundation is of an entirely 'different order'.[10] By way, then, of emphasising the fictitious nature of the archives generated by the Atlas Group, Baird stresses that 'the Arab Image Foundation's archives are *real* archives, documenting the history of the representation of Arabs by regional photographers'.[11] Here, Baird implies that, since the foundation's collections are not only *actual* but generally represent what they purport to represent, they provide a kind of factuality more concrete and therefore more documentary than the documents that Raad (as the Atlas Group) creates or appropriates and reassigns. While this supposition is typical of attempts to read the AIF in relation to the Atlas Group, it radically misconstrues not only what it is about Raad's work that marks its most serious interventions into those structures of authority that construct and legitimise history, but also the conceptual framework that motivated *Mapping Sitting*.

For this installation/exhibition, Zaatari and Raad collected images from the AIF's extensive archive and exhibited them in groupings that reflect what they claim are the four most prevalent genres of studio photography: identity, group, itinerant, and 'surprise'.[12] While these images were presented as a representative totality, the installation emphasised the ease with which the organisation and selection of some images over others is always already determined by the desire of those doing the organising and collection. On one wall of the exhibition, for example, Zaatari and Raad

Akram Zaatari and Walid Raad, *Mapping Sitting: ID*, 2002, photos from Studio Anouchian, 1935–1970, detail of the installation, dimensions variable, collection AIF/M Yammine, courtesy the artists and the Arab Image Foundation, photo: Musée Nicéphore Niépce

pinned some four thousand of six-by-nine-centimetre contact prints of ID photographs from the Foundation's vast holdings from Antranik Anouchian's Tripoli studio to spectacular effect. But beyond the shimmering appeal of this mega-mosaic lay the point: an order that was evoked but never fully revealed. The organisation drew attention to the ways in which images suggest their own relationships and logical associations. Of these, some were easily discernible, such as the groups in which moustache styles or scarf patterning corresponded to suggest distinct typologies. Others, however, remained less transparent, the product of the artists' own often invisible desires. The installation, in sum, worked as both an exercise in classification and a testimony to its inevitable failures.

As in Rossellini's film in *Mapping Sitting* the emphasis fell on the arbitrariness of certain narratives, even as they were derived from the factual record provided by the archive. Consider, for example, the artists' installation of a collection of 1950s photographs of male swimmers taken by el Madani, in whose archives Zaatari has been working for several years independently of this collaboration. These photos were grouped by Zaatari and Raad to exemplify 'itinerant photography', the practice wherein a studio photographer would roam the city and its leisure spots to locate paying subjects. While the itinerant photographer was explicitly and perhaps exclusively engaged in the material practice of his trade, his images, repositioned and regrouped by Zaatari and Raad, are made to perform conventions of masculinity and self-presentation, just as the figures within perform the identities to which they aspired. As fragments of one photographer's work introduced into the body of two artists' own collaboration, these images traverse the borders that separate author from audience, research from production, and creation from consumption. As such, they insist that photographic truths are as contextual and desire-based as any fictive practice. As is the case in many of Raad's and Zaatari's independent investigations, the artist's role as author, fabricator, inventor and interpreter is highlighted precisely by his (or in the case of *Mapping Sitting*, their) retreat. More than operating according to simplistic binary oppositions, such as truth *or* falsehood, history *or* memory, public *or* private, *Mapping Sitting* functions simultaneously as *both* and *neither*. As Roland Barthes long ago advised, the story photographs tell makes sense only when contextualised (though I revise him to note that the contextualising information may come in forms not limited to text or linguistic inscription).[13] How otherwise might we make sense – even incorrectly, as we are often instructed by the artists to do – of the digitally corrected images of vernacular Beirut architecture in Raad-as-Atlas-Group's *Sweet Talk*, the coloured dots that indicate the national origins of bullets shot during the Civil War in *Let's be honest, the weather helped*, or even that glittering wall of mugshots in *Mapping Sitting*?

Contrasting the archives of the Atlas Group to those of the Arab Image Foundation, which Baird does by implication in the passage cited above, is therefore not as simple as stating that one archive is true and one is not. It would be better to suggest that they represent different experiential approaches to history, neither fictional nor real. Both, in fact, are concerned with how the past and the identities it is thought to conjure are not only represented but also constructed, if not deliberately performed by a multiplicity of desires – not the least of which are the original subjects or the archiving authorities. Like Raad's imaginary

Mapping Sitting: On Portraiture and Photography, which, in recognition of the importance that design and layout have in determining meaning, is credited to the collaborative efforts of the designers Karl Bassil and Zeina Maasri alongside Akram Zaatari in collaboration with Walid Raad, Fondation Arabe pour l'Image and Mind the Gap, Beirut, 2002.

11. Baird, op cit, p 40

12. 'Surprise' photography designates the urban practice wherein photographers from a studio would take unsolicited and unposed snapshots of pedestrians in order to lure them to the studios.

13. See 'The Photographic Message', 'Rhetoric of the Image', and 'The Third Meaning: Research Notes on some Eisenstein Stills', in Roland Barthes, *Image, Music, Text*, trans Stephen Heath, Hill & Wang, New York, 1978.

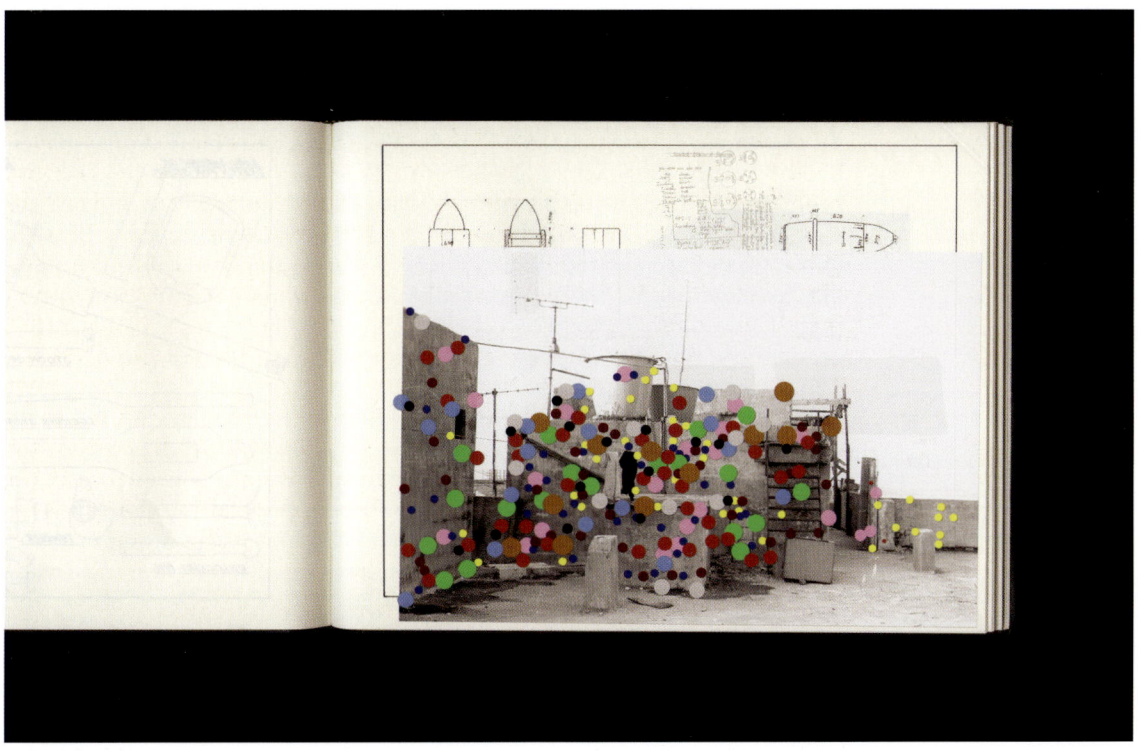

Walid Raad, *Let's Be Honest, The Weather Helped, US*, 2006, framed digital prints, 45 × 72 cm, ed 7 + 1, Photo: courtesy of the artist and Sfeir-Semler Gallery

Atlas Group, the Arab Image Foundation enables art projects that undermine the neutrality of photographic curating, archiving and documentation. If the archive is a static entity, rooted in institutional power, then these projects are better thought of as the archive's antitheses in that they constantly draw attention to their constructedness, as well as to their gaps and, therefore, the ways in which they are organised as the obverse of power. In *Mapping Sitting*, what was nominally a display from the archives of the AIF was arranged and presented according to a schema that unmoored the archive's claims to self-sufficiency – a schema more properly associated with conceptual art practices than with straightforward archival exhibition. Here, however, unlike traditional conceptual art, the schema spoke of the artists' own desires; its hybrid form insisted that the real fiction is that imaging can avoid the document and that the document can similarly avoid fiction.

FOSSILS ARE NOT READYMADE

In This House, 2005, finds Zaatari once again in the south and once again attending to the territorial conflicts the region has come both to represent and to occasion. In this split-screen, single-channel digital video, one side of the screen shows the literal excavation of a garden in Ain-el-Mir, while the other displays documentary-style footage of Ali Hashiso, a photojournalist and former member of the Lebanese secular

14. The 2005 single-channel version condenses what was originally displayed in installation on five monitors in 2004 onto a single screen.

15. Although Zaatari also sites both conversations with Laura Marks, and Janet Walker and Diane Waldman's *Feminism and Documentary*, University of Minnesota Press, Minneapolis, 1999 as sources for his thinking on the fossil as a metaphor for appropriative practice, his initial investments in the term were revealed to him through the surprising reference of Egyptian cinema. For him, the model of the fossil's function is best illustrated in Shadi Abdel Salam's popular film *El Mumia (The Mummy)*, 1976, a story about the commercialisation and trading of ancient Egyptian antiquities in upper Egypt. In the film, the director cast an ageing Egyptian film icon, Nadia Lotfi, to play a

resistance, talking about his experiences while his group was stationed in a house abandoned during the Israeli occupation.[14] Intercut between segments of Hashiso's interview are photographs, including those Hashiso took 'at the front' for his own memories and those he sold as a professional photojournalist. Zaatari's voiceover explains that while he had originally approached Hashiso to talk only about this latter category of image in relationship to what he calls the 'dynamics that govern the state of the image in situations of war', it was Hashiso's diary that led him to the garden of the house in Ain-el-Mir to find a letter of gratitude Hashiso had buried there. Zaatari builds the project on the expectation that, if found, the letter would become the discernible trace of Hashiso's occupation, much as Hashiso's photographs constitute the south's indelible mark on his own memory.

Zaatari here acts literally as the kind of archaeologist that his work otherwise metaphorically figures. Indeed, whether the research he conducts concerns a specific photographic archive or, as in this case, the secret traces of a site's history and the different adaptations to which it is put, there is no better way to understand the objects he manipulates in order to reintroduce these places and collections into the present than by following the logic of the archaeological metaphor developed above and situating them as 'fossils'.[15] By definition, fossils are entities hidden inside other matter until they are unearthed. Unlike 'document' or its artworld correlate, 'readymade' – both of which direct analyses towards questions of originality, authenticity and authorship – the metaphoric reach of 'fossil' imputes to the object a history: it has not only been

Akram Zaatari, *In this House,* 2005, single channel digital video, dimensions variable, photo: courtesy of the artist

created but subsequently forgotten, and only later unearthed, rediscovered and endowed with a new sense. As such, the object is preserved in its original integrity but also contains the evidence of its transformations *over time*. It resists belonging to the present until a conscious act seeks to use it for a particular purpose, to reassign it a new function. Hashiso's letter, originally meant as a note of gratitude to the family whose house he made his home during the war, becomes testimony to the continued persistence of old conflicts into the present. This redirection of meaning, however, depends on the very fact of the object's dormancy, here on the letter's having been transformed from a communication into a secret, invisible in the decade-plus since the Taef accord had enabled the original occupiers of the Ain-el-Mir house to return home.

The significance of the work that Zaatari does within the AIF archive, expands considerably when considered in light of this archaeological metaphor. In *Studio Practices: Hashem el Madani*, an ongoing project that runs parallel to but is nonetheless distinct from the artist's involvement both with *Mapping Sitting* and with the AIF, Zaatari restores, collects, researches, incorporates, films, exhibits and restages photographs by Saida-based commercial photographer el Madani. Manipulated by Zaatari's intervening hand and the contemporary desire that guides it, el Madani's archive is reorganised to expose something of photography's economy, conventions and even conflicting relationship with the social and the political. Aspects of an otherwise invisible Lebanese history are re-materialised through a cast of characters who reveal borders – national, perhaps, but to a greater extent cultural – precisely through their ambitions to cross them as tourists, idealists, resistance fighters, workers and a whole genre of other aspirants and performers. As with Hashiso's letter, excavated like a fossil, the artist's intervention here renders the past and the stories it guards active, alive and yet changed. A photographic portrait of a paying sitter in 1957, for instance, intended to capture that woman as she chose and paid to be pictured. A 2004 hanging of the original silver print, now reactivated as part of Zaatari's own practice, tells a different story. Deep scratches cut across the woman's face trace her husband's jealous rage. Angered that his wife had taken the portraits, the husband insisted el Madani destroy the negative. Unwilling to destroy the integrity of an entire film roll, el Madani refused, finally agreeing to scratch the emulsion so that the photograph likeness could never be reprinted whole. As such, the image not only suggests the social mores regarding women's standing in a modernising Lebanon, but also tells us about the studio photographer's determination to protect his livelihood.

Similarly, when we look at assembled collections of el Madani's portraits of young men dressed in the uniform of Palestinian militants taken during the 1970s, we see signs of a nascent military resistance, *not* because the photographs necessarily document an actual rise in the numbers of militia, but because the images capture the young men performing their *desire* to be seen as such (and also to be seen in other guises, such as that of husband-and-wife partnerships, muscle-men, etc). Zaatari's excavation encourages us to ask at what point we discover that what we have been looking at *as history* or as a *document* of a repressed truth is also a performance of resistance or indeed, in other instances, of conservatism. Not only is the representation of history questioned

---

bit part as a high-class prostitute. Within the narrative, Lofti's presence – her identity easily and immediately recognisable to any Egyptian viewer – comes subtly to suggest an uneasy settlement between Egypt's ancient past and its current popular culture. Her silence and her iconicity seem to call for a temporary muting of the present in order to hear the narratives of past civilisations, precisely those of the actual fossils being traded and destroyed with the film's narrative. Without Lotfi's presence, inserted fossil-like as an integral entity within an external structure, Abdel Salam would not have been able to make this critique as concisely.

Akram Zaatari, *Objects of Study/ Hashem el Madani/ Studio Practices/ Scratched portrait of Mrs Baqari Saida (Lebanon) 1957*, 2004, silver print, 29 × 19 cm, photo courtesy of the artist and Sfeir-Semler Gallery, copyright the Arab Image Foundation

These are negatives that were scratched because of a jealous husband from the Baqari family, who never let his wife out by herself. She used to come frequently to be photographed with her sister before meeting him. After they got married, he was upset to know that she came to be photographed in my studio without telling him. He came asking for the negatives. I refused to give them to him, because they were on a 35 mm roll that had portraits of other clients. In the end we agreed that I would scratch the negatives of his wife with a pin, and I did it in front of him. Years later, after she burnt herself to death to escape her misery, he came back to me asking for enlargements of those photographs, or other photographs she might have taken without his knowledge.

Hashem el Madani

through the reception and interpretation of the documents that both participated in and witnessed it, but so too are questions of meaning and intention, authorship and institutionality, as it is Zaatari who presents the re-orchestrated archive as his own artistic intervention. As is the case with an archaeologist or palaeontologist who literally unearths a fossil by smashing a stone, the artist enriches our understanding of the fabric of everyday life in the region by unearthing, recoding and circulating these images to a broad public. At the same time, he is able to do so only because the tradition that originally framed these images has, as a consequence of time passing, also disappeared. Appropriation reactivates the fossil, and with it the past, the present, and perhaps the future. As fossils, these artefacts – be they Hashiso's letter or el Madani's photographs – maintain an ambivalent autonomy, speaking simultaneously in two different tenses.[16]

As a result, the temporal order – normally implicit in the understanding of both photographic representation and history as related to things that have already passed and are thus absent – fractures. Even though still fully engaged in traditional media, the resulting emphasis on simultaneity mimics locutions enabled by dominant trends in new media, the networks of which themselves are essential to understanding contemporary art from the region or any other now hailed as 'emergent' according to the logic of globalisation. Such concomitant pasts, presents and futures might, in addition, function as a productive template for better locating the multiple strains of modernity we now recognise across the globe as being in fact always interconnected in ways far more complicated than outdated models of influence and adaptation have been made to suggest.

BORDERS IN AND OF REPRESENTATION

Such a shift in chronology suggests a corresponding shift in formulations of space, leading away from the inclusive and uniform totality implied by terms like 'atlas' and toward the simultaneously metaphorical and concrete phenomenon of the 'border' or 'partition', both of which emphasise divisions and misidentifications instead of similarities, and the latter of which emphasises the arbitrary human-made aspects of these separations. While the critical reception of recent Lebanese art projects often stresses the way this work expands the field of representation to include psychological or individual truths otherwise unaccounted for by more official histories – as is true, for instance, with Lamia Joreige's video series *Objects of War 1–4*, 2000, 2003, 2006, Joana Hadjithomas's and Khalil Joreige's *Khiam*, 2000, or even Raad's more individualised representations – this is, at best, an incomplete interpretation. Limiting these works to such analysis understands them strictly as what Zaatari has described as 'mobilisation images' – pictures that aspire to motivate viewers to act in accordance with a specific agenda or that solicit empathic identifications. Instead, it is important to see how these projects foreground contradiction, irreconcilability and multiplicity, as well as how they locate the importance of the narratives they weave therein.

Zaatari's earlier documentary, *All Is Well on the Border*, 1997, a feature-length video produced in collaboration with the Beirut Theatre

16. Nowhere is this more poignant than in Zaatari's latest el Madani work, *Hashem el Madani: Itinerary*, 2008, in which he focused on Madani's portraits of people at work in shops and merchants in Saida's souk. Zaatari has collected forty-one such portraits, framed them, and installed them at the original site where they were shot. While there is not adequate space here to discuss this project more fully, it should be noted that the project is unique in Zaatari's oeuvre in that it is sited in public and makes viewing the photographs a participatory event. When I saw the installation during *Homeworks IV* in 2008, this meant art tourists from around the world descended on Saida's ancient streets in a kind of goose hunt for the discreetly installed photographs. Becoming conscious of ourselves looking for evidence of the past as others looked at us in our quest was only one of the ways in which the experience resonated with Zaatari's longstanding interest in discreetly combating the multiple manifestations of Orientalism that still pervade the cultural expectations of the West.

(then administered by Elias Khouri), provides an excellent case in point.[17] Taking as its subject the myth of popular resistance during the Arab–Israeli conflict, the film systematically interrogates assumptions about the southern Lebanese border and the militias who protected it. To this end, *All Is Well on the Border* broaches not only the different stories then current in early civil war remembrances, but also the different categories of representation that were integral to the codification of certain images of resistance and the exclusion of others. In the 43-minute single-channel video, Zaatari presents three interviews with militia members who had been imprisoned in Israel during the nearly ten years of conflict, intercut with both archival television footage of the 1982 Israeli invasion and passages read from letters written by a Lebanese detainee in an Israeli prison. The resulting montage enables an examination of both the incomplete documentation of the mainly leftist and secular militias that fought against Israeli occupation as well as the issue of representational strategy, demystifying the former while implicating the latter in its originary codification. On one level, it is true that *All is Well on the Border* articulates an alternative history of the Lebanese Wars from the vantage point of those excluded from its dominant representations – the prisoners, the traitors, the exiled, the coerced and the opportunistic. Yet, more importantly, the video avoids the fate of 'mobilising images' by refusing to make victimhood a source of empathetic identification or to use the documentary as an argument for a 'just cause'.

One of the interviews, for example, describes the paranoia that plagued the border following Israel's 1982 invasion. Due to shifting and multiple allegiances, the identity of the enemy was perpetually unclear, and everyone from the shopkeeper to the mayor of the village was equally suspected of collaboration. This uncertainty was only enhanced by the restricted movement imposed by the occupation. Being confined to one's own village or home meant losing contact with the outside world and its entertainments. Intercut with the representations of the ensuing boredom, however, haunting testimonies by several Lebanese actually incarcerated in Israeli prisons attest to the psychological abuse inflicted by their captors. Rather than abandon the representation there, which would encourage a sympathetic response to the detainees' plight, the sequencing culminates to reveal a more fraught relationship to the politics of armed resistance, emphasising that the men's allegiance was often determined less by ideological certainty than by the enduring circumstances imposed by the borders built and fought for around them.

Just as Zaatari cites a Rossellini film as the source for some of the lessons that inspired his interventions within el Madani's archive and an Abdel Salam film for prodding his interest in the model of the fossil, it is Jean-Luc Godard and Anne-Marie Miéville's *Ici et ailleurs* (*Here and Elsewhere*), a film also about borders – both real and imagined – that he cites as inspiration for much of his video work, including *All is Well on the Border*. Commissioned in 1970 by Al Fatah, then the largest faction of the Palestinian Liberation Organisation, to document their struggle against Israeli imperialism, Godard and Miéville travelled to Jordan to make what they then called *Jusqu'à la victoire*, and which they forecast would document the triumph of the PLO against the Israeli army. History, however, had other plans. By the time Godard and Miéville

17. Chad Elias has reminded me that the video was shot using the resources of Prime Minister Hariri's television station, Future TV, thus subtly extending Zaatari's exploration of media culture. Beyond this specific reference, Elias merits special thanks for his research assistance on *All is Well on the Border* and *Ici et Ailleurs*.

returned to France in 1971, their working title was already ironic: far from celebrating victory over Israel, the Palestinian militias had found themselves forcibly expelled from Jordan.[18] Unsure how they should position the footage shot in Jordan, Godard and Miéville began weaving together images of Palestinian refugees conducting drills and reciting revolutionary slogans with contemporaneous pictures of a French family eating dinner and watching television. Alternating between these two worlds, Godard and Miéville put their own initial investment in the Palestinian revolution and their relationship to its failure on display. The image of armed struggle in the Third World that they eventually produced was thus ultimately paralleled by a counter-investigation into the politics of media circulation in the First. Their point was a rigorous critique of French consumer society – built around the images of bourgeois pleasure and satisfaction – as inextricably implicated in the proliferation of mass-media images of terrorism. The problem, so to speak, might be located elsewhere, but, the film suggests, it is here (in France, of course, but also, more metaphorically, within the circulation of images) that we need to look for its roots. *Ici et ailleurs* rejects, therefore, not only the false neutrality of conventional documentary, but so too the original mandate to represent the Palestinian cause from the point of view of those directly engaged in it. To have done anything otherwise, Godard and Miéville reasoned, would have pre-determined what and whom a politics of the image might address, whereas, in fact, these were precisely the stakes of the issue at hand.

As if responding to the provocation of Godard and Miéville's chosen title some twenty years later, the philosopher and curator-critic Stephen Wright has opined that 'we live in partitioned times'.[19] Unlike or even in opposition to the sequential descriptors postcolonial, neocolonial, global, etc, the notion of the partition – which Wright uses to introduce the French artist Jean-Luc Moulène's astounding indictment of internationally sanctioned erasures of Palestinian visibility in his *48 Palestinian Products* – is useful in that it emphasises the arbitrariness of our separation around the lines drawn or imagined to keep populations, nations and identities disconnected. By extension, it also suggests the resulting isolation not only of people, but of ideas, genders, classes, actions; in fact, what Wright suggests is 'virtually every field and discipline of contemporary human activity'. Thus separated and fragmented, our identities are made more available to control and supervision, our actions to diffusion and dismissal.

To some degree, Zaatari's *All is well on the Border*, and even more markedly the work with which this text began, *This Day*, must be thought of as attempting to straddle this partition precisely in order to assess what and how the image is used to uphold these borders and what they might do to contest them in an age marked precisely by an over-saturation of images. As we have been reminded again and again in the years following 9/11, or by the scandal at Abu Ghraib, or even, to bring it back to Lebanon, the July War of 2006, war usually occasions not the kind of refusal-to-image upon which so many trauma studies are based, but instead an actual surge in image circulation.

Never innocent of their context, these images are the subject of the final sequence in *This Day*. In this section of the film, Zaatari weaves together a disparate chain of digital photos that he received on a daily

18. By 1970 at least seven Palestinian guerrilla groups had been established in Jordan. Initially, King Hussein of Jordan had sought to accommodate these militias, or fedayeen, by providing training sites and financial assistance. But the groups obtained additional funds and arms from other Arab states as well as from Eastern Europe, developing a quasi-state-within-a-state and openly flouting Jordanian law. After a series of assassination attempts on King Hussein, and following the hijacking of three civilian aircraft in Amman in September of 1970, the Jordanian Army drove the fedayeen out of the country. The most important factions wound up in Lebanon – setting the stage, according to many historians, for the civil war. Once established in Lebanon, they were joined by a number of Lebanese parties and became the dominant military power in south Lebanon until the Israeli invasion of 1982.

19. Stephen Wright, 'Products of Partition', *Jean-Luc Moulène: 48 Palestinian Products*, exhibition brochure produced in association with PhotoCairo 3, the Townhouse Gallery, and the Contemporary Image Collective, Cairo, 2005. Wright credits the Indian philosopher Ranabir Sammaddar with having introduced him to the phrase.

basis in two years' worth of emails soliciting support for the Palestinian cause during the al-Aqsa Intifada. Rather than support this cause as its advocate, which he no doubt does elsewhere, Zaatari takes a cue from Godard and Miéville and attempts to understand this new form of imagistic communication as related to the larger history of image production and circulation in the region and across its borders. In pairing these digitally transmitted, low-res internet images with the other kinds of photographic depictions that the video features, Zaatari endeavours to 'slow down' the stream of representation in order to ponder what the images communicate beyond the pure information coded as content. In other words, he excavates this digital archive from the dormancy of an already read and archived email in order to give these images new life as young fossils. To a degree, all three sets – personal, illustrative and propagandistic – of the images he probes speak cogently to the experiences of war, including displacement, voluntary nomadism and the involuntary movements of a refugee. No photographic genre, the video concludes, is free from the distortions of desire or the imprint of history. And none, especially not those of the Intifada, the militant implications of which were meant to resonate as political with a capital P, is actually more political than the others. Juxtaposed across the partition that usually separates these different types of photography, each is revealed in the complexities of its constructedness. In this way, the work refuses to be part of 'an uninterrupted chain of images over which we have lost all power' (*Ici et ailleurs*) and is transformed into a tool for investigating how, and in whose interests, images are assigned meaning in the world.

Analogue and Digital Anecdotes and Artworks from South Africa

Marcus Neustetter

My intention with this text is to reflect critically on a complex dialogue I experience between the influx of the ICTs (Information and Communication Technologies), their creative and alternative uses and the underlying experiences that are constructing a landscape of appropriated content, form and function. Focusing on my experiences and findings as an artist in my own research, production and feedback, and on that of my creative collaboration and production platform, the Trinity Session, the anecdotes and critical reflections of successes and failures will construct a narrative that reflects the South African context and its emerging systems.

I am focusing on South Africa as it is a unique mix of the First and the Third World. Through its complex history of apartheid and a relatively young democracy finding its cultural, political, social and economic foundation, it holds potential for those who are inventive due to a need for survival. The sharp contrast between the infrastructural development during apartheid and the ongoing changing social and political conditions in a country of reconciliation of differences produces a wide spectrum of experience. This adds particular critical perspective to a people constantly reminded of the contrasts between the wealthy and the impoverished, those educated in Western civilisation and those informed by traditional knowledge and rituals, and those who choose to embrace the resources, tools and modes of exchange with their new neighbours and those who do not. It is a space of juxtapositions where the prolific use of VHS and audiotapes in many parts of Africa are still in divergence with the latest MP3 sales points in music stores or pirated CDs and DVDs sold by street vendors. It is a space of inventiveness, where a children's merry-go-round gets used as a water pump and a corporate billboard doubles as a solar panel to power the low-cost housing below.

In this space, where one person's redundant or old technology is the next person's dream gadget, technology is recycled. Companies test their products, users appropriate what is offered to them and someone is still happy to use my first old mobile phone, which resembles a brick, as it is better than no phone at all. The juxtaposition is amplified by the identity and image portrayed by the advertisers of the latest technology. We want to look cool with a slim and slender super-sexy phone; but wait, the sexier the phone, the more risk of it being stolen in this crime-ridden country; we will need to take out insurance. It almost seems as though crime is one of the factors that ensure a good flow of affordable phones, part of the dissemination, connectedness and effective communication of local society.

FINDING A LOCAL CONNECTEDNESS

There are those without phones, but their streetwise skills keep them connected. A recent visit to a community art school in the inner city of Johannesburg proved this. One of the mentored lecturers asked me whether he could use my phone. I gave it to him, hoping he would not be on the phone for long. Instead of dialling a number, he asked me if I knew my pin number. I nodded, mentally extracting it from the myriad of other important numbers I know I have to memorise. He turned my phone off, took out my battery and SIM card and replaced it with one of the three SIM cards he pulled out of a small compartment in his wallet. Handing me my SIM for safekeeping, he turned on the phone, thumbed in his pin and started reading his text messages (SMSs). He dialled into his voicemail, listened and replied with an SMS. Satisfied, he put my SIM card back into the phone, thanked me in a casual manner. After returning my phone, he headed over to the next takeout roadside public phone to make a call.

This habit of SIM swapping is not unusual in certain parts of Johannesburg. A SIM card, the size of a thumbnail, is the only thing that connects the lecturer to the power of the communication world. He had a phone but gave up a long time ago trying to prevent it being stolen and has instead perfected his streetwise understanding of the local systems.

He knows different SIM cards give him access to different services and even reduced rates in certain cases. He understands that the local public phone vendor, a call metre and a handset powered by a car battery connected to some phone line (legally or illegally), is still the cheapest way to make a phone call. And he understands how to make use of all of these methods to stay connected.

The impact of the local mobile phone market has hit the sophisticated video-conferencing and GPRS/3G market, but the inventiveness of a large portion of the population has challenged the companies and their offerings. It is thought that in response to the large mobile phone and SIM-card use, the local landline telecommunication service is developing a public phone system in which one can insert one's SIM card to access messages and telephone numbers. Mobile service providers have realised that they need to cater for the streetwise communicators and lower income bracket. An example of this is their offering a free 'please call me' SMS from one user to another, which enables communication and will get them eventually to call each other. Just like the 'missed call' these have become everyday communication tools that are born out of a need to keep each other informed but not spend money.

I have made use of this service many times. On one particular occasion I had made an arrangement with a painter who was assisting me on a large installation. We arranged that when he ran out of paint he should send me a 'please call me', knowing that he would not have credits to call me. Later, when I called him back, I found out that he was illiterate, since he could not read the type of paint over the phone to me. But he knew how to use this communication service to get me to call him. He explained that he did not need to be able to write, and that knowing the sequence of the buttons on his phone was sufficient to get a message to me to call him back: an inspiring moment where text-based systems break down literacy boundaries for communication. Yet I am not convinced that the streetwise use of the system provides a solution for the current extreme difference between those who can contribute to the connected society and those who cannot.

CONNECTEDNESS AND REPRESENTATION

The examples I mentioned might be appropriations of the local system for contextually relevant use that enable more people to start to understand the interaction with technology, but it is still in strong contrast to the misrepresentation I see of many African online contexts. Similarly the internet cafés, second-hand email use and donated connectivity projects that are popping up all over Africa might enable the first steps of communication and exchange. However, if they are not relevant to local use, they are hardly successful in changing the perceptions of the continent of people actually experiencing them. The systems are used to communicate for social or business purposes or survival such as the Advance Fee Fraud, 419 scam letters or Nigerian scam letters,[1] but beyond this alternative users are not able to compete with the global powers that present their perspective on the African continent and so change perceptions. While in the urban centres there is hype around the internet and the possibility of using this space, many of the internet stations I have visited are used for checking email and, judging by the history bar of the browsers, mostly used to go to popular American and European culture, brand, music, celebrity and film sites. This seems to be an extension of what is culturally presented on global TV, in cinemas and on the music circuit. While an effort is being made to develop local content from local governments, businesses and NGOs, in order for these institutions to have an online presence, the culture of using these sites and creating buy-ins and ownership by the local community requires a cultural hype and motivation that is currently being usurped by the flashy images of the foreign media powers.

With the information technology industry now active in South Africa, I wonder whether there is not more potential to create a content platform that not only presents local information for local consumption, but also questions the current sources of content that impose their totalising view of our context on us. Much as the reports on the War on Terror in global news are questionable due to political agendas, the economic powers seem to be far ahead of the information race in the global mass media. Unfortunately, on the African continent, there is no global power as measured by European and American standards. The

---

1. 'An *advance fee fraud* is a confidence trick in which the target is persuaded to advance relatively small sums of money in the hope of realising a much larger gain. Among the variations on this type of scam are the *Nigerian Letter* (or *419 fraud*)', http://en.wikipedia.org/wiki/Advance_fee_fraud

Public phone service, Johannesburg, photo: Marcus Neustetter

global capitalist hold over consumer culture and the mass media or, as I like to refer to it, the 'Coca-Colanisation', needs to be questioned. This should set up a critical dialogue and attempt to introduce pride in traditionally relevant beliefs, local consumables and local culture, in order to create an understanding of the power of the local consumer to guide the global partner to be more sensitive to our heritage, culture, image and dialogue as a developing context.

Challenging issues, such as language differences in online communication, can alienate potential contributors. In South Africa, with its eleven official languages, I am very aware of my own shortcomings since I am fluent in only two and do not know any of the indigenous languages. It is an alienating experience, especially as the languages I do speak, namely English, Afrikaans, German and French, are all colonial languages that were imposed on the African continent. In a recent work I drew parallels between this and the context of the online alienation in a space where limited knowledge of a language prevents access. I extracted keywords that related to this very debate on language and the connection barrier between the First and Third World such as 'communication', 'access', 'technology', 'internet', etc. I then found an online Zulu (a local language often spoken in South Africa) translation program into which I placed these words. Some words could be translated and others could not. With a German reading program I had downloaded, I then allowed a computer voice to read out these partially translated words. The result is a strange series of words with recognisable sounds, which echoes my daily experience in public spaces in South Africa. During the conference 'UNESCO between two Phases of the World Summit on the Information Society in St Petersburg' (17–19 May 2005)[2] I found the perfect opportunity to use this sound experiment. Issues around language differences were addressed by the keynote speaker Adama Samassékou,[3] who was President of the WSIS Preparatory Committee for Geneva Phase. Frustrated by the feeling that the issues he raised fell on deaf ears, I found my way to the translation booths and played the sound piece off my laptop directly to the audience's headsets in order to disrupt and challenge the listeners. During panel discussions I raised the issue again and I hope persuaded some people to reflect critically on the experience of the divide when you are on the 'other side'.

RELATED TO THE ART INDUSTRIES AND NETWORKS

Introducing alternative perspectives and, where possible, educating the audience seem to be essential approaches for the survival of the local art industries in South Africa. In 2001 the Trinity Session embarked on a research document for the International Labour Organisation on the Visual Arts and Craft Industries in the SADC (Southern African Development Community) Region.[4] On analysing the fourteen countries of the region it soon became clear that there were major gaps in the structure that might create a successful visual arts and crafts industry capable of sustaining itself and its producers. Amongst other conclusions, findings indicated that the local creative producers, industry players and audiences were challenged by the imposed notion of art in Africa. The boundary between the crafter and the artist seemed more often than not

2. International Conference: UNESCO between two phases of the World Summit on the Information Society, 17–19 May 2005, St Petersburg, Russia. 'The Conference is organised with a view to clarify the next steps and key decisions of UNESCO with regard to the building of the global information society. One of the main objects set by the conference is drafting recommendations for determining UNESCO's position on further implementation of provisions of the main documents adopted at the World Summit on the Information Society.' http://confifap.cpic.ru/conf2005/eng/info/

3. H E Mr Adama Samassékou, President of WSIS Preparatory Committee for Geneva Phase, President of the African Academy of Languages, Former Minister of Education of Mali (1993–2000)

4. *SME Development and Employment in the Cultural Sector in the SADC Region: The Visual Art and Craft Industries,* research report prepared for the International Labour Office (ILO), Geneva, 2002

to be blurred. The main patrons of the visual arts were foreign diplomats and tourists who, because of their very 'foreignness', impose their perception of what art from Africa should look like and what purpose it serves. This results in the perpetuation of the stereotypical artefact that represents the region, whether it be for their personal home decoration or as gifts. While some contemporary art producers are profiled on platforms on the continent, such as at the Dak'Art Biennale 2006, production and intention is mostly geared to an industry that can cater for and support this type of intellectual pursuit – a rare occurrence on the African continent.

One of the findings was that the local longing for international recognition (following the market) has motivated artists to set up their own websites, in the hope of causing a sensation attracting foreign interest and being given a break on the international platforms. However, the internet hype has created false hope. Strangely enough this need to connect with others is rarely shared within the region or even within the same city. The concept of participating in a local initiative using technology has not been effective in encouraging communication with neighbouring countries that might be able to deal with local issues and problems, as opposed to looking to the First World for the solution.

A Trinity Session project presented at the Arts Electronica Festival 2002 attempted to look at the exchange and communication network possibilities in South Africa amongst creative individuals who use the internet regularly and are technologically knowledgeable. This project, called 'Search', invited nine South Africans from two cities to Linz to workshop a common creative technology communication base with the aim of developing exchange and collaboration in the ICT and creative industries in South Africa. While the project was a success during the discussions and interactions in Linz, and was personally very rewarding for individuals who attended from an educational and networking point of view, when it confronted the reality of setting up the network in South Africa it did not succeed. Similar network attempts, such as sanman (southern African new media art network) and DigiArts Africa (in collaboration with UNESCO DigiArts),[5] while they are continuously being improved and adapted, have also proved that the idea of online exchange and interaction on the African continent is exceptionally difficult to develop in terms of a communication network that might enable us to combine our resources and make an impact.

When reflecting on the informal nature of the appropriated uses of technology in the examples mentioned, there is merit in understanding the local systems that are currently informing the uses of these technologies. For example, word-of-mouth dissemination of information, people meeting socially, and family and friend networks seem to overshadow the formalised and structured approach to disseminating information and generating participation. In South Africa, there is a strong preference for direct interaction rather than mediated interfaces. Personal connections are of great importance for business transactions. Cultural rituals and collective experience are forms of learning and exchange preferred to virtual discussions and alienating lectures. Easily accessible and usable technologies, such as the mobile phone, become tools for these transactions and connections. This has become an obviously interesting space for creative experimentation.

5. http://portal.unesco.org/digiarts

With strong emphasis on low technology and easy accessibility, I have launched a series of downloadable picture-message SMS artworks. Following on from a body of work that uses old dot-matrix computer paper and printers, I retained the dot or the pixel as it is found on the first mobile phones that had limited image resolution. Since many of the old phones are still being used, the images can still be downloaded. Today, the content-provider industry largely caters for high resolution, colour and animated graphics. Keeping it pixelated and simple, I have produced a series of images for mobile phones that are a commentary on the system. They are black pixel drawings that reflect connectivity and communication using icons from the computer and invented symbols in a web of connections. These easily downloadable system images were tweaked and released in different cultural contexts in South Africa so that they could be downloaded on any phone with a simple SMS. Tracking the number of downloads and the response from the public, from the gallery audience and club culture to the street traders, I was able to watch and measure the enthusiasm and interest in the project and the impact it had. While print-media campaigns, electronic mails and websites were created to publicise the project, it was through word of mouth and social activities, such as image and ring-tone sharing, that it managed to reach a relatively large audience in quite remote places.

FITTING IN CREATIVE TECHNOLOGY-BASED PRODUCTION

As with much screen-based production, due to the fleeting nature of the virtual and momentary experience, it is a constant challenge to integrate this type of work into the art industry and gallery context. The terms 'new media art' and 'digital art' categorise this type of production. Local institutions still struggle to integrate this technologically based production into their infrastructure and programmes. Various exhibitions focusing on art and new technologies in the last six years have been invaluable in highlighting the importance of these types of shows. In a context where the art audience has always been relatively modest, the inclusion of technology-based artwork has not only attracted new audiences but has also sparked interest from different industries. Mass media and entertainment-content providers, technology suppliers, production companies in moving image and design and advertisers are entering the art environment through the interest that has been generated in the creative use of technology. Art educational institutions realise they are losing students because they do not offer technological tool training. Students interested in creative production are choosing design and multi-media production schools since they stand a better chance of getting a job with these skills. In response art schools are becoming more competitive and are opening new-media departments to offer training based on art and technology skills.

While this is an important step in the development of the local art scene in order to further its involvement with different industries, students are mainly taught to be competitive in the market and learn how to use the latest technology and software they will use in the workplace. The challenge is how to balance this acquired knowledge with the need to engage local context and produce work with appropriate content. They should be able to produce work that does not simply reflect the technology itself or the latest international design trends, but that presents their personal voices and styles with content of local significance.

Enjin Magazine has a modest print-run and reviews the latest technology and presents creative projects in the print, design and screen-based industry. The magazine's aim was to challenge its readers and position its relevance beyond just the latest gadgets. The result was the launch of an Enjin Museum of Dead Media (EMODM)[6] in collaboration with Hobbs/Neustetter. This became an ongoing project page in the magazine that challenged the notions of redundant technology in the South African context. Launched with an exhibition of a collection of 'old' technology at the Design Indaba in 2005, it developed into an installation at a new-media university in Johannesburg: the City Varsity Newtown in 2006. This is accompanied by an ongoing virtual museum concept where details of people's personal collections in drawers, garages or on their office walls are published so that one can view them when travelling to that part of the world. EMODM not only poses questions about the recycling of seemingly redundant technology, but asks critical questions about the nature of a contemporary museum. Many museums are not only faced with the challenges of integrating technology into their research, displays and archiving, but locally also of educating audiences on the use of the museum. While interviewing people walking past the inner-city Johannesburg Art Gallery about what they thought might be inside the building, the general response was that it was a post office, city offices or a court. One person even said it might be a prison.

MOVING OUT OF THE GALLERY
TO MEET LOCAL CHALLENGES

Notions of decentralising the gallery or museum, moving into the public realm and introducing popular culture to attract audiences underpin attempts to produce programmes and projects that are more socially aware and audience focused. As in the current fields of user-orientated design and consumer-focused marketing, institutions and producers are looking for alternative platforms and approaches. Projects such as Africastudio.net are currently trying to achieve this.[7] With its recent launch at the Africom (African Museums Network) conference in October 2006 in Cape Town, the project outlined its objective of setting up studio experiences for creative production in museums in African centres to stimulate local-interest traffic and debate. With the use of locally relevant technology, from the radio and VHS recorder to the mobile phone, creative adaptations of local content and the appropriation of popular culture and mass media, a new approach to the public and production process is being addressed.

Local approaches to consumers using the electronic media have an impact on the culture of production. In Lusaka (Zambia) in 2003 a group of artists who were generating income through hand-painted

6. EMODM (Enjin Museum of Dead Media), http://onair.co.za/emodm/

7. http://www.africastudio.net/ (discontinued); for more information on Africom installation go to: http://www.onair.co.za/pdf/africomstudio.pdf

billboard advertising were losing business. Because of new LED billboards that were being used in different parts of the city, advertisers were offered competitive rates for rotating adverts. The question was whether the consumer not used to the digital presentation format would respond as well to the electronic image as to the hand-painted sign. In order to get round this and to support the local producer again, proposals were presented to commission sign-writers to paint the advertised products, and then scan them in for the electronic screen. While I am not sure if that project was ever executed, hand-painted advertising on an electronic screen creates an odd image that illustrates current attempts to integrate the skills of producers with the advancement of technological platforms. As an extension of this experience, Nathaniel Stern and I were commissioned by Turbulence.org in 2004 to create the project getawayexperiment.net.[8] The aim was to motivate Johannesburg artists and sign writers to hand paint jpgs and gifs of popular sites. These images then replaced the original digital images online. Just as awkward as reading the resulting handmade images on the net, the large electronic flashing billboard presented itself towering above the shacks and stalls. This contrast is one that reflects the struggle of incorporating the First and the Third World, but is also a constant reminder of the human experience within the technological advancement accompanying globalisation.

In current research and production areas such as locative media the focus is on the audience and his or her position in relation to the reach of the technological network. So for example, a South African service provider is using the locative qualities of mobile technologies as a business opportunity. Responding to fear within crime-ridden communities, the locative services are now being offered with a 'find-me' option. This enables one phone user to locate another accurately. While this may border on the illegal invasion of privacy, it is a valuable tool enabling concerned South African parents to locate their children. Inspired by this local service, Hobbs/Neustetter[9] explored projects that mimicked this high-tech resource through low-tech devices. The first of the locative projects, entitled *TangoCity*, was a process during which Stephen Hobbs and I had to find each other, equipped with a mobile phone and a camera in the inner city of Johannesburg. One was on top of the Carlton Centre, the highest point in the city, while the other was navigating the streets, waiting to be located by camera using the mobile phone service. This simple experiment stimulated ideas around 'locativeness' using this kind of technology. While the project achieved its goal of exploring a low-tech version of locative media, we were further interested in exploring the human network and interaction for navigating a city.

In response, Hobbs/Neustetter produced a project 'UrbaNET Hillbrow-Dakar-Hillbrow'[10] for the Off Programme of the Dak'Art Biennale 2006. While the original intention was to produce the project technologically, the result was an experiential approach that made use only of documentation technology. Yet it connected the artists directly into different communities in Dakar and made 'locativeness' possible through interaction with people. Already with the first encounter, which inspired the project, we were reminded of our location. Photographing a public area on the border of Hillbrow, a neighbourhood of Johannesburg's inner city notorious for its state of urban decay and influx of African immigrants, we were warned in French by a francophone immigrant

8. http://turbulence.org/Works/getawayexperiment/

9. The meeting of Stephen Hobbs and Marcus Neustetter in an artist's collaboration fuses their interests in urban social change and virtual culture. Over the years their artistic practice has resulted from experimentation with the juxtaposition of high and low tech, dead and new media interventions. These experiments manifest in public space, galleries and museums and in the arena of their artist lab the Trinity Session. Taking into consideration the exclusivity of the museum and gallery context, current projects focus on social research and mobile platforms enabling their artistic expression. See http://www.onair.co.za

10. http://www.onair.co.za/pdf/urbanethillbrowdakar.pdf

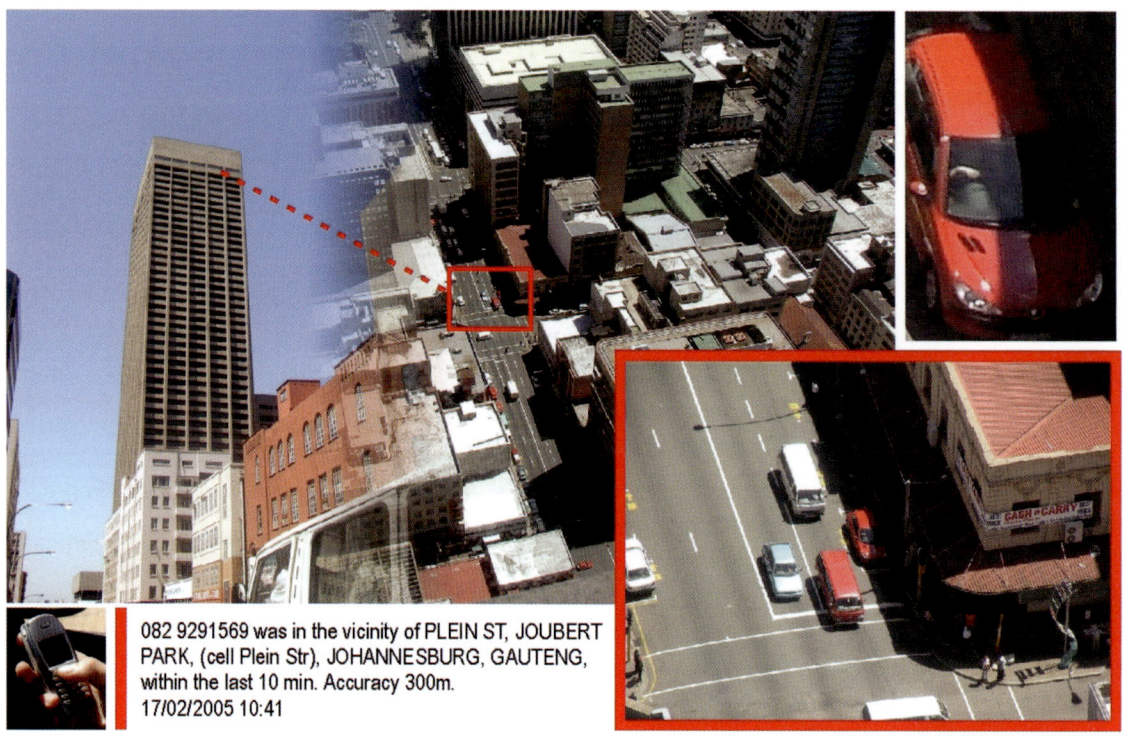

Hobbs/Neustetter, *TangoCity*, locative mobile experiments in Johannesburg, 2005

where it was not safe to photograph, defining a boundary not only for our safety but also through the use of language. This project developed into an exploration of the neighbourhood we were warned about and its immigrant Senegalese community. While interviewing Senegalese immigrants, they drew us maps of Dakar, which we used to navigate the city during a two-week residency at Kër-Thiossane in Dakar. The immigrants described the places and people we should visit and told us stories of a city that some of them had not been to in twelve years.

The most intriguing aspect of navigating Dakar was the interaction and exchange with people as we tried to make sense of the information we had received in Hillbrow. We were not aware of any other maps or information on the city, and our navigation became dependent on asking for the next landmark or area name so we could, recalling the stories, eventually create our own map to find the people and places we were asked to locate. The resulting video and photographic documentation, as well as the hand-drawn maps, was exhibited in a home in Dakar and then presented to the immigrants in a night club in Hillbrow on our return, which in turn has allowed us to access a network of people who have helped us understand the activities in our own city.

IN CONCLUSION

To summarise the experiences presented here, as cultural producers from South Africa move out of the gallery context and away from the imposed

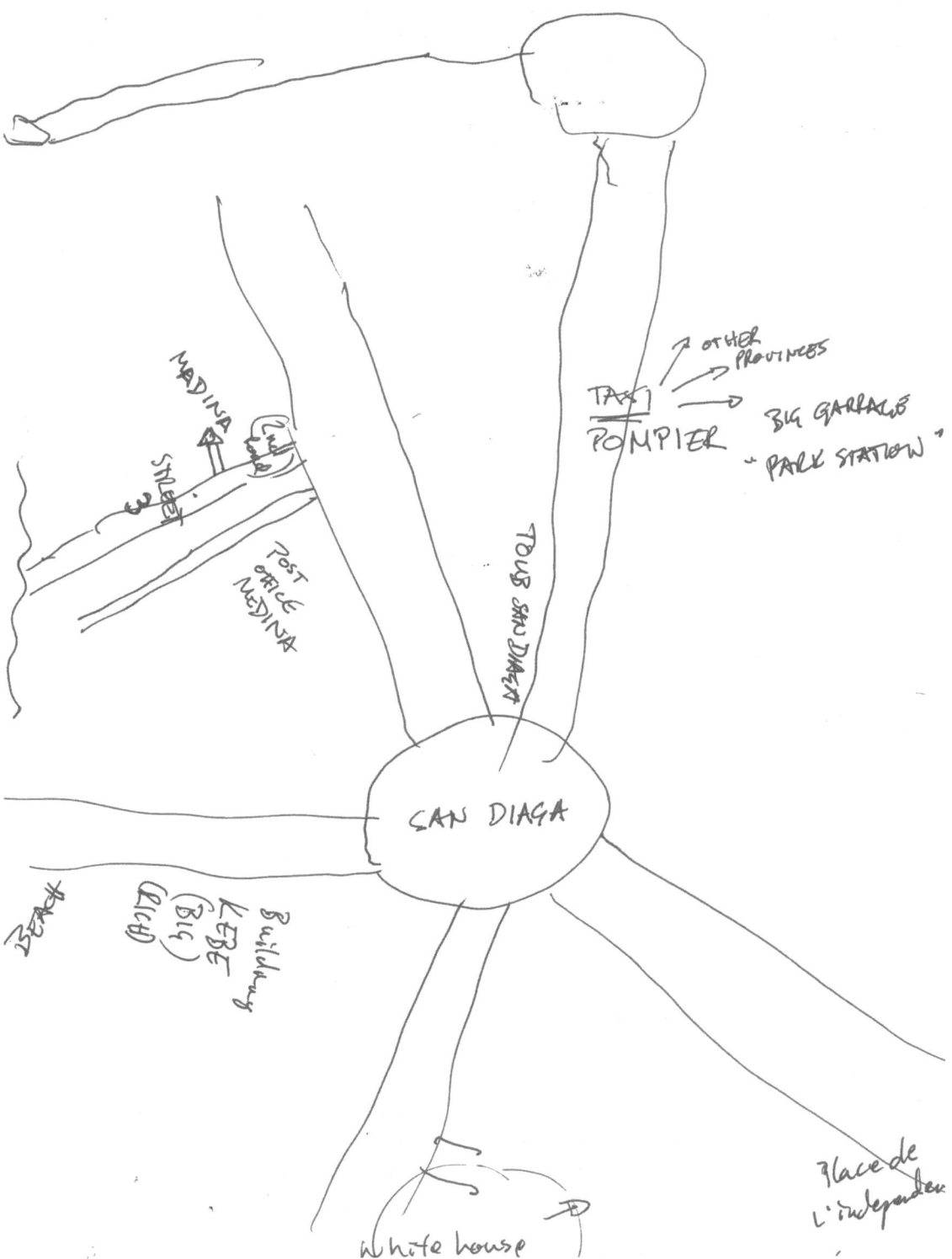

Map of Dakar drawn by Senegalese immigrants in Hillbrow for Hobbs/Neustetter's *UrbaNET Hillbrow-Dakar-Hillbrow* project, South Africa, 2006

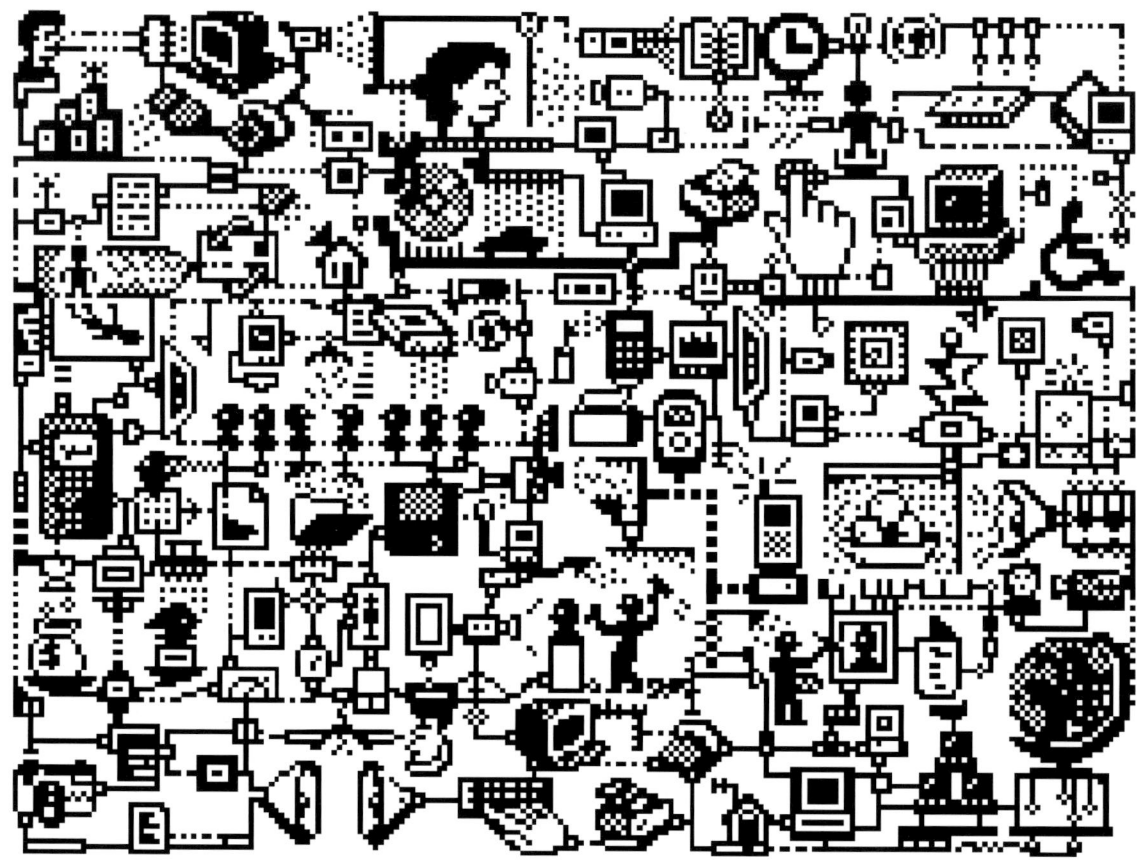

Marcus Neustetter, *System*, assemblage of mobile phone picture graphics 2003–2006

perception of art from the African continent they are employing new tools and approaches in their production. Digital technology and its connectivity have been combined with locally relevant strategies and methodologies of communication and exchange in everyday interactions in South Africa. As local artists look for ways of challenging the way in which they are being represented, they are naturally tapping not only into the global mass media tools, but into creative local ways of dealing with them.

So the example of 'UrbaNET Hillbrow-Dakar-Hillbrow' presents an alternative to the GPS device, a connection with an alternative information and knowledge system outside global technological control. It illustrates well the local and human information system, in contrast to that of second-hand appropriated knowledge from the net or an electronic tour guide. It maintains everyday human contact and does not confine us to the screen and the keyboard, ensuring that we are constantly reminded of our physical presence in a 'context' and that technology is merely a tool to be appropriated for local needs. When it comes to using this tool for broadcasting, we need to remain critical and patient, as the translation of the experience from everyday survival activities to the intake of mass media global information is not only difficult to digest, but even more difficult to present as relevant to the global viewer.

Revisiting the Pirate Kingdom

Ravi Sundaram

The body is a thing among things[1]   Maurice Merleau-Ponty

In an essay entitled *Theatrum Philosophicum*, Michel Foucault made one of his now widely cited predictions – that this century may well be known as 'Deleuzian'. Less is known of the exact occasion of this statement – Foucault's discussion of Gilles Deleuze's two books, *Difference and Repetition* and *The Logic of Sense*. After Deleuze, Foucault suggested that 'the philosophy of representation – of the original, the first time, resemblance, imitation, faithfulness is dissolving; the arrow of the simulacrum released by the Epicurians is headed in our direction'.[2] Since Plato's time, the relationship between the real and the copy has been framed where the simulacrum has existed almost entirely as a negative mode of comparison, a false claimant to the real. Plato's hierarchy was that of the model, the copy and the copy of the copy, designated as the simulacrum. In the *Republic*, Plato had displayed his hostility to the 'imitator' who as the 'creator of the phantom, knows nothing of reality'.[3] In *The Logic of Sense* Deleuze argues for the equality of representations, in a philosophy that abolishes classical distinctions between essence and appearance: 'The simulacrum is not a degraded copy. It harbors a positive power which denies the *original and the copy, the model and the reproduction.*'[4]

Plato's philosophical distinction had became significant by the seventeenth century when Western modernity refashioned itself through the lenses of creativity and authorship, tied to an emerging theory of cultural property. The establishment of a widespread discourse on authorship has by no means been easy. From the seventeenth century mass reproduction techniques inaugurated by print rendered Plato's philosophical distinction increasingly suspect through the proliferation of more versions of the Same and the Different.

POSTCOLONIAL URBAN PROLIFERATION[5]

The 'crisis of the real' referred to in *The Logic of Sense* marked Western cultural and philosophical debates in the 1970s. At the same time

---

1. Maurice Merleau-Ponty, *The Visible and the Invisible*, trans Alphonso Lingis, Northwestern University Press, Evanston, IL, 1968, p 137

2. In Donald F Bouchard, ed, *Language, Counter-Memory, Practice: Selected Essays and Interviews*, Cornell University Press, Ithaca, NY, 1977, pp 65–96

3. Plato, *Republic*, X, 601c. Cited in Robert S Nelson and Richard Shiff, eds, *Critical Terms for Art History*, University of Chicago Press, Chicago, IL, 1996, p 36

4. Gilles Deleuze, *The Logic of Sense*, trans Mark Lester and Charles Stival, Columbia University Press, New York, 1990, p 262

5. My use of the term postcolonial is completely pragmatic – to indicate a successor to the nationalist enterprise. The terms 'Third World' and 'South' make no sense today in their original formulation.

post-Fordist global production in the capitalist world economy set up vast networks of factories, semi-autonomous affiliates, distribution techniques, technological capabilities that soon moved regionally and in a non-linear fashion.[6] This is a space–time cluster commonly collapsed in the phrase called 'globalisation', a period that saw both urban expansion and crisis in all parts of the postcolonial world. Proliferation, endless proliferation marks the new postcolonial urban. Home workshops, markets, hawkers, small factories, small and large settlements of the working poor now spread all over the planned metropolis, or in regions where it would have been impossible some years ago. Productive, non-legal proliferation has emerged as a defining component of the new urban crisis in India and other parts of the postcolonial world. These urban proliferations, sometimes called 'informal', have remained ambivalent about the law. As Timothy Mitchell's work on Egypt shows, urban populations identified as informal tended to stay away from legal regimes of property as the latter could potentially destroy local knowledges and bring the informals into the extractive monetary structures of urban government.[7] In Delhi, Solomon Benjamin found out that the East Delhi neighbourhood of Vishwas Nagar, called a slum by planners, in fact emerged as the main centre of electronics hardware production in North India in the 1980s.[8]

It is increasingly clear that this unhinged proliferation of urban life is enclosed in a world of media urbanism. Postcolonial cities are today also *media cities*,[9] a tag typically reserved for the 'global city'. Saskia Sassen and Manuel Castells have recognised that international technological networks of finance and communication produce new geographies of concentration and dispersal. Sassen argues that financial centres concentrate in certain core cities with a large, increasingly disenfranchised low-end workforce helping to provide services and back-up.[10] Manuel Castells's network society thesis focuses on how a new space of flows draws producers of information goods everywhere into powerful communication networks.[11] Elite urban enclaves service and house these classes, simultaneously marginalising other forms of labour in the city. Positioning in the new space of flows becomes part of the strategies of new info-elites. The global network society also produces a range of spatial entities of generic environments: software parks, outsourcing hubs and data parks. New technological urban peripheries emerge around global concentrations. Despite its obvious insights, global city literature has preferred to map its own geography onto that of mainstream development theory: here the postcolonial urban is implicated in a theory of the 'digital divide' where technological effects are concentrated in elite enclaves.

An increasing range of research from Mexico to Nigeria and now Asia suggests that contrary to more *simpliste* digital divide arguments, postcolonial cities are also vibrant hubs for new media productions, spurred on by a range of low-cost infrastructures: mobile telephony, video and digital technologies, and parallel distribution circuits.[12] This produces a media experience that assumes constant breakdown, recycled assemblages, serial dispersal and endless proliferation of multiple forms and sites. Breakdown and productive life are enmeshed in a dynamic constellation. Experiencing of this media city produces a complex hyperstimulus: an escalation of the senses along with the increasing speeds of

6. See Giovanni Arrighi, *The Long Twentieth Century: Money, Power and the Origins of Our Times*, Verso, London, 1994

7. Timothy Mitchell, 'The Properties of Markets: Informal Housing and Capitalism's Mystery', Institute for Advanced Studies in Social and Management Sciences, University of Lancaster, Cultural Political Economy Working Paper Series, Working Paper no 2, http://www.lancs.ac.uk/ias/polecon/workingpapers/2mitchell.doc

8. Solomon Benjamin, 'Touts, Pirates and Ghosts', in *Sarai Reader 05: Bare Acts*, Sarai, The New Media Initiative, Delhi, 2005, pp 242–54

9. A growing literature is beginning to document this. See Brian Larkin, 'Degraded Images, Distorted Sounds: Nigerian Video and the Infrastructure of Piracy', *Public Culture*, 16:2, Durham, NC, 2004, pp 289–314.

10. Saskia Sassen, *The Global City: New York, London, Tokyo*, Princeton University Press, Princeton, NJ, 2001

11. Manuel Castells, *The Rise of the Network Society: Economy, Society and Culture*, Blackwell, London, 2000

12. Distribution now comes from a transformed and radically expanded bazaar that moves beyond the hegemony of older merchant communities and loses its 'traditional' shape.

the city, and a relentless circulation of things, images and people. Proliferation has produced a diversity of media experiences, but also unsettled classic boundaries of consumption and circulation, drawing urban populations into a dynamic but addictive loop.

With globalisation, Indian cities saw unending waves of new commodified technological objects entering markets, homes and offices. Pirate production and circulation was a publicly acknowledged sphere in this new world of things. It encompassed most consumer products but was particularly significant in media goods whose surfaces spread in every part of the city. These goods took on life as counterfeits, fakes or copies, or, in popular language, the 'pirated', the 'local' or 'duplicate'. When the new media boom began in India and other parts of Asia around the introduction of the cassette deck, the VCR and the home computer, the old regime of media property and control went into a spin.

By the mid-1980s piracy had become technology's cultural kingdom of the Many, and the source of mass cultural ambiguity in the regime of authorship and originality conferred on things. This has increased rapidly with the coming of the digital era and high-quality reproductions. As with early modern print culture, piracy is again at the centre of the debate over access and authenticity. Low-cost digital reproduction in the late twentieth century both recalled and radically expanded early modern conflicts. In twentieth-century global terms, the radical 'everywhereness'[13] of this new reproducibility is not confined to the digital alone, but seems increasingly to allegorise the production of industrial and consumer goods. Counterfeit culture is here to stay. Corporations have sought to defend their markets with brand protection and vast advertising budgets. In a world where Asian factories export vast quantities of consumer goods globally, a commodity sold as an expensive label in Paris could equally appear as a low-cost surplus item from an Asian factory in a street market in Lagos. Piracy affects debates on medicine, biotechnology, international trade disputes, trademarks, youth culture, indigenous knowledge and corporate 'bio-piracy', sovereignty and property. Piracy, along with terrorism, is now included in the favoured language of global fear with its consequent attractive/destructive semantic overflow. For liberals and old-style Marxists, piracy seems to allegorise an impure transgression, tainted by commerce and an inability to produce a discourse on itself. Pirate production of commodities and media objects fits neither a narrative of resistance nor normative critique, nor does piracy seem to fit received models of creativity or innovation. Piracy today produces a series of anxieties from states, transnational capital and media industries, and even among some liberal proponents of the public domain. The efflorescence of non-legal media production and circulation exists as a series of publicly articulated facts, constantly referred to in media panics, national security discourses and everyday conversations.

High-speed networks of the 1990s have seen the deployment by the media industry of tracking and controlling architectures that attempt to resolve the historic tension between intangible private property and its material circulation in the Thing – the very tension that has plagued the copyright regime from the outset. This has been paralleled by some of the most draconian laws against piracy, legal cases against individuals

13. I owe this phrase to Nitin Govil, 'War in the Age of Pirate Reproduction', *Sarai Reader 04: Crisis, Media*, Sarai, The New Media Initiative, Delhi, 2004.

and small shops, and raids by enforcement agencies against 'infringers'. The discourse against piracy as morally reprehensible and illegal is in a large part shaped by this campaign. A spectral zone of infringement statistics, pirate P2P (peer-to-peer) networks, factories in Southeast Asia, and the supposed link between terrorism and piracy enacts the anti-piracy campaign on a global scale. The very expansion of contemporary copyright's power has been challenged at each step – by hackers who break every digital encryption used by the industry, by peer-to-peer networks that dodge enforcement and provide a platform for users to share media files, and most importantly by hundreds of millions of ordinary buyers of pirated media who seem not to share the media industry's vision of the world today.

I want to suggest that there is more to piracy than its illegality or economic potency, destructiveness or radical alterity. The debate around authorship and the shrinking public domain that has emanated from Western critiques of the property regime is an important one, but limited by its axis: the split personality of modern liberal individualism and personhood that modernity inaugurated. In their critique of the current property regime, public domain theorists have variously mobilised the category of the information commons, the right to share and reinterpret cultural material, and a domain of creative authorship through collaborative P2P networks. These are surely important and significant resources for a critique of the current property regime. However, as Lawrence Liang points out in his excellent critique, there is an embarrassed silence on piracy in the entire public domain debate.[14]

Piracy's absence from this debate is significant,[15] perhaps because it fundamentally disrupts the categories of the debate of property, capitalism, personhood and the commons that have moved the debate in the past decade. Postcolonial piracy is typically a post-liberal (if not a post-Marxist) cultural effect. Piracy destabilises contemporary media property and, working through world markets and local bazaars, both disrupts and enables creativity, and evades issues of the classic commons while simultaneously radicalising access to subaltern groups in the Third World. Postcolonial piracy works more through dense local networks of exchange and face-to-face contact, rather than individual online downloads.[16] In an earlier essay in *Third Text*, I termed this phenomenon a pirate or recycled modernity,[17] unconcerned with modernity's classic search for originality. More pragmatic and viral than the avant-garde or tactical, pirate culture allowed the entry of vast numbers of poor urban residents into media culture. The metaphor of the virus suggests parasitic attachments to larger structures, with rapid replication, disruption and transformation of official networks through non-linear communication. 'Recycling' is not a process of more of the same, ie, simple replication, but works as a complex difference engine – each copy is different from its predecessor, through variation and recombination. Piracy therefore occupies a field the edges of which move all the time, margin to centre, international to local. Governments and industry have been publicly repelled and secretly fascinated by media piracy, a sure sign of the latter's corporeal power. This is piracy's great public secret – and the reason for the relative ease with which it has withstood severe attacks from industry-sponsored enforcement campaigns.[18]

14. Lawrence Liang, 'Beyond Representation: The Figure of the Pirate', in *(Con)texts of Invention*, eds Peter Jaszi, Martha Woodmansee and Mario Biagioli, University of Chicago, Chicago, IL, 2007. Liang argues that, in the eyes of the liberal public domain, piracy neither suggests a model of creative authorship, nor does it fall within the normative claims of the public domain. For Liang, legalism and liberal constitutionalism limit the application of mainstream public domain discourse in postcolonial contexts of unmarked populations.

15. See James Boyle, *Shamans, Software and Spleens: Law and the Construction of the Information Society*, Harvard University Press, Cambridge, MA, 1997; Yochai Benkler, *The Wealth of Networks: How Social Production Transforms Markets and Freedom*, Yale University Press, New Haven, CT, 2006; Lawrence Lessig, *Free Culture: How Big Media Uses Technology and the Law to Lock Down Culture and Control Creativity*, Penguin Press, New York, 2004.

16. Online downloads through P2P networks have been increasing among middle-class internet subscribers in India.

17. Ravi Sundaram, 'Recycling modernity: Pirate electronic cultures in India', *Third Text*, no 47, summer 1999, pp 59–65

18. I do not deal with the complex process of enforcement in this essay, but for a wider discussion see Ravi Sundaram, *Pirate Modernity: Media Urbanism in Delhi*, Routledge, London, 2009.

For urban populations long used to more stable sites like the cinema theatre and the radio, piracy's decentralised proliferation induced a narcotic disorientation of the senses. Populations conceived by state media policy as spectators and listeners now entered piracy's landscape of infinite attractions, where images, sounds and objects moved rapidly through networks of proliferation: small shops, bazaars, friends. Piracy escapes the boundaries of space, of particular networks, of form, a before and after, a *limit*. Though it has complex strategies of deployment and movement, piracy is like no other form of expression, and respects no formal barriers. The lines between the surface and the inside, original and copy that transfixed the Western modernist archive and its postmodern reformulations are subject to question in piracy. What appears is a subjectless subjectivity; there is no being behind doing, or as Nietzsche said, *the deed is everything*.[19]

THE CASSETTE ASSEMBLAGE: NORTH INDIA 1980–

In January 1984 the journalist Ayesha Kagal travelled around India to examine the spread of video, which had been introduced to the country on a wide scale barely a year earlier. Kagal painted a picture of booming makeshift video theatres and thriving cassette libraries in small towns and villages all over the country. Showing the latest releases from Hindi and regional cinema, as well as a reasonable selection of pornography, video drew people from all walks of life – youth, working people, businessmen, women and children. The classic landscape of picturesque India – the great cattle fair in Puskhar in Rajasthan, the hill station in Panchgani in central India, Leh in Ladhakh – all bore witness to the turbulence unleashed by video: closing film theatres, bankrupting distributors and placing a film industry under siege. 'We're sunk', film industry producer Gul Anand told Kagal. 'Cinema simply can't face the competition. Our prints are bulky, our processing charges are going up while the prices of cassettes are going down and will drop further... I sometimes feel the 35 mm projector is going to be a museum item.'[20] The main problem for video was identified as piracy – libraries and theatres sourced the latest movie from an international circuit almost immediately, bypassing local laws and film industry prohibitions. This was then distributed through low-cost VHS cassettes – in local video libraries and makeshift theatres. New parallel infrastructures of distribution arose rapidly – cable networks, video libraries and small video theatres. A significant expansion of the media public was under way, at the same time as the decline of older cinema theatres and exhibition spaces.

The situation in the audio market was even more dramatic. Audio cassette technology had spread rapidly and easily by the early 1980s, spawning an army of small music producers all over the country. Conservative estimates, which tend to privilege the legal industry (including smaller players), show that the turnover of the music business increased *twentyfold* in the decade of the 1980s.[21] The music scholar Peter Manuel hazarded a guess of 250 producers in North India alone based on his research – a figure that *excluded* pirate and unregistered players. Small and medium players ripped through the main monopolies like HMV and opened up a large hitherto untapped market of regional

19. I refer to the cultural experience. To be sure there are loosely organised pirate networks and coalitions; their staying-power has been limited due to harassment and raids by the police.

20. Ayesha Kagal, 'As the Video Virus Spreads', *Times of India*, Bombay, 22 January 1984

21. Harini Swamy, 'In the big music bazaar', *Times of India*, 21 July 2001

and local music and, as in the case of video, also set up a low-cost geographically diverse distribution network. The spread of cassettes in the 1980s as a dominant form was rapid. Peter Manuel's standard work on that period summarises the situation well: 'By the mid-1980s cassettes had come to account for ninety-five per cent of the recorded music market. The recording-industry dominance formerly enjoyed by GCI dwindled to less than fifteen per cent of the market, as over three hundred competitors entered the field.'[22] The share of film music dropped to a minority position in the market, replaced by a combination of regional, devotional and non-film pop.[23] Manuel's study of that period calls this the cassette 'revolution' where a mix of new producers and technologies responding to regional and local genres overturned the classic music monopolies and the star system of singers they created. Small labels, argued Manuel, were responsive to local tastes and now offered their diverse audiences an equally diverse range of musical forms. In ownership, in content and in the circulation of a musical form, argued Manuel, cassettes democratised the audio experience. New artists emerged as a new pool of talent came into the business all over the country, some of whom entered the music star system in the 1990s. Despite Manuel's own ethical discomfort with piracy, there was no hiding the fact that pirate production was a critical part of the emergent world of audio production. Says Manuel, 'Until the late 1980s pirate producers dominated the industry in terms of turnover and profits, and they continue to claim a significant share of the market'.[24] Piracy's structure of law-bypassing techniques marked almost all emergent enterprises in audio.[25]

The video explosion and the audio cassette boom stand out, but not just for the rapidity of their expansion in Indian media history. They marked new parasitic media geographies, a vast spatial expansion of media life. Drawing from a growing infrastructure of small enterprise and emerging classes of entrepreneurs, cassette culture of both audio and video let loose a series of conflicts around piracy – between large and small companies, between pirates and copyright enforcement detectives, and between large and small pirates. As a form that bypassed the law, media piracy was not unique to social and cultural forms in postcolonial India. Nor was piracy new, for it dated back to the coming of print. By shifting the material and spatial registers of copy culture into an uncertain sphere of disturbance, the cassette era opened up a new phase in Indian media history.

Piracy produced a novel form of panic in the media industry, which had always been used to a certain manageable chaos. Piracy suggested not just a permanent loss of space and corporate markets for the industry, but also a model of dispersal where 'distribution' took on a productive form. Distributor pirates also produced more media, piracy bred further piracy. This was a breakdown of cultural management impossible for the industry to fathom – even to this day. Industry panic in the 1980s went through a series of cycles: initially the film industry declared noisy war on video piracy. No person in the Bombay industry was allowed by the main association to sell national video rights. The implication was that, by default, any video cassette sold in the country was 'illegal'. Regular press campaigns, court battles, delegations to Delhi to convince the government to change copyright laws to incorporate video,

22. Peter Manuel, *Cassette Culture: Popular Music and Technology in North India*, Oxford University Press, New Delhi, 1992, p 63

23. Ibid

24. Ibid, p 78

25. Innovative replication of film music was central to the audio boom, along with the commodification of local and regional music.

and an industry-wide strike against 'piracy' marked the first half of the 1980s. Behind all the façades of unity the industry was actually deeply divided, with many producers wanting to break rank and sell video licences to local distributors. The association was already tearing at the edges and there was a growing demand to move to an 'adjustment' with the new network.

After a bruising battle, analogue cassettes finally entered the industry's definition of a market segment in the 1980s, with rights management, regional distribution and a staggered temporal cycle where the cassette would come in after the film had its initial run. The idea was that with adequate management the industry could expand its profits and produce a new widening of publicity. The model, if it could be called that, provoked immense anxiety about leakage and non-compliance right from the outset. In the event, these were reasonable intimations.

A LANDSCAPE OF PEOPLE AND THINGS

By the late 1980s and early 1990s Indian cities were swarming with small entrepreneurs and migrants who took part in the pirate trade, along with older communities of traders. In Delhi they flocked to the small factories of East Delhi and the media markets of Nehru Place, Lajpat Rai market and Palika Bazaar. Some became cable operators, others joined the booming music business, and still others tried their hand in the computer trade. Lamington Road in Bombay, Burma Bazaar in Chennai and National Market in Bangalore were other similar media markets that developed at that time. By the 1990s travel to Southeast Asia by small businessmen in Delhi and other cities to source computer parts and electronic goods was standard;[26] in Delhi's old city a whole business of travel agents grew up around booking tickets for Asian travel for small business. The shifting cultural landscape of the media networks built in the 1980s and 1990s was in remarkable contrast to the more abstract state-sponsored discourse around computers during the Rajiv Gandhi era, which sought to graft new technology onto a modernised nationalist model. Popular knowledge about breakdown, assembly, duplication, hardware, software dominated conversations in the pirate zone of this period, shot through with a almost counter-tactical model – assembly rather than attack, evasion rather than resistance. In his work on Nigerian video Brian Larkin argues convincingly that pirates produced a viral infrastructure of media: generating both the speed of globalisation and the noise of postcolonial cultural production: used equipment, assemblages, decentralisation. At a time when the world economy has seceded from Africa, piracy has brought a globalisation of recycled technological artefacts to Nigeria, and has provided media products to a subaltern population: Indian and Hollywood films, Hausa dramas and Islamic religious cassettes. Says Larkin, 'Instead of being marginalised by official distribution networks, Nigerian consumers can now participate in the immediacy of an international consumer culture – but only through the mediating capacity of piracy'.[27]

In the early years of piracy in Delhi a complex network of production sites, which produced low-cost hardware for TV and music networks, connected media markets and local dealers in the neighbourhood. Today

26. In 1999, on a trip for an architectural conference to Taiwan, I met two Delhi small businessmen who did this regularly. They showed me their suppliers' directory and a list of small budget hotels in Southeast Asia printed in the Old City of Delhi. Bangkok, Singapore, Taiwan, Hong Kong and Shenzen were on the travel circuit. The Taiwan connection began with T-series importing equipment from there for its factories in the 1980s.

27. Larkin, op cit, p 297

copying is part of a vast Asian network of procurement. Bombay films for example are sourced from Dubai and Malaysia, mixed in Pakistan, and sent on the internet and by courier to India. Master disks (from which more copies can be made) are made in factories outside Delhi (safe from enforcement raids). Sales agents then go to neighbourhoods on scooters with album covers and pitch to local shops. In the case of mainstream releases this entire operation takes 24–48 hours before people have access to it through the local cable network or neighbourhood shops. To be sure, pirate practices ranged from the straightforward reproduction of mainstream film/audio releases, remix and remake of audio/video, local and regional music and video. The latter were part of a more complex mutation, sometimes feeding off successful film and audio releases, but usually dispersing into a series of multiplicities, where the cultural 'supplement' takes on a life of its own, making new connections and staging new disruptions.

THE PUZZLE OF THE 'ORIGINAL'

'Is this an original?', asked an article in the Bombay music industry magazine *Playback and Fast Forward* in 1988, referring to the confusion among buyers of audio cassettes as to whether the international brand (Sony, TDK) stamped on most blank cassettes was indeed the original.[28] The magazine went on to conduct a test and found that just about all cassettes branded and pirated were in fact produced in India, despite international labels. 'And whether it's HMV, CBS, MIL or Weston or any of the pirated music available on the streets, all cassettes are 100 per cent Indian.'[29] *Playback* was in fact addressing the anxieties of a turbulent landscape of media life in the first half of the 1980s when piracy was the dominant form through which populations experienced new media. These were the wild years of the cassette era, when a cluster of piracy, local media production and neighbourhood copy shops set the benchmarks for media culture at the edge. For most early users, it mattered little that the cassette was not 'original'; it simply had to be available.

From the late 1980s companies began rapidly catching up with copy techniques: price cuts, strengthening of distribution and design changes to mimic pirate aesthetics. With the movement to digital in the mid-1990s, this situation became even more fluid, and producers, shopowners, discerning consumers and enforcement agents produced complex but temporary classifications to distinguish between original, pirate and local. What emerged was a materiality that disclosed popular ideas of authenticity and surface within the context of a bazaar economy well nigh integrated in a regional global technological constellation.

In the 1990s, when pirate distribution and reproduction of mainstream film and music releases were localised, the differences between the 'original' and its copy were twofold: the latter typically preceded the original release and was marked by a modest cover, screen printed or even handwritten. By 2002 the entry of larger players into the pirate business took mainstream releases away from the locality, but the quality of the cover and the disk improved substantially. Digital printing and cardboard designs came in, and camera prints, a phenomenon of early piracy, now declined in market share, with more high-quality reproductions coming

28. *Playback and Fast Forward*, May 1988, p 56

29. Ibid

from Dubai and Pakistan. While the hierarchy of master disk and copy has remained in the pirate market, it is something that has been subject to considerable techno-cultural flux since 2000. In the past decade shopowners in Palika Bazaar and Lajpat Rai market in the old city have prided themselves on identifying 'original' and 'pirate' versions. Pirate CDs were distinguished not just by their early release time, and their slim cover, but by a particular holographic sheen on lower quality disks.

Piracy has emerged as the perceived culture of the urban edge, inflected with a certain materiality that ranks it differently from the 'original'. This edge space is marked by surface effects: over-informationalised and tacky designs, a specific quality of inlay cards and CD covers. Strangely, this perception carries over to sections of the media industry that sell to the pirate market along with legal releases – in the case of a flop or for tax evasion. In an interview with media researcher Ankur Khanna, Meghna Ghai of Mukta Arts candidly described this process, as allegedly followed by a rival company Eros:

> So Eros releases limited copies of the official DVD (as per the contract), as well as larger numbers of the pirated version which are priced at one-fourth the cost of the official DVD. Special care is taken to ensure that the pirated DVD possesses all the characteristics of what is perceived to be the prototypical pirated disc. In other words, an attempt is made to deliberately downgrade the packaging of the disc so that it subscribes to a certain notion of a pirated disc cover: soft sleeves (as opposed to a hard case) containing high grade colour printouts of original disc covers. The disc itself is of exactly the same quality as that of the original.[30]

Piracy remains a zone of infinite attractions for users, for pirates, and for the very people who are its imagined antagonists – the property holders of the media industry.

SURFACES

The pirate surface rested on a particular corporeal economy of emotions and things – assuming a tactile movement of the city dweller between touch, vision and operation of media objects. In short, the surface of the media object was not simply a window that exposed a broader set of exchanges on subjectivity and representation. The surface further 'bled' into multiple media objects (CDs, cassettes, videotapes) and screens (TV, computer and mobile phone), deploying its concentration of commerce and information to produce a space of apperception that paralleled the street signs of the city. From the late 1980s Indian companies were selling technology that allowed local cable operators to insert neighbourhood advertising in film and video releases. This technology had become fairly refined by the 1990s, producing a cluttered viewing screen, bordered with advertising and transgressing the classic rules of disembodied television spectatorship, which used to separate the commercial from the main feature. This video's informationalised, overcommodified frame typically enters the home through the local cable network.[31] Viewers trained their senses to adjust to the cable video screen crowded with moving local advertising, the price of partaking in the pirate aesthetic. The claustrophobic space of the screen existed in a force field with

30. See *Sarai Reader 05: Bare Acts*, op cit, p 285.

31. See Larkin, op cit, for a fascinating enquiry into the Nigerian experience of pirate video.

crowded urban spaces in the city, producing a periodic warping of media experience.[32] The commodified mingling of surfaces and objects recognises no limits today: paper flyers in local newspapers, television channels that implore their viewers to call in on shows or text their opinion, impossible-to-remove stickers on walls and newspapers, SMS and text solicitations, a hyperstimulus that presumes an active anthropology of the senses – of readers, consumers, viewers, participants.

Piracy was the wild zone of this constellation, sometimes occupying the centre stage as in the 1980s and then moving to the edge as in recent years when the media corporations moved rapidly to try to discipline and stabilise the arrangements of space and image through authorised sites like malls and multiplexes. Piracy's disruptions ranged from media property, secular cultural arrangements, older image economies, media distribution, stardom and consumption – the very fabric of urban social life. The a-spectacular nature of the pirate zone is the key to the corporeal constellation. Piracy set up a zone of attractions that drew from the vernacular and the modern, the regional and more mainstream cultural fare. Piracy's participants did not suffer that paralysis of disembodiment that Debord had so famously claimed that the spectacle produced.

One can say that piracy is that practice of proliferation after the demise of the classic myth of modernism. Piracy exists in commodified circuits of exchange, only here the Same disperses into the Many. Dispersal into viral swarms is the basis of pirate proliferation, disappearance into the bazaar's hidden abodes of circulation is the secret of its success and the distribution of profits at various points of the network. Piracy works within a circuit of production, circulation and commerce that also simultaneously suggests many simultaneous time zones – Paul Virilio's near instantaneous 'time of light', the industrial cycle of imitation and innovation,[33] the retreat of the commodity from circulation and its re-entry as another. Media piracy's proximity to the market aligns it to both the speed of the global (particularly in copies of mainstream releases) and also the dispersed multiplicities of vernacular and regional exchange.

In cinema the pirate market follows the journey of the film closely. If a film does well at the box office, the more likely are the pirate editions and supplements. Speed is central to the race between distributor and pirate. Just as distributors now plaster the market with many prints in simultaneous time, so pirates release camera print prequels and high-quality sequels. The race between industry and copier is a small part of the cultural story of the pirate story. The larger story is one of endless imitative frenzy: media company copying company, remixed versions in local music and cinema. While media companies fight it out in court, outside copyright's formal legal sphere a vast cultural universe of small regional cinema re-releases and remixes are produced. 'True copies' of the original are filtered through the 'noise of the real'[34] – pirates cut longer films, insert advertisements, and sometimes add censored scenes to releases. Each version becomes a new one, with camera prints in the first release, advertisements in the next, and hundreds of versions of popular film and audio hits.[35] This proliferation of near-copies, remastered versions, re-visions refract across a range of time–space shifts, moving between core and periphery of the media-city almost phenomenologically, rather than spatially. Versions of popular numbers are

32. The recent crowding of the mainstream TV screen with moving information and advertising in US and Indian TV networks was actually introduced in the pirate video in India way back in the 1990s.

33. In the small industries of East Delhi there was usually a six-month lag before products were copied by competitors.

34. Jane Gaines, 'Early Cinema's Heyday of Copying', *Cultural Studies*, 20:2/3, 2006, pp 227–44

35. The research by Bhagwati Prasad showed that there are at least thirty-seven versions of the explicit tune *Kaante Laaga*, ranging from dance to devotional forms. See his 'Piracy: Judte Rishte, Phaylta Bazaar', *PPHP Laghupatrika*, Sarai, Delhi, 2003.

produced by the pirate market, fade from the big city and return in devotional music, or local videos from the states of Bihar, Haryana and Western UP – back to the city, brought by migrants and travellers. In short, piracy does not dwell only in objects or spaces, it enacts them momentarily. Its materiality consists in its mix of place, time and thing, a mix that dissolves and reconstitutes itself regularly. Piracy *an sich* seems to have no end, just as it had no particular point of beginning.[36] Piracy produces a surplus of cultural code which fractures the surfaces of media spectacle through a tactic of dispersal. For the new Indian elites alarmed at the ruination of the Asian growth dream, there has been a nervous, attempted flight from piracy to controlled spaces of consumption – multiplexes, malls and branded stores.[37]

In place of a spectacular urbanism, or the classic site of alterity, pirate culture suggests a constant overflow and an unhinging from contemporary property regimes. Its combination of bazaar commodification and a-spectacular techniques posits a new urban edge, which evades both classic radical redemptive hopes and the discipline of modern capital. Piracy is a desire, a promise and a threat, depending where you stand in the world today.

36. 'This indefinite life does not itself have moments, close as they be to one another, but only between-times, between-moments...' Gilles Deleuze, *Pure Immanence: Essays on a Life*, Zone Books, New York, 2001, p 29

37. Delhi alone is building forty-seven malls with multiplexes. In addition, controlled media delivery direct-to-home satellite platforms are being retailed to middle-class customers.

Communication Monographs

Published on behalf of the National Communication Association

EDITOR:

Mike Allen, *University of Wisconsin, Milwaukee, USA*

Communication Monographs reports original, theoretically grounded research dealing with human symbolic exchange across the broad spectrum of interpersonal, group, organizational, cultural and mediated contexts in which such activities occur. The scholarship reflects diverse modes of inquiry and methodologies that bear on the ways in which communication is shaped and functions in human interaction.

The journal endeavours to publish the highest quality communication social science manuscripts that are grounded theoretically. The manuscripts aim to expand, qualify or integrate existing theory or additionally advance new theory. The journal is not restricted to particular theoretical or methodological perspectives. Manuscripts reflecting diverse issues, scholarly modes of inquiry, and innovative thinking about the ways in which communication is shaped and functions in human interaction are presented.

2007 Impact Factor: 1.512
Ranking: 4/45 in Communication
©2008 Thomson Reuters, Journal Citation Reports®

NATIONAL COMMUNICATION ASSOCIATION

To sign up for tables of contents, new publications and citation alerting services visit www.informaworld.com/alerting

Register your email address at www.tandf.co.uk/journals/eupdates.asp to receive information on books, journals and other news within your areas of interest.

For further information, please contact Customer Services at either of the following:
T&F Informa UK Ltd, Sheepen Place, Colchester, Essex, CO3 3LP, UK
Tel: +44 (0) 20 7017 5544 Fax: 44 (0) 20 7017 5198
Email: subscriptions@tandf.co.uk
Taylor & Francis Inc, 325 Chestnut Street, Philadelphia, PA 19106, USA
Tel: +1 800 354 1420 (toll-free calls from within the US)
or +1 215 625 8900 (calls from overseas) Fax: +1 215 625 2940
Email: customerservice@taylorandfrancis.com

View an online sample issue at:
www.tandf.co.uk/journals/cm

Contributors

Ernesto Calvo is studying Visual Culture at the University of Barcelona. He was director and chief curator of the Museum of Contemporary Art and Design (MADC) in Costa Rica (2002–2008), where he organised several exhibitions of video and digital art as well as other curatorial projects related to contemporary art and public spaces. He has collaborated with many publications on art in Latin America, the United States and Europe.

Sean Cubitt is Director of the Program in Media and Communications at the University of Melbourne. His publications include *Timeshift*, *Videography*, *Digital Aesthetics*, *Simulation and Social Theory*, *The Cinema Effect* and *EcoMedia*. He is series editor for Leonardo Books at MIT Press, and a member of the editorial advisory board of *Third Text*.

Nina Czegledy is an artist, curator and writer, who works internationally in media and electronic art. She has exhibited widely and has led and participated in workshops, forums and festivals worldwide. She has curated and presented numerous video programmes internationally and published extensively. Czegledy is a Senior Fellow, KMDI at the University of Toronto, Associate Adjunct Professor at Concordia University, Montreal, and co-chair of the Leonardo Education Forum.

Mauricio Delfín is an anthropologist, producer and director of Realidad Visual, an arts and new media association. Since 2004 he has directed the organisation of the International Festival of Video/Arte/Electrónica (VAE Festival). He has been a member of the editorial committee of the magazine *Distancia Crítica*. He is currently developing a social research project on the relationship between cultural development, cultural policies and globalisation in Peru.

Hannah Feldman is an assistant professor of art history at Northwestern University. At present she is in residence as a fellow at the Getty Research Institute where she is completing a book about the aesthetics of decolonisation.

Olga Goriunova is currently lecturing in Interactive Media at Goldsmiths, London and working on a book on art platforms and aesthetic organisation on the internet. She has been involved in the field of software art, co-organising Readme software art festivals (Moscow, Helsinki, Aarhus, Dortmund) and Runme.org software art repository (still running).

Eduardo de Jesus is a professor at Pontifícia Universidade Católica de Minas Gerais (PUC Minas) and member of the Associação Cultural Videobrasil. He has a master's degree in Communication from the Universidade Federal de Minas Gerais (UFMG) and a doctorate degree in Arts from the Universidade de São Paulo (ECA-USP).

Pi Li is a lecturer at the School of Humanities, Central Academy of Fine Arts, Beijing and a doctoral student of Art Theory After World War II. He is also an independent curator, and in 2005 he co-founded a hybrid-space named universalstudios-beijing, and worked for Boers-Li Gallery.

José-Carlos Mariátegui is a scientist – with a combined degree in Biology and Mathematics and a MSc on Information Systems – and a media theorist and researcher. He is a founding member of Alta Tecnología Andina. He has taught, researched, published and curated extensively on the themes of art, science, technology and society, particularly in relation to Latin America. He is currently a doctoral student of Information Systems at the London School of Economics and Political Science (LSE).

Laura Marks is a theorist and curator of independent and experimental media arts and author of *The Skin of the Film: Intercultural Cinema, Embodiment, and the Senses*, *Touch: Sensuous Theory and Multisensory Media*, and *Enfoldment and Infinity: An Islamic Genealogy of New Media Art*, forthcoming from MIT Press. She is the Dena Wosk University Professor in Contemporary Arts at Simon Fraser University, Vancouver.

Maree Mills joined the Hastings City Art Gallery in Hawke's Bay, New Zealand as its new Director in January 2008. She previously lectured at the University of Waikato on video production and experimental video practice. Her own art practice explores communication of ethereal and cosmological concepts inherent in a Maori world-view from a female perspective.

María José Monge has an MA in Anthropology with emphasis on Cultural Policies. Since June 2008 she has been the director of the Museum of Contemporary Art and Design (MADC) in Costa Rica, coordinating programmes and events dedicated to the stimulus and promotion of Central American contemporary visual arts.

Gunalan Nadarajan is an art theorist and curator from Singapore. He is currently Vice Provost for Research at the Maryland Institute College of Art, USA.

Marcus Neustetter is an artist based in Johannesburg. Over the past ten years he has been consistently developing international networks, platforms and local art-industry strategies, realising public art projects, producing art, science and technology experiments and exhibiting art in Africa and Europe. In partnership with Stephen Hobbs, he has been active with the Gallery Premises, the Trinity Session and in their collaborative capacity as Hobbs/Neustetter.

Ravi Sundaram is a Fellow at the Centre for the Study of Developing Societies (CSDS), Delhi. In 2000 he co-founded the Sarai programme. Sundaram has co-edited the critically acclaimed Sarai Reader series, *The Public Domain* (2001), *The Cities of Everyday Life* (2002), *Shaping Technologies* (2003), *Crisis Media* (2004), and *Frontiers* (2007). He is the author of *Pirate Modernity: Media Urbanism in Delhi* (2009).

Andrea Szekeres, with a background in literature and linguistics, worked with the Budapest Soros Center for Contemporary Art (SCCA) from its founding in 1985 as an assistant director, and from 1996 as a programme director of C3: Center for Culture and Communication. Between 1999 and 2001 she was a founding member and president of ICAN: International Contemporary Art Network. At present she is web content editor at the Ludwig Museum of Contemporary Art, Budapest.

Miguel Zegarra is a curator at the Vértice Art Gallery in Lima. Since 2004 he has been co-curator of the itinerant international exhibition, 'Vía Satélite: Panorama of Photography and Video in Contemporary Peru'. He also acted as curator of the video installation by artist Patricia Bueno that represented Peru at the 52nd Venice Biennale, 2007. He is a member of the team behind the MAC-Lima Project, which aims to promote the realisation of the Museum of Contemporary Art of Lima.

Submitting a paper to THIRD TEXT

Before preparing your submission, please visit our web site for a complete style guide (contact details are given below) or send an e-mail inquiry to thirdtext@btconnect.com

Papers for consideration should be sent to the Editors, address given below. Please send an original and three photocopies. Submissions can also be made via e-mail.

Papers are accepted for consideration on condition that you will accept and warrant the following conditions. In order to ensure both the widest dissemination and protection of material published in our Journal, we ask authors to assign the rights of copyright in the articles they contribute. This enables Taylor & Francis to ensure protection against infringement.

1. In consideration of the publication of your Article, you assign Third Text with full title guarantee all rights of copy right and related rights in your Article. So that there is no doubt, this assignment includes the right to publish the Art in all forms, including electronic and digital forms, for the full legal term of the copyright and any extension or renewals. You shall retain the right to use the substance of the above work in future works, including lectures, press releases and reviews, provided that you acknowledge its prior publication in the Journal.
2. We shall prepare and publish your Article in the Journal. We reserve the right to make such editorial changes as may be necessary to make the Article suitable for publication; and we reserve the right not to proceed with publication for what ever reason. In such an instance, copyright in the Article will revert to you.
3. You hereby assert your moral rights to be identified as the author of the Article according to the UK Copyright Designs & Patents Act 1988.
4. You warrant that you have secured the necessary written permission from the appropriate copyright owner or authorities for the reproduction in the Article and the Journal of any text, illustration, or other material. You warrant that, apart from any such third party copyright material included in the Article, the Article is your original work, and cannot be construed as plagiarising any other published work, and has not been and will not be published elsewhere.
5. In addition, you warrant that the Article contains no statement that is abusive, defamatory, libellous, obscene, fraudulent, nor in any way infringes the rights of others, nor is in any other way unlawful or in violation of applicable laws.
6. You warrant that any patient, client or participant mentioned in the text has given informed consent to the inclusion of material pertaining to themselves, and that they acknowledge that they cannot be identified via the text.
7. If the Article was prepared jointly with other authors, you warrant that you have been authorised by all co-authors to sign this Agreement on their behalf, and to agree on their behalf the order of names in the publication of the Article.

There are no page charges in *Third Text*.

Corresponding authors can receive 50 free reprints, free online access to their article through our website (www.informaworld.com) and a complimentary copy of the issue containing their article. Complimentary reprints are available through Rightslink® and additional reprints can be ordered through Rightslink® when proofs are received, or alternatively on our journals website. If you have any queries, please contact our reprints department at reprints@tandf.co.uk Additional copies of the journal can be purchased at the authors' preferential rate of £15.00 per copy.

Editorial Office:
2G Crusader House, 289 Cricklewood Broadway, London NW2 6NX, UK
Tel: +44 (0)208 830 7803
e-mail: thirdtext@btconnect.com

Please refer to the following website for the journal style guide:
http://www.tandf.co.uk/journals

For more information on our journals and books publishing, visit our Taylor & Francis website:
http://www.tandf.co.uk

If you are unable to access the website please write to: Journals Editorial, Taylor & Francis, 4 Park Square, Milton Park, Abingdon, Oxfordshire OX14 4RN, UK.

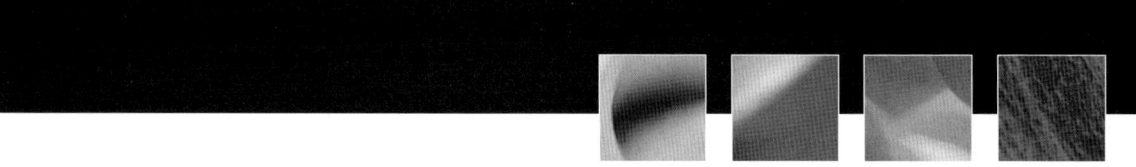

AUTHOR SERVICES

Publish With Us

   **informa** healthcare

The Taylor & Francis Group Author Services Department aims to enhance your publishing experience as a journal author and optimize the impact of your article in the global research community. Assistance and support is available, from preparing the submission of your article through to setting up citation alerts post-publication on **informa**world[TM], our online platform offering cross-searchable access to journal, book and database content.

Our Author Services Department can provide advice on how to:

- direct your submission to the correct journal
- prepare your manuscript according to the journal's requirements
- maximize your article's citations
- submit supplementary data for online publication
- submit your article online via Manuscript Central[TM]
- apply for permission to reproduce images
- prepare your illustrations for print
- track the status of your manuscript through the production process
- return your corrections online
- purchase reprints through Rightslink[TM]
- register for article citation alerts
- take advantage of our i*OpenAccess* option
- access your article online
- benefit from rapid online publication via i*First*

See further information at:
www.informaworld.com/authors

or contact:
Author Services Manager, Taylor & Francis, 4 Park Square, Milton Park, Abingdon, Oxon OX14 4RN, UK, email: authorqueries@tandf.co.uk

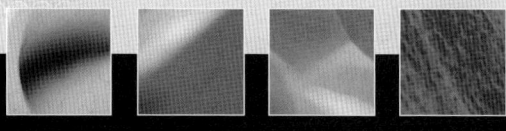